Contingent Computation

MEDIA PHILOSOPHY

SERIES EDITORS
Eleni Ikoniadou, Lecturer in Media and Cultural Studies at the London Graduate School and the School of Performance and Screen Studies, Kingston University
Scott Wilson, Professor of Cultural Theory at the London Graduate School and the School of Performance and Screen Studies, Kingston University

The Media Philosophy series seeks to transform thinking about media by inciting a turn towards accounting for their autonomy and 'eventness', for machine agency, and for the new modalities of thought and experience that they enable. The series showcases the 'transcontinental' work of established and emerging thinkers whose work engages with questions about the reshuffling of subjectivity, of temporality, of perceptions and of relations vis-à-vis computation, automation, and digitalisation as the current 21st century conditions of life and thought. The books in this series understand media as a vehicle for transformation, as affective, unpredictable, and non-linear, and move past its consistent misconception as pure matter-of-fact actuality.

For Media Philosophy, it is not simply a question of bringing philosophy to bear on an area usually considered an object of sociological or historical concern, but of looking at how developments in media and technology pose profound questions for philosophy and conceptions of knowledge, being, intelligence, information, the body, aesthetics, war, death. At the same time, media and philosophy are not viewed as reducible to each other's internal concerns and constraints and thus it is never merely a matter of formulating a philosophy *of* the media; rather the series creates a space for the reciprocal contagion of ideas between the disciplines and the generation of new mutations from their transversals. With their affects cutting across creative processes, ethico-aesthetic experimentations and biotechnological assemblages, the unfolding media events of our age provide different points of intervention for thought, necessarily embedded as ever in the medium of its technical support, to continually re-invent itself and the world.

'The new automatism is worthless in itself if it is not put to the service of a powerful, obscure, condensed will to art, aspiring to deploy itself through involuntary movements which none the less do not restrict it'.

—Eleni Ikoniadou and Scott Wilson

Software Theory: A Cultural and Philosophical Study, Federica Frabetti
Media After Kittler, edited by Eleni Ikoniadou and Scott Wilson
Chronopoetics: The Temporal Being and Operativity of Technological Media, Wolfgang Ernst, translated by Anthony Enns
The Changing Face of Alterity: Communication, Technology and Other Subjects, edited by David J. Gunkel, Ciro Marcondes Filho and Dieter Mersch
Technotopia: A Media Genealogy of Net Cultures, Clemens Apprich, translated by Aileen Derieg
Recursivity and Contingency, Yuk Hui (forthcoming)

Contingent Computation

*Abstraction, Experience,
and Indeterminacy in
Computational Aesthetics*

M. Beatrice Fazi

ROWMAN & LITTLEFIELD
Lanham • Boulder • New York • London

Published by Rowman & Littlefield
An imprint of The Rowman & Littlefield Publishing Group, Inc.
4501 Forbes Boulevard, Suite 200, Lanham, Maryland 20706
https://rowman.com

6 Tinworth Street, London SE11 5AL, United Kingdom

British Library Cataloguing in Publication Information Available

Library of Congress Cataloging-in-Publication Data
Names: Fazi, M. Beatrice, 1981– author.
Title: Contingent computation : abstraction, experience, and indeterminacy in compu-
tational aesthetics / M. Beatrice Fazi.
Description: Lanham : Rowman & Littlefield International, 2018. | Series: Media philos-
ophy | Includes bibliographical references and index.
Identifiers: LCCN 2018023183 (print) | LCCN 2018033860 (ebook) | ISBN
9781786606099 (ebook) | ISBN 9781786606082 (cloth : alk. paper)
Subjects: LCSH: Computers—Philosophy. | Aesthetics.
Classification: LCC QA76.167 (ebook) | LCC QA76.167 .F39 2018 (print) | DDC
004.01—dc23
LC record available at https://lccn.loc.gov/2018023183

ISBN 9781538147061 (pbk. : alk. paper)

Contents

Acknowledgements   vii

Introduction: Novelty in Computation   1

Part 1: Aesthetics   **21**

1   Continuity versus Discreteness   23

2   Computation   47

3   Processes   61

Part 2: Abstraction   **81**

4   Computational Idealism   83

5   Axiomatics   97

6   Limits and Potential   113

Part 3: Experience   **141**

7   Computational Empiricism   143

8   Factuality   157

9   Actuality   173

Conclusion: Computational Actual Occasions   203

Bibliography   213

Index   223

About the Author   239

Acknowledgements

I would like to thank the editors of the book series Media Philosophy, Eleni Ikoniadou and Scott Wilson, as well as Sarah Campbell, Isobel Cowper-Coles, and Natalie Linh Bolderston at Rowman & Littlefield International, for believing in this project and for their valuable assistance.

Many colleagues and friends have offered advice and support during the writing of this book. In particular, I wish to express my gratitude to Caroline Bassett, David M. Berry, Trine Bjørkmann Berry, Giulia Bozzi, Tom Bunyard, Howard Caygill, Antonella De Santo, Michael Dieter, Mike Featherstone, Jonathan Fletcher, Matthew Fuller, Andrew Goffey, Olga Goriunova, Graham Harwood, N. Katherine Hayles, Caroline Heron, Tim Hitchcock, Michael Jonik, Tim Jordan, Giuseppe Longo, Celia Lury, Lorenzo Magnani, Sally Jane Norman, Eleonora Oreggia, Kate O'Riordan, Jussi Parikka, Luciana Parisi, Ben Roberts, Darrow Schecter, Brian Cantwell Smith, Rachel Thomson, Nathaniel Tkacz, and James Williams.

In 2017, the British Academy funded the research project *Digital Culture and the Limits of Computation*, which allowed me to test and develop further my conceptualisation of indeterminacy in computation. I am grateful for this support.

The Sussex Humanities Lab has been the ideal place in which to complete this study. I would like to extend my thanks to everybody there, as well as to the School of Media, Film and Music and the University of Sussex for having established this unique interdisciplinary research programme.

Finally, I wish to thank my parents for their trust and love. This book is dedicated to them.

Introduction

Novelty in Computation

> The Analytical Engine has no pretensions whatever to *originate* any thing. It can do whatever we *know how to order it* to perform. It can *follow* analysis; but it has no power of *anticipating* any analytical relations or truths. Its province is to assist us in making *available* what we are already acquainted with.
>
> —Ada Lovelace, 'Notes' (1843)

CONTINGENT COMPUTATION

This book offers a philosophical study of *computation*. Computation is understood here as a method of systematising reality through logico-quantitative means. The systematisations of computation are generally considered to be 'simple formulae' that are geared towards capturing the dynamism and complexity of the world. From this perspective, computation is assumed to be something that merely appropriates and represents reality through the binary calculation of probabilities. In consequence, it is also assumed that there is no novelty in computation, but only the iterative repetition of the preprogrammed. The aim of this book is to challenge that view. I propose that computation is dynamic and complex: that one can find *within* the preprogrammed, logico-quantitative operations of computational processing something akin to what the mathematician and philosopher Alfred North Whitehead described as 'process'.[1] This is because an ontology of *contingency* should be identified at the formal level of the computational system. Computation is a process of determining indeterminacy. This indeterminacy, however, is internal to the process itself, and a condition for computation's ontological production.

1

To argue that contingency is to be found at the formal heart of computation is a radical and original claim that concerns the modes of being and becoming of computation. It is also an admittedly counterintuitive assertion: computational systems would seem to work by means of logical necessity, rather than through contingency. After all, computing machines are 'engines of logic'.[2] That is to say, they are the technological realisations of those strategies of formal abstraction that deductive thought has developed over many centuries in order to respond to human reason's attempts to organise or simply make sense of reality. It is important, therefore, to stress that this book does not discard the formalist origin of the computational method, nor does it reject the logical self-sufficiency of that method's deductions. By engaging directly with the formal character of computational systems, I aim to conceptualise computation's internal potentiality to actualise itself. This potentiality, I will argue, is inherent to the abstractive operations of discretisation that are specific to computational formalisms and to their functioning.

This argument concerning the contingency of computation is a response to the urgent need to assess philosophically the promise of quantification and rationalisation afforded by computational systems in the twenty-first century. My conceptualisation of *contingent computation* is also a response to the need to address theoretically the growing centrality of automated modes of formal systematisation within the contemporary world. Today, debates on computational culture find themselves in a strange predicament. On the one hand, there is much excitement about the possibility that algorithmic processing could exhibit a 'conceptual capacity'. The latter expression refers to an alleged capacity to produce modes of knowledge, understanding, and reasoning. On the other hand, however, there remains a sense in which this supposed computational conceptual activity is inferior to the thinking that originates from lived experience. This is because the modes of thought associated with the formal logic employed in computation involve a matrix of *discrete* relations, in which there is no room for the generative potential of indeterminacy that comes from the *continuity* of life and lived experience. Computation's matrix of discrete relations is understood as an epistemic reduction in which everything is preset and preprogrammed: a matrix that returns, as output, only what one has put into it as an input. This is something that was perhaps clear from the very early attempts to design an algorithm that could be run by a machine, as demonstrated by this introductory chapter's opening epigraph from the computer programmer *ante litteram* Ada Lovelace.

This strange predicament in computational culture echoes familiar philosophical concerns regarding the mechanisation of thinking and being, as exemplified, for instance, by critical theory's accounts of technological and instrumental reason, or by poststructuralist arguments against representation. From this perspective, computation is a representational tool in the hands of cognitivism, as well as in those of technocapitalist apparatuses of instrumentalisation. These concerns, however, pertain not only to philosophy: science, too, must confront the disparity between formal systems and life on a daily basis. In an attempt to respond to that disparity, within the specific context of computer science, the basic algorithmic model of computation has been challenged by new conceptualisations of the computing machine. According to the interactive paradigm in computing,[3] the deductive algorithmic rule has to be complemented with the unpredictability of the environmental input so as to bring the indeterminacy of the real world into the computational system. Similarly, experiments in ubiquitous, pervasive, embedded, and physical computing also highlight the question of how computation can be rendered more akin to an empirical situation. In this respect, the technical—as much as the cultural—rhetoric associated with *situated* forms of computing focuses on the mediated availability of computational devices towards a phenomenal reality. This availability, in turn, is mainly acted out in the physical relationship between the user and the machine. Interaction, then, is to be performed and lived through in a material or embodied context. It becomes an operation concerning the orientation of computing machines in the world, and our relation with them.

These attempts in computer science echo what has happened in some strands of cognitive science too, where algorithmic programmability has been rejected, in part, on the basis that formal rules cannot engage with the environmental complexity that makes us intelligent, and which should, presumably, inform the putative intelligence of any machine that would simulate us. Post-computationalist trends in neurosciences, artificial intelligence, and robotics have made it clear: to think is not the same as to compute. Rather, it means to do or to behave, to act upon the environment, and to have a body that feels. This has prompted a search for 'mind in life',[4] 'intelligence without representation',[5] and 'action in perception'.[6] Finally, it is important to mention here that 'unconventional', 'natural', and 'non-classical' computing are just some of the broad labels assigned to current explorations of computability that attempt to endow computational formalisms with the dynamism and complexity that pertain to the biological and physical realms, and which prefer the inductive approaches of the empirical sciences to the deductions of logic. Opportunities are thus pursued for computational formalism to deviate from predetermination towards the ambiguities and intermediary states of life, of ordinary languages, and of multiagent operations.

The different contexts and modes of scholarship that have been mentioned above will be referenced and mapped out throughout the book as my argument proceeds, and they will also be considered in relation to the specific fields that are brought together and addressed in each chapter. On the basis of what has been said so far, however, we can note here that these instances attest to the growing belief that, in today's computing, the formal has to be made as empirical or factual as possible. One aspect of the research that I have conducted for this book grew from considering this multifaceted philosophical and scientific condition, and the consequent questions that that condition gives rise to are as follows: despite the operational success of its general validity and comprehensive applicability, should computational formalism be discarded altogether? If we want to find true ontological production in computation, should we expect the latter to be more like life and nature, and thus withdraw into a qualitative translation of its logico-quantitative character? Or, as I propose in this book, should we rethink what this logico-quantitative character means for computation, so as to consider if it has its own ontological means of generating being and becoming? In order to address this problem fully, and to prove the significance of rethinking the logico-quantitative character of computing, I had to enter, figuratively speaking, the formal matrix of computation so as to understand what computation is and what it does. By engaging with formal logic, I took computing machines for what they are: *formal axiomatic systems.* An axiom is a self-evident truth; it is the postulate from which consequences are inferentially derived. Computational systems are axiomatic because they too implicate a starting point that is self-evident and which defines the inferential steps that can be taken from it towards a result. From this perspective, computer programs, just like axioms, return to us only what is already known. They provide an output that is already implicit in the input. This would seem to imply that if computation is truly unable to generate anything new, then this must be due to its axiomatic nature.

One of the central and more distinctive propositions of the study offered in this book, however, is that in order to find the realisation of new actuality in computation we need look no further than the axiomatic method of computation itself. My aim is not simply to propose a revision of computational axiomatics. Instead, I will advocate its reconceptualisation. I will consider the axiomatic determinism of computing—something that would, paradoxically, seem to be very removed from contingency—so as to study its limits. I will be addressing those limits, however, not in order to have done with the axiomatic in computation, but rather to rethink the significance of the former for the ontology of the latter. Understanding computation vis-à-vis the formal determinism of logico-mathematical sciences is therefore a key stage in advancing my contentions. It will be proved, in the course of this book's arguments and demonstrations, that the computational matrix is dynamic and complex because it is infinite and processual, and that axioms cannot be seen to be reductive. There is more to computational axiomatics than a mere set of predetermined instructions, and in order to demonstrate that point I have turned to computability theory's foundational papers—specifically, those of Gödel and Turing—so as to consider the core idea that everything that is computed is deductively determined.

Although many histories of computing are possible, I develop my argument by engaging with the most 'molar' (to use a Deleuzian term) of these historical accounts. In 1931, the logician Kurt Gödel determined the *incompleteness* of formal axiomatic systems by demonstrating that there are propositions that appear to be true when viewed from the outside of the system, but which cannot be proved or disproved within the system in question.[7] In 1936, Alan Turing built on Gödel's discovery to show that some functions are *incomputable*, thereby describing the limits of computing machines before any such machine was built. Turing's formalisation phrased the computational method in terms of a procedure (that is, an algorithm) that would solve a problem in a finite number of sequential steps. This formalisation of computation, however, also revealed the challenging existence of incomputable problems—namely, problems that cannot be solved via algorithmic means because the steps involved in their processing are infinite.[8] We just do not know, for instance, if a program will halt unless we run such a program, and we cannot tell which inputs will lead to an output.

Incompleteness and incomputability have been traditionally read as evidence of the failure of formal axiomatic systems, and of the automated mechanisations of thought and being that rely on them. In contrast with this popular view, however, it is my contention that the incomplete and the incomputable are not errors or stopping points for axiomatics. Rather, they show that indeterminacy pertains not only to the empirical realm but to the formal too. Computation is an abstractive procedure of determination that always confronts indeterminacy. This indeterminacy does not need to be qualitatively translated by (or coupled with) a body, a biological substratum, or an empirical referent, because it is already expressed, in its logical and quantitative nature, by algorithmic procedures. Although it remains incalculable, this formal indeterminacy is hence not outside computation but intrinsic to its axiomatic character. By engaging with the incomplete and the incomputable, I aim to rethink indeterminacy within computation's formal axiomatic systems and to understand it as predicated upon the logico-quantitative specificity of computation itself. Against what I call the *metacomputational* perspective (in other words, the belief that rational calculation can explain every element of reality deterministically), I will demonstrate that, with its processes of *abstractive discretisation*, the computational function itself manifests the inexhaustibility of computational processing. Of the formalist origin of the theory of computability, and of the cognitivist projects that stem from it, we must thus challenge not the technique per se, but rather the belief that computation corresponds to a simple matrix of total determinism. This book aims to do so by reassessing the ontological significance of operations of discretisation in computation. While metacomputation would imply that the quantities that characterise the discrete nature of computational systems compose a pattern of closed logical necessity, I claim that the incomplete and the incomputable demonstrate that this pattern is in fact open to quantitative infinity and to formal indeterminacy. Consequently, I can challenge the conception of computation as an all-encompassing formula—a conception that is predicated on the postulation of computation's striving for total determinism.

What, then, is contingent computation? The concept of contingency is often slippery and hard to circumscribe. This is due to its precariousness, which mutates, just as the ontological status of the contingent itself seems to do. I contend that the contingent should be viewed as maximally *indeterminate*. In this respect, a key conceptual operation accomplished by this study is the divorce of the contingent from the empirical. Computation might encompass, or be modelled upon, the empirical mutability of the real world, and through interactive and embedded operations it might become more powerful and adaptable. Algorithms might also be enmeshed with the empirical plane by means of application, implementation, and performance. However, a crucial assertion of this book is that computation is *already* contingent, before any implication with the empirical dimension of sensible reception, because of the maximal indeterminacy of its axiomatic character.

The perspectives that I have taken issue with so far can be schematised as attempts to bring the formal abstractions of computation into contact with the indeterminacy of material existence. In this respect, these attempts employ an interpretation of computation that casts the latter as being capable (or as nearly capable) of experiencing the mutability of sensibility. The notion of *contingent computation* that I propose affords a different view. Computation, it will be argued, might already possess a mode of experience, one that is not limited to the sensible input of empirical reality or the simulation thereof. Consequently, this book not only attempts to divorce the contingent from the empirical; in addition, it also extracts the analysis of experience from its current purviews. On the one hand, I will separate the analysis of experience from the traditional, early modern empiricism of the senses and of matters of fact (as in Hume's philosophy, for example); on the other, I will detach it from the transcendental empiricism of abstract sensation and virtual matter (as in Deleuze's work). The notion of contingent computation that these separations afford also supports my attempt to advance an unusual empiricism of computational processes. This empiricism is not focused on Humean habits and customs, or on the phenomenal, reflexive, and existential experience of a user or a programmer. Nor is it focused—to phrase this in a more Deleuzian register—on the intensive vibrations of matter that are experienceable through affects or through an unmediated relation with the 'being of the sensible'.[9] Instead, the empiricism that I advance is focused on the experience of the computational process itself: an experience that corresponds to a process of determination that is always ingressed by indeterminacy, and which is based upon the abstractive and quantitative nature of the computational method. I thereby claim that computation possesses its own mode of experience, although it should be noted that the term 'experience' must be understood in a very particular sense that pertains solely to the computational processes' *self-actualisation*.

This brings me to the third separation that this book attempts: that of differentiating actuality from factuality or, rather, from the manner in which factuality is commonly conceived within computing. Factuality is typically associated with the empirical world, and thus with the modes of sensibility that some of the perspectives outlined above seek to connect to the abstract formality of computation. However, the factuality of the real world does not need to be conceived as a mere sequence or concatenation of bare facts, and thereby as something that stands opposed to the formal abstractions of computation. I draw on the work of Alfred North Whitehead, who presents reality as an activity of self-actualisation: as a process that involves the interrelation of forms, or schemas of abstraction, with factual existence. I will adopt this view, yet I will relate it to the self-actualisation of computation itself: for computation, I will argue, entails just such an interrelation of *form* with *fact* (although not just the factuality of empirical reality, but that of the actual elements and moments of computation itself). It is a key aspect of my argument for contingent computation that computational processing must be conceived as being actual and, therefore, in act, fully realised in space and time. At this point, it can be explained that the notion of contingent computation highlights the indeterminacy that underpins all computing, but also the *eventuality* of computation itself. My use of the term 'eventuality' does not refer to the merely accidental but to computational processes that are to be conceived as *actual events*. This means that they should be understood as unique occurrences or occasions that will never be ontologically repeated in exactly the same way. Following Whitehead's philosophy of actuality, I will propose that a computational event (or a *computational actual occasion*) is the end result of a process of self-determination. This self-determination starts from a physical reception of data. Still, it is never concluded in the absence of a conceptual determination too. The actuality of computation is thus not a simple bare fact in the world, and it should not be predicated uniquely upon a principle of sense reception of this factuality. We should thus resist naturalising computation into what will be referred to here as an 'empirical phenomenon among empirical phenomena'.

This book ultimately contends that ontological production in computation results from a process of actualisation involving both physical and conceptual functioning. In this sense, computation is a process of determination that entails operations upon the sensible and upon the intelligible alike. However, I will argue that this process of determination is a becoming that also has a moment of permanence. Achieving this moment is the *finality* of the computational procedure, which can be fulfilled thanks to the presence, in the procedure, of a formal indeterminacy that can only be grasped, as Whitehead would phrase it, conceptually; or rather, to put this in terms of my engagement with computing, it can only be grasped logically. The maximal indeterminacy that I identify with contingency in computation is therefore the essential condition for computation's self-actualisation.

WHY AESTHETICS?

My claims concerning the contingency of computation are presented in terms of the theoretical implications that they pose for computational aesthetics. Why, the reader might ask, am I proposing an *aesthetics of contingent computation* and not, for instance, an epistemology, or perhaps an ethics? Why, in other words, does my argument for the contingency of computation inhabit an aesthetic dimension and not some other arena of intellectual enquiry? This is a legitimate question, and I will answer it here by outlining the origins of this research and by thereby introducing and explaining three statements that are key to its development.

1. The aesthetic investigation of computation should aim to uncover computation's potential for self-actualisation.

This book originates from a desire to respond to the difficulty of establishing an aesthetics of computation. This difficulty is rendered all the more acute by what I identify as two pertinent contemporary problematics: the crisis of formalism in science and the critique of representation in philosophy. In this study, I am taking up the challenge of assessing whether aesthetics is a viable mode of investigating contemporary computational systems. This challenge is inscribed within particular debates about the aesthetics of digital media, according to which aesthetics is not a theory of art and is not tied to traditional tenets such as beauty, taste, and judgement. In these debates, which will be directly addressed in the first part of the book, aesthetics is understood in a manner that is more in keeping with its etymological roots—which lie in the term *aisthesis*—and it is thus conceptualised as a theory of sensory knowledge, or, more specifically, as a theory of knowledge that is predicated upon the immanence of thought and sensation. From this point of view, the difficulty of establishing an aisthesis of computational systems pertains to the disparity between the relational and perceptual character of lived experience (understood as the origin of such immanence between thought and sensation) on the one hand, and the informational, instrumental, operative, and technologically mediated features of computation on the other.

In the book, I characterise the relatively recent development of an aisthetic attention to digital culture as a position that draws upon the philosophy of Gilles Deleuze. I will then argue that, for Deleuze, any attempt to establish a computational aesthetics would be a contradiction in terms. According to Deleuze, aesthetics is an immersion in the field of infinite qualitative transformation that constitutes what he called 'a life'.[10] Aesthetics thus concerns unmediated affective relations that possess ontological continuity with the matter-flow of the real. In contrast, Deleuze understood computation (and discrete formalisation, in general) as a finite instrument of quantitative calculation, ruthless prediction, and empty communication: as something that breaks with the immanence of thought and sensation in order to provide us with a cognitive representation, or to use Deleuze's terms, an 'image of thought'. Despite the fact that, from a strict and orthodox Deleuzian perspective, the aesthetic and the computational are two divergent modes of relating to the real, it is my contention that aisthetic accounts of computational systems have adopted Deleuze's aesthetics of ontological continuity and extended it to account for what is not continuous: digital computation. I believe, however, that there is an inherent risk in arguing for an aisthesis of digital computation—the risk of subsuming, or flattening down, the logical within the aesthetic, upon the premise that the former can share (with a bit of adjustment and an injection of sensibility's flexibility) the latter's attention to the qualitative. To put it otherwise, the implicit assumption would be this: if we want to address computation aesthetically, we cannot rely on the formal character of computation. Instead, we need to rework computation's logico-quantitative functions in terms of vectors of modulation and differentiation, or through the insertion of intensive materialities (such as, for instance, those of art or of society at large) that combine with the operations of computational logic.

This dichotomy between the matter-flow of things and computation might be interpreted as a different yet somewhat parallel version of what I have earlier described as the popular separation between the empirical variability of the 'real' world on the one hand, and the static formalisms of computational systems on the other. Both dichotomies highlight a supposed defeat of the relation between the aesthetic and the logical in computation. This apparent defeat reveals, in turn, an impasse in digital culture that needs to be addressed at a rigorous theoretical level. This book's argument for the contingency of computation is an attempt to respond to that need. My goal is to repair the fracture between the aesthetic and the logical, and I will do so by demonstrating that the indeterminacy and eventuality of contingent computation highlight how computing's formal logic is able to step out of its representational mode not solely through the affective plane of sensation (the importance of which, however, I do not deny), but through its formal operations of abstraction and discretisation too. By understanding computation as an event of self-actualisation that is always ingressed by formal indeterminacy, I aim to show that closing the gap between the aesthetic and the logical involves refusing to conceive computation as static and finite. An aesthetics of contingent computation thus points to a processuality and an infinity that are proper to the actualisation of computation.

From Deleuze—and from the perspective of a pursuit of an aisthesis of the digital—I retain a profound insight: aesthetics concerns becoming and creation. As such, aesthetics pertains to ontological questions about the *potentiality* of the real and to how this potentiality can engender the production of new actuality. An aisthetic perspective on computation would maintain that computation's potentiality might lie in that inexhaustible field of potential generation that Deleuze called the 'virtual', and that becoming thus corresponds to the intensive differentiation of the affective plane that, for Deleuze, records and transduces virtuality. In contrast, this book argues *against* the ontological virtualisation of digital computation and explicitly calls for the examination of a potentiality that is instead inherent and specific to the capacity of computational processes to actualise themselves. I am differentiating, therefore, between virtuality and potentiality. If we explain the potentiality of computation in terms of virtuality, we always need to presuppose an associative ground between the mechanised operations of computation on the one hand, and lived experience (i.e., what the mechanised and the computational are not) on the other. In this way, we risk missing the specificity and autonomy of computational processing. Moreover, we also risk missing the fact that computation might have its very own conditions of experience, which differ from those of the user or of the associative ground itself.

To sum up: the challenge of establishing an aesthetics of contingent computation is, in my view, that of investigating computation's potential for self-actualisation. The question as to what account can be given of such a potentiality of computation is one of the principal questions that drives this study: how does it differ from that of the continuity of life and sensation?

2. Thought is aesthetic. That is to say, aesthetics concerns thinking processes, and vice versa.

While this is not a book on Deleuze or on 'Deleuze and computers', the hypothesis that aesthetics concerns thinking processes is borrowed from his philosophy, which opened up the prospect of resolving the question of what thought is through aesthetics. However, my intention is to radicalise Deleuze's aestheticisation of thought so as to examine that which Deleuze would not have considered to be either aesthetic or a legitimate form of conceptual activity: computational processing.

Deleuze wanted to bring the question of what a thinking process is and does beyond any identity of thought with being. This is why aesthetics is so important in his philosophy. Thought is understood as immanent to sensation; thinking is a process that cannot be represented via formal or symbolic reductions, and which can only be expressed through the affective level of the real, and thus grasped in the fullness of lived experience. For Deleuze, this lived experience is the field of aesthetic enquiry. Although I wish to take up the same challenge of Deleuze—namely, that of thinking thought beyond being and, in fact, in its becoming—I have already mentioned that, from a strictly Deleuzian perspective, the aesthetic investigation of digital computation poses a difficulty. Computational thinking processes cannot be addressed aesthetically because they are outside of lived experience. One can assume, therefore, with a certain degree of confidence, that Deleuze would not only have rejected the view that computation is aesthetic; in addition, he would also have objected to the claim that computation constitutes a form of thought, or that it has a conceptual capacity of any sort.[11] Paradoxically, then, it can be remarked that my aim to close the gap between logic and aesthetics means accepting the Deleuzian premise that aesthetics is not only about ontology but, more particularly, that it is also about reconsidering the ontology of thought. This is a paradox, because this very same premise would seem to have initiated the gap in the first place. Having acknowledged this debt to Deleuze, however, closing the gap between logic and aesthetics also involves stressing that computation's conceptual capacity is quite different from the abstract thought that originates, in Deleuze, from a clash with the being of the sensible. I will briefly explain why here.

It is my contention that Deleuze assigned the status of *abstractness* to thought, with its virtual infinity and indeterminacy, and dismissed techniques of *abstraction* as epistemic reductions of such boundless virtuality. For Deleuze, computation is an example of this reduction, because it is a technique of abstraction. Contra this view, I argue that it is by virtue of abstraction that infinity and indeterminacy enter computation. These are, however, a *quantitative* infinity and a *formal* indeterminacy. As such, they are not predicated upon virtual life but are instead specific to the computational system. The study advanced in this book, then, not only intends to overcome the Deleuzian critique of computation; in doing so, it also intends to demonstrate that computation exhibits a legitimate mode of conceptual activity and that, although this mode is not immanent but consequent to sensation, it can still be approached in aesthetic terms.

The ontological schema proposed by the mathematician and philosopher Alfred North Whitehead will prove to be key to advancing this argument. It should be stressed that, while I acknowledge that Deleuze and Whitehead can be read in harmony with each other, I will not attempt to do so. My aim of radicalising Deleuze's aesthetic ontology of thought does not entail emphasising the undeniable connections between Deleuze and Whitehead but rather their equally profound disparities. I thus read Whitehead as a post-Deleuzian, even though the chronological relation between the two philosophers would imply the opposite. It was stated earlier that this is not a book on Deleuze (or on 'Deleuze and computers'); it might now be added that this is not a book on Whitehead (or on 'Whitehead and computers') either. From Deleuze's work I will develop a series of speculative challenges. Vis-à-vis Whitehead, I will formulate a set of ontological speculations to cope with these challenges. However, neither the problems that this study addresses, nor the propositions that it will offer, fit perfectly with either the Deleuzian or the Whiteheadian philosophical project. This is to say, I am not interested in tailoring a bespoke reading of those projects that would suit my own; I do not apply Whitehead to solve Deleuze, nor do I pick and choose between the two in an attempt to overcome the conceptual difficulties of this kind of investigation. Instead, I use Whitehead's ontological schema to push my speculations beyond the positions that Deleuze is capable of bringing me towards. The overall aim of this work is to offer an ontological perspective on the aesthetics of computational processes that could stand independently of its Deleuzian or Whiteheadian conceptual underpinnings.

Having clarified this, we can now signal the greatest contribution that Whitehead's philosophy makes to this book's radicalisation of a Deleuzian aesthetics of thought. This contribution consists in extending aesthetics from the sensible to the intelligible. In Deleuze's work, thought is aesthetic because it concerns a virtual abstractness that can only be felt metaphysically. By contrast, Whitehead envisaged an aesthetics that I define as operating at two levels. For him, aesthetics is not only about a bodily transduction and a physical reception, or about the thought that comes from sensibility. Instead, aesthetics is about mental processes too. In Whitehead's philosophy, this mental activity pertains to actuality. It is aesthetic because it is not a representational reduction or mediation but a *conceptual prehension*: it is a grasping, seizing, or holding of the pure potentiality of an ideal. This characteristic of Whitehead's ontology makes his philosophy particularly interesting for this book's aims. It affords a means of advancing an aesthetic ontology of computation that would not discard the logico-quantitative operations of computational systems expressed through formal abstraction, but which would instead interpret such formal abstraction through Whitehead's description of conceptual prehensions. By constructing a computational aesthetics at two levels, it will become possible to show, against the cognitivism that prevails in the computing field, that computation is not just a mere method of reduction via a priori representation. However, it will also become possible to rethink the undeniable abstractive capacity of computation in a manner that goes beyond the representational but remains within the formal and the quantitative.

3. The aesthetics of contingent computation concerns the investigation of the conditions of computation's own experience.

Drawing on Deleuze, I take aesthetics to be an investigation into the conditions of *real experience*. Consequently, I propose that, in order to address computation in aesthetic terms, a conceptualisation of computation's *own* experience (in other words, not that of a user or a programmer, of a biological substratum or of a material transducer, but that of a computational process itself) should be developed. Insofar as it addresses computational formalisms, this speculative attempt will have to consider experience beyond the confines of an empiricism of the senses, and it must accommodate the view that computation has a level of experienceability that is tied to the logico-quantitative specificity of the formal axiomatic system.

While I also draw on the Deleuzian view according to which real experience extends beyond the psychological and intentional territories of conscious human experiencing, and that its investigation thus concerns metaphysics, it is however the case that, from my perspective, the conditions of this experience should be understood in a rather different manner from those that Deleuze advocated. The differential changes of the virtual are, for Deleuze, intensively registered by affects and sensation as the only conditions of real experience. In contrast, this book develops the unexplored hypothesis of a *computation that experiences* by arguing that this experiencing is tied to quantitative processes that are not expressions of virtual sensibility but are in fact the actual and yet formal operations of computation itself. I phrase this proposition as an empiricism: what I am after is an elucidation of the computational process, according to which everything that can be elucidated, and indeed thought or spoken of about this process, is predicated upon the fact that the latter is an occurrence or an occasion of experience itself. However, since the objects of its enquiry are computational procedures, this empiricism will have to offer an account of the activity of experiencing that is somewhat weird and radical. The empiricism that can meet these requirements is, in my view, that of Alfred North Whitehead.

Whitehead's philosophy should be read as an attempt to provide a new conception of structural organisation in which science and philosophy are reconciled—while remaining distinct—into an account of *immediate experience* that aims to accommodate being and becoming, subjectivity and objectivity, permanence and change. Whitehead did not restrict his investigation of experience to human conscious experience, nor did he limit a capacity for experiencing to that which is strictly alive. For Whitehead, as for Deleuze, the experiential thus has a much wider connotation than its common usage would imply. Yet, in a manner that contrasts with Deleuze, Whitehead's notion of experience does not suggest any existential connotation, related to what is lived, nor is it circumscribed to the sensible either. Whitehead's metaphysics has sometimes been described as a 'panexperientialism'. This expression denotes the view according to which all actuality experiences. In my opinion, such a label might conceal vitalist, panpsychist, and often theistic undertones that I wish to avoid in my reading of Whitehead. Nonetheless, the point that needs to be made is as follows: for Whitehead, all actuality experiences because experience, in his philosophy, is equivalent to the process of self-determination of actuality. In this book, I follow Whitehead's characterisation of experience as self-actualisation to argue that computation's own experience can be understood to correspond to computation's own process of self-determination. However, if one wants to establish the extent to which computation's activity of self-determination can be understood as the experience of computation itself, the conditions of such self-determination need to be investigated, together with the degree to which they can be understood as those of computation's experience. Reciprocally, if such experience corresponds to an ontological operation of determination (specifically, that of computation), then the conditions of that experience are also those that allow this operation of determination.

Drawing on Whitehead, to experience is to produce oneself as a new actuality; yet it should also be stressed that all actuality, for Whitehead, carries out both physical and conceptual operations, and that these operations convey distinct (albeit related) ontological determinations. Consequently, experience corresponds to a construction that is just as 'dipolar' as actuality itself.[12] It follows from these comments that the aesthetic enquiry into computation's conditions of experience is strictly connected to the investigation of this double determination and to a consideration of how computational procedures require not only physical (and therefore sensible) indeterminacy but also conceptual (and therefore intelligible) indeterminacy in order to develop their full potential for actualisation.

STRUCTURE OF THE BOOK

The book is organised into three parts (each of which is composed of three chapters) and closes with a separate conclusion. As indicated above, the question that initiates this study concerns the ontological significance of computational aesthetics: is aesthetics a viable mode of investigating the being and becoming of computation? The three parts of the book are arranged in relation to a series of contemporary debates that I will show to pertain to this question.

Part 1, 'Aesthetics', unfolds the rationale of my proposition and the book's core philosophical setting. Chapter 1 discusses the disparity between an ontology of discreteness, which pertains to the logico-quantitative character of computation, and an ontology of continuity, which pertains instead to qualitative concerns for perception and sensation that characterise aesthetic investigations. I describe the status quo of computational aesthetics in terms of an impasse between these two ontological registers. This impasse is phrased as a deadlock that I relate to Deleuze's argument for the metaphysical superiority of affect over discrete formalisations. The chapter differentiates this Deleuzian attention to sensation from other aesthetics of continuity, such as phenomenological ones. It also suggests that this Deleuzian advocacy of sensation has entered digital culture as an aesthetic consideration of the ways in which the computer meshes with material forces and intensities. In contrast, the chapter argues that we should resist the virtualisation of computation that such an affective perspective would propose. The risk, in fact, would be that of overlooking the logico-quantitative character of computational systems. This book aims to assign an aesthetic legitimacy to this logico-quantitative character, albeit a legitimacy that is distinct from that of affect.

Chapter 2 explains why I focus on the category of the computational rather than on that of the digital. Computation and digitality are both based on discretisation. However, I focus on computation because of the systematising character of its discretising: to compute, in my view, involves a systematisation of the real through quantitative abstractions. Following on from these considerations, chapter 2 addresses the rejection of the ontological significance of these formal abstractions. In particular, I consider the philosophical and scientific critique of the computational theory of mind. I also understand this critique as dismissing the logico-quantitative character of computation. While I agree with the motivation and the target of this criticism, I do not agree with this dismissal. My proposed reconsideration of what aesthetics in computation might be is intended to take up the challenge of rethinking the logico-quantitative character of computation beyond cognitivism and representational understandings of computing, and it aims to do so without conflating the intelligible and the sensible.

To this end, chapter 3 introduces the significance that Whitehead's philosophy of actuality holds for the book's aims. I explain why I do not read Deleuze and Whitehead in harmony with each other, and I analyse the differences between the two philosophers. The technical vocabulary of Whitehead is also clarified here. In particular, I introduce the book's core proposition of understanding computational processes in the Whiteheadian terms of actual occasions. Such understanding is key to the establishment of an aesthetics of computation that would include computational systems' abstractive character. This discussion of Whitehead is framed in relation to the following argument: because of computation's inherent contingency, the abstractive character of computation can be understood as central to the possibility of a computation that experiences. In this respect, chapter 3 clarifies how turning to Whitehead helps, on the one hand, to conceptualise this contingency as computation's indeterminacy and eventuality, and on the other to address computation's experience in non-existential terms. Moreover, the chapter's discussion of Whitehead begins to consider the question of the potentiality of

computation and emphasises that theorising this potentiality vis-à-vis Whitehead offers a means to overcome the impasse between discreteness and continuity in computational aesthetics.

Part 2 of the book, 'Abstraction', presents my theorisation of computational processes as processes of self-determination. Chapter 4's initial focus
rests on the alleged beauty of the supposedly static and mathematically ordered character of computation. The chapter tackles a specific view on the
aesthetics of computation that I intend to evaluate critically: a view that I
name 'computational idealism', and which recalls notions of elegance, harmony, and beauty in order to establish an equivalence between logical truth
and aesthetic value. Computational idealism is an aesthetics of discreteness,
yet it is quite different from that which this book is aiming for. This discreteness is that of the 'simple formula': computational procedures are considered
a priori forms that indicate a more fundamental type of reality than that
which is gained through sensibility. The primary philosophical reference for
computational idealism is the Platonic top-down schema in which an ideal
plane transcends and orders the empirical world. Addressing this Platonic
orientation of computational idealism provides a means of engaging with a
common conception of aesthetics in computation, but also for focusing on
the centrality of formal abstraction to computational systems. This is because
the equivalence between truth and beauty identified by this orientation is
based on a model of axiomatic reasoning that corresponds to the formal
abstractive discretisations of the Turing machine. In addition to Platonism,
the other philosophical tradition that chapter 4 takes into consideration is that
which has descended from Leibniz's project for a *mathesis universalis*. What
I call 'Universal Computation' is a contemporary reworking of this rationalist project for a comprehensive science of deductive reasoning. The Platonic
a priori of logico-mathematical formalisation is key to the Leibnizian rationalisation of being and thought and to the twentieth-century instantiation of
this rationalisation in the computing machine. Considering these issues is
also a central step in this book's theorisation of the contingent character of
computational systems: I can only prove that the formal matrix of computation is complex and dynamic, indeterminate and eventual, provided that I
have also shown that the systematisation of reality via a simple method of
abstraction (an endeavour that I call *metacomputation*) cannot be accomplished.

Chapter 5 begins to develop my critique of the metacomputational view.
The axiomatic preprogramming of computing fits well with the idealist and
functionally determinist scenario of metacomputation, for Turing's notion of
computability is a formalisation according to which a finite set of rules
accounts for the full predictability of a mechanical system. Chapter 5 addresses such a deterministically closed character to describe and assess the
conformity between axiomatic systems and computational systems. In ad-

dressing this isomorphism, the chapter contends that computational idealism pursues an 'aesthetics of necessity', which is best encapsulated in the notion of the algorithm. Chapter 5 acknowledges that algorithms can be seen as having a non-necessary dimension too, for they are applied to many specific empirical situations, thus performing in world-making processes. I consider how these characteristics can be interpreted as indicating that algorithms have a degree of contingency. I argue, however, that while approaches that focus on the algorithmic contingency of applications, implementations, and performances would object to the metacomputational view, they do not manage to fully confute it. This is because these views indirectly reinforce the equivalence between the empirical and the contingent as this is established by the aesthetics of necessity of computational idealism. What chapter 5 proposes, then, is that we should understand the contingency of computation as being predicated not upon the latter's empirical dimension, but upon its formal one.

In order to do this, I must place the logical formalisation of the notion of computability within the larger debate about the limits of formal reasoning. This forms the starting point of chapter 6, where my critique of computational idealism and of the metacomputational view is reinforced by some key speculative propositions. I suggest a novel reading of the onto-aesthetic significance of computability theory's foundational papers (specifically, those of Kurt Gödel and Alan Turing). In a manner that goes beyond the views presented by Gödel and Turing, this reading affirms the self-sufficiency of computation's formal axiomatic systems, as well as their open-endedness, and characterises computational procedures as always leaning towards quantitative infinity. More specifically, via a close engagement with Turing's notion of incomputability, the chapter shows that computation's preprogrammed procedures should be understood as processes of determination that are always ingressed by indeterminacy. This indeterminacy is inherent to the activity of discretisation that is carried out by computational formalisation; it thus highlights the status of contingency in computation while also showing that this status is not predicated upon an empirical dimension. The chapter's ontological reworking of incomputability shows that formal abstraction is not an enframing or a reduction, but rather the way in which a non-representational yet logical relation with the maximally indeterminate can be established within computation. Via the proposed understanding of incomputability, I can begin to demonstrate that computational processes may be addressed in terms of Whitehead's 'actual occasions'. The axiomatic autonomy of computational procedures can in fact be understood as computation's striving for self-actualisation. Via Whitehead, moreover, it is possible to theorise computation's capacity to address the maximally indeterminate logically and to understand this maximally indeterminate as a conceptual capacity to grasp the pure potentiality of ideality. In this sense, chapter 6 also begins to describe how computation, because of its contingent status, involves the potential for genuine ontological production.

Part 3 of the book, 'Experience', expands on this theorisation of computation's self-determination and develops the possibility of understanding this self-determination as a complex and dynamic process of self-actualisation. Part 3 then speculates on the conditions under which ontological novelty might be produced in computation and on the sense in which a computational aesthetics should be concerned with this ontological production. In chapter 7, my focus is still on the logical matrix of computation. While I attended to the deductive character of this matrix earlier in the book, in this chapter I tackle those approaches that propose an inductive reworking of what it means to compute. I thus address those computational techniques that go under the name of unconventional, natural, and non-classical computing, and which propose alternatives to Turing's formalisation of computation. These techniques aim to make computation as close to empirical reality as possible in order to develop non-standard architectures able to simulate its mutability. In chapter 7, the expression 'computational empiricism' is coined to describe this outlook. The primary reference point here is early modern British empiricism, which understood experience in terms of a reception of sense-data. In particular, I take Hume as the philosophical frame of reference for computational empiricism, since alternative computing recalls, in my view, the associationism between abstraction and experience and the externality between thought and sense-data that Hume advocated.

Chapter 8 addresses the notion of emergence because the latter is, in my opinion, the powerful explanatory framework through which these alternative approaches to computing account for empirical novelty. Computational empiricism and its underpinning emergentist ontology are, however, problematic, for they understand contingency in terms of the chance occurrences of the physical world. Moreover, they predicate the possibility of indeterminacy in computation upon the assumption that computational procedures can be dynamic and complex only because they belong to the empirical plane of facts. In this respect, computational empiricism reiterates the conflation of the contingent upon the empirical that this book intends to dismantle. Chapter 8 recounts my effort to expose these problems and to offer a speculative hypothesis that might lead to surpassing them. Whitehead's philosophy is again a means through which I can advance my arguments. I turn to his critique of Hume and of what he calls the 'sensationalist principle' of British empiricism because this can help us to dispute computational empiricism's reduction of experience to sense experience, together with its elaboration of change as accidental variability.

Drawing on Whitehead, I can thus rethink the dynamism of the formal procedure as a processual becoming engendered by an internal principle for the realisation of computation's actuality. In chapter 9, the Whiteheadian notion of causal efficiency is introduced so as to offer an explanation of the physical reception of data by way of a causal connection among the *res* of reality. In a computational context, focusing on causal efficiency involves stressing the way in which algorithms order and objectify data as causally constitutive of the computational occasion itself. Chapter 9, however, does not stop its investigation at this physical level of data reception. It shows that the conditions of computation's own experience (or, in a Whiteheadian sense, those of computation's self-actualisation) include a conceptual determination too. In order to theorise computation's potential for actualisation, I stress the finality of the computational procedure: computational processes express a becoming with an end—that is, with an accomplishment and an aim. Both accomplishment and aim are the self-actualisation of the procedure. However, insofar as it is possible to say, following Whitehead, that such a final cause emphasises the role of ideality within the construction of reality, I contend that the 'real' potentiality of computation has to include the 'pure' potential of the incomputable in order for the computational process to determine itself fully. In developing this argument, my intent is to show that a computational aesthetics at two levels (the physical and the conceptual) can be constructed.

The aesthetic investigation of computation is an investigation of computation's self-determination: of how the latter is engendered by physical and conceptual indeterminacy, and also of how it achieves completion with a form or structure of actualisation, which is not a priori or a posteriori but is inherent to the actual event of computation. In the conclusion to the book, I recapitulate this contention and discovery and also expand on its significance vis-à-vis the question, how do we live with contingent computation? I make evident there that such an enquiry can only be conducted on the basis of a foundational ontological work such as that advanced within this book.

NOTES

1. See Alfred North Whitehead, *Process and Reality: An Essay in Cosmology* (New York: Free Press, 1978).

2. Martin Davis, *Engines of Logic: Mathematicians and the Origin of the Computer* (New York: Norton, 2000).

3. See Peter Wegner, 'Why Interaction Is More Powerful than Algorithms', *Communications of the ACM* 40, no. 5 (May 1997): 80–91, https://doi.org/10.1145/253769.253801.

4. Evan Thompson, *Mind in Life: Biology, Phenomenology, and the Science of Mind* (Cambridge, MA: Belknap Press of Harvard University Press, 2007).

5. Rodney A. Brooks, 'Intelligence without Representation', *Artificial Intelligence Journal* 47, nos. 1–3 (January 1991): 139–59, https://doi.org/10.1016/0004-3702(91)90053-M.

6. Alva Noë, *Action in Perception* (Cambridge, MA: Harvard University Press, 2004).

7. See Kurt Gödel, 'On Formally Undecidable Propositions of the Principia Mathematica and Related Systems I', trans. Elliott Mendelson, in *The Undecidable: Basic Papers on Undecidable Propositions, Unsolvable Problems and Computable Functions*, ed. Martin Davis (Mineola, NY: Dover, 2004), 4–38.

8. See Alan M. Turing, 'On Computable Numbers, with an Application to the Entschei-dungsproblem', *Proceedings of the London Mathematical Society* 42 (1936): 230–65, https://doi.org/10.1112/plms/s2-42.1.230.

9. Gilles Deleuze, *Difference and Repetition*, trans. Paul Patton (London: Continuum, 2004), 176.

10. See Gilles Deleuze, 'Immanence: A Life', in *Pure Immanence: Essays on a Life*, trans. Anne Boyman (New York: Zone, 2001), 25–33.

11. 'Closer to our own time, philosophy has encountered many new rivals. . . . Finally, the most shameful moment came when computer science, marketing, design, and advertising, all the disciplines of communication, seized hold of the word *concept* itself and said: "This is our concern, we are the creative ones, we are the *ideas men*! We are the friends of the concept, we put it in our computers." Information and creativity, concept and enterprise: there is already an abundant bibliography. . . . Philosophy has not remained unaffected by the general movement that replaced Critique with sales promotion. . . . Certainly, it is painful to learn that *Concept* indicates a society of information services and engineering.' Gilles Deleuze and Félix Guattari, *What Is Philosophy?*, trans. Graham Burchell and Hugh Tomlinson (London: Verso, 1994), 10–11.

12. Whitehead, *Process and Reality*, 45.

Part 1

Aesthetics

Chapter One

Continuity versus Discreteness

AN IMPASSE

Contemporary aesthetic enquiries into digital media are stuck in an impasse. On the one hand, this impasse attests to the relentless expansion of modes of thinking, acting, and perceiving that have been enabled by digital technologies and which are, in fact, specific to them. On the other hand, however, it also reflects the widespread belief that these digitally native experiences are imperfect or flawed if they are not validated by a biological substrate, a human referent, a body, or simply by 'life', which—in its multiform organisations and configurations—expresses and catalyses the affects and sensations that are central to aesthetic experience. This impasse in digital aesthetics thus concerns the difficulty of attributing those perceptual and relational features that are the object of aesthetic enquiry to the strictly informational and operative character of the computer or the digital device. This is a difficulty that poses a genuine problem for present-day notions of aesthetics, given that contemporary society is in large part structured by such informational operations and machines.

The deadlock that I am bringing to the fore here lies at the heart of aesthetic elaborations in the field of digital media theory and digital media studies. However, this deadlock is not limited to the cultural analysis of computational media but is informed by much older and broader philosophical questions. The impasse can be conceived as a standoff between two seemingly irreconcilable ways of relating to the world. A mode of relation that is said to be aesthetically primary, insofar as it concerns the *qualitative* features that belong to the perception and receptivity of lived experience, is thus opposed to an alternative view, which is, by contrast, mediated, technological, instrumental, and, most importantly, dictated by digital technologies' *quantitative* modes of formal organisation. As a result of this impasse, the very possibility of an aesthetics of the digital becomes a contradiction in terms. While media and cultural theorists, computer scientists, and philosophers might disagree on an exact definition of 'digitality', they accept *discreteness* as its fundamental feature. The digital is, in this sense, intrinsically discrete or, in other words, characterised as a data technology that uses discontinuous values to access, represent, and manage information.[1] Conversely, philosophical, cultural, and social accounts of aesthetic activities describe a universe of percepts and perceivers, the reciprocity of which is established by a rapport of *continuity* with what is given or encountered in experience. Aesthetics, in this respect, concerns the perceptual understanding of what counts as sensuous experiencing: its proprieties, features, and qualities and, subsequently, the prospect of its expression all rely equally on the continuity of perceptual and sensuous relations.

In the light of these considerations, I wish to propose a model to interpret this impasse. This model frames the deadlock as an opposition between continuity and discreteness. The continuous and the discrete are antagonistic ontological registers, or two antithetical modes of being, which concern conflicting modes of grasping and recording reality. Digital technology, with its binary elaboration of reality through quantifiable mechanical operations and quantitative inputs and outputs, attends to the real by discretising it. Aesthetics, however, being predicated upon perceptual relations and sensations, would seem to require a continuous—and thus analogue—association with the world. One can see that, from the standpoint of the model of the impasse offered here, the conceptual challenge of any aesthetic investigation of the digital pertains to the problem of pinpointing what constitutes the aesthetic dimension of digitality itself. What are the foundational elements that concern such a dimension, and what ontology do we need in order to account for the disparity between that which is supposedly continuous (perception and sensation) and that which is not (digital technology)?

It becomes evident, through taking up the challenge of thinking about these questions, that the possibility of establishing a digital aesthetics extends beyond the traditional disciplinary boundaries of a theory of art (in general), or of art made with or by computers (in the specific). The impasse between continuity and discreteness calls the etymological roots of the term 'aesthetics' into question. These roots lie in the ancient Greek *aísthēsis*, meaning 'perception from the senses', 'feeling', and 'sensation'. If we return to this original sense of aesthetics, the term could be said to denote *sensory knowledge*, and thus knowledge that is prior to any artistic meaning and judgement of taste.[2] From the perspective of aesthetics-as-aisthesis, the difficulty of having an aesthetic account of the digital entails the effort of conceiving of a digital perception or of a digital sensation. Aesthetics, here, is no longer just a theory of art but, more broadly, a *theory of sensory relations*, aimed at the investigation of how we relate to things, and how these things in turn relate to other things. From this point of view, what is continuous is not only the recording of reality, but also reality itself, in its relational infinity of variations, modulations, and transformations—relations that aesthetics aims to register through the sensible. Moreover, in this sense, it should already be apparent that the impasse that I am sketching between continuity and discreteness has profound Deleuzian connotations.

It is not an overstatement to say that the French philosopher Gilles Deleuze was not keen on computers. Although Deleuze engaged, both independently and in partnership with Félix Guattari, with media such as television, radio, and—above all—cinema, he wrote little, and not fondly, about computing machines. Still, the little that he did write on the topic has influenced the critical investigation of digital technologies, the ubiquitous proliferation of which was just beginning at the time of Deleuze's death in 1995. These sparse comments have framed, with a degree of prescience and great philosophical rigour, the limitations and dependencies of the digital medium, exposing how computing is inherently ancillary to the regimes of communication and representation, and how it relies upon the axiomatic infrastructures and informational goals that fuel contemporary society's systems of control.[3] In a sense, it is thus somewhat paradoxical that, despite Deleuze's overt suspicion towards the computational, his metaphysical vocabulary of rhizomes, assemblages, bodies without organs, and abstract machines abound in media theory syllabi as a means of explaining the condition of living in a networked information society. The influence that Deleuze has exerted over the cultural study of digital technology can, however, be explained by considering how a conceptual apparatus of intensities, multiplicities, and affirmations would seem particularly apt to describe a technomediated society that is, and whose media and modes of production are, without a centre and in continuous flow. In this respect, Deleuze's theoretical language has indirectly facilitated attempts to legitimate a philosophy of digital media. These are attempts that aim to mobilise Deleuze's famous conceptual tool kit in order to advance novel fields of engagement with the technological.

We should now return to the impasse between continuity and discreteness with these concerns in mind. In order to do so, it is crucial to stress that, while the status quo of contemporary digital media studies is *not* unanimously and universally informed by the philosophy of Gilles Deleuze, issues pertaining to aesthetics-as-aisthesis have entered digital media theory (partially but influentially) through an appropriation and elaboration of Deleuze's argument for a 'logic of sensation'.[4] This is a relational knowledge in which the forces in play are prior to cognitive descriptions of the world and are thus '*freed from the model of recognition*'.[5] Such a Deleuzian setting in digital aesthetics might be explicitly acknowledged, implicitly asserted, or also openly bypassed. Nonetheless, it remains the case that, when dealing with aesthetics-as-aisthesis in the digital realm, the Deleuzian problem, according to which what is mechanical and codified is able to generate neither sensation nor thought, is brought to the fore.

Of course, Deleuze is not alone in posing this problem. The disparity between the limitations of the technological (with its representational and cognitive character) on the one hand, and the irreducibility of the thinking that comes from lived experience and sensation (which both surpass cognitive representation) on the other, has been addressed frequently in contemporary philosophy and critical theory, mostly via critiques of instrumental reason or oppositions to the mechanisation of life. One might think here of the Frankfurt School as a clear example of such criticism.[6] Interestingly, one can also count Gilbert Simondon among those who share a critical stance towards the mechanisation of thought and being; obviously, one cannot omit Martin Heidegger from this list either.[7] Moreover, although they afford very different premises, aims, and outcomes, poststructuralism, postmodernism, and post-Marxism similarly emphasise particularities rather than the abstract universals that might subsume them, thus questioning the usefulness and validity of automating and systematising that which is lived.[8] Finally, as another figure in this list, I should mention Alain Badiou, who—like Deleuze—made irreducible multiplicity the central point of his thought. Despite his aversion towards the affective and the perceptual, and despite his passionate defence of the discreteness of events that do not relate to but rather break with the quotidian, for Badiou as well thought and being ultimately remain beyond formalisation.[9]

This account of philosophical suspicions of the mechanical qua the instrumental is not meant to be exhaustive. However, the heterogeneity of the voices mentioned above demonstrates that the aesthetic impasse between the continuous and the discrete should be contextualised vis-à-vis a broader intellectual aversion to the modern technological 'enframing' (to use a well-known Heideggerian term) of thinking and feeling into preprogrammed structures of reasoning that can be replicated automatically. From this standpoint, aesthetics is less the ultimate citadel of the Luddite than the sharpest tool in the box of those scholars concerned with saving the singularity and specificity of the lived, whether this latter is a practice, language, art, man, or existence itself. Yet, although other entry points to the impasse in digital aesthetics are thus possible, and although aesthetics itself can be mobilised in different manners in order to respond to this situation, I maintain that the setting of the ontological model of the deadlock between continuity and discreteness that I am proposing in this chapter remains characteristically Deleuzian. This is also the form in which it has, in part, entered the cultural theory of digital media. From Deleuze, one can draw the conclusion that a digital aesthetics (that is, an *aesthetics of discreteness*) is perhaps impossible. This is not to say that Deleuze himself claimed that. My point, rather, is that the association of aesthetics with a field of continuity can develop directly from Deleuze, and that this affinity between aesthetics and continuity leaves the aesthetic investigation of the digital with a difficulty that cannot be dodged or avoided, but which needs to be fully addressed.

Ontological continuity is a key feature of Deleuze's elaboration of aesthetics-as-aisthesis. Drawing upon Bergson's notion of duration (which is about qualitative rather than quantitative multiplicity) and upon differential calculus,[10] Deleuze's continuity is an asymmetric synthesis of the sensible. The continuum is the ontological plane of transformation of what is prior to individuation, of what is not logically predetermined, of what instead invents and creates through difference. This differentiation, however, is never fully realised: it always demands the occurrence of tendencies, vectors, lines of flight, and infinite speeds, which remain pure differential affirmations. For Deleuze, aesthetics is exactly what offers us the opportunity to address these unactualised conditions, insofar as it concerns one's unmediated relation with the sensuous dimension upon which these unactualised conditions find expression. Although he also addressed art and artists extensively, Deleuze did not centre his aesthetics upon notions of the art object, or upon traditional aesthetic values or definitions of spectatorship. Deleuze's aesthetics is, primarily, a theory of sensibility. Following a post-Kantian legacy, and transversally linking Bergson with Nietzsche, Deleuze defined sensation as what strikes us before meaning is trapped into figuration and signification. Operating beyond stable or fixed subjectivity, sensation is characterised not as a merely sensory reaction triggered by the qualities of a certain object, but as constituted by differential relations in intensity, which in turn endow reality with its transcendental conditions of existence.

From this Deleuzian perspective, the discreteness of digitality is evidently problematic, for it epitomises yet another development of the *representational*: in other words, a development of that which breaks the unmediated relation with the sensible and separates thinking from affect and intuition—the former to be understood in the Spinozist sense of a variation in the *potentia agendi* of a body,[11] and the latter in the Bergsonian sense of a method of unmediated and immediate 'sympathy' with things.[12] Deleuze's reworking of the traditional notion of aisthesis presupposes instead the immanence of thought and sensation. In this respect, Deleuze's aesthetics is truly an aisthesis insofar as it can be described as a sensory knowledge: there is thought in aesthetics, yet this thinking is enmeshed, inextricably, with the sensibility of the real. Consequently, it is useful to frame the contemporary impasse of digital aesthetics in terms of a mismatch between, on the one hand, the finitude of logico-mathematical techniques of systematisation of thought and being and, on the other, that infinite reality of thinking and feeling that moves in what Brian Massumi has called the 'missing half second' of what is too spatiotemporally compressed and, as such, cannot be cognised or represented but only felt.[13] The impasse of digital aesthetics can thereby be phrased as a problem concerning the *infinity* and continuity of thought and sensation against the *finitude* and discreteness of those strategies that want to bind both thinking and feeling into an automated mechanism. From this standpoint, the finitude in question is not only that of the medium or of the tool, in their historical and material instantiations, but also that of the inherent limitations of formal sciences and of those disciplines that attempt to channel the continuity of thinking and feeling into a self-contained structure of reasoning. This claim can be expanded by phrasing the impasse between aesthetics-as-aisthesis and the digital as an impasse concerning the dynamism and generative power of life as opposed to the static nature of the formal, finite, and binary means through which the digital machine harnesses the living and the lived. The richness and density of sensation, at the core of aesthetics-as-aisthesis, is thus in conflict with the digital machine, understood as both product and producer of cognitive and logocentric abstractions.

In conclusion, this aesthetic deadlock is a contest that is to be fought in an ontological ring: the competition is between the indeterminacy of the lived and the determinism that the digital machine needs in order to operate and function. From this perspective, what seems more challenging is the relationship between the separateness attributed to formal abstraction (as a procedural technique or a method considered to be the norm of reasoning, and therefore also of the information processing that digitality stands for) and the viscosity of life and perceptive experience. Finally, identifying the impasse between continuity and discreteness emphasises the sense in which an attempt to describe what an aesthetics of the digital might be and might do implies a commitment to determining the ontological conditions of the real. It thus requires us to assess whether the digital can indeed be a character of these conditions, and if so, how.

AESTHETIC FLUX, LOGICAL MATRIX

The impasse between continuity and discreteness in digital aesthetics emerges from, but also reshapes, previous issues in the critical assessment of digital media. Stressing the occurrence of this impasse can thereby illuminate digital culture's present, but it can also advance new perspectives on its past. For instance, the aesthetic deadlock between the continuous indeterminacies of life and the discrete determinism of digital technology inherits late twentieth-century cybercultural elaborations of the eternal debate about the integration or separation of body and mind, technoscientific discussions about the nature-culture divide, and views as to the possibility of overcoming such oppositions. Yet, in my opinion, worries about losing the body in what science fiction famously described as a cyberspace wherein 'there were no shadows',[14] as well as concerns about authenticity and simulation, are subordinated to the key challenge of accounting for the ontological gap between analogue experience and digital abstraction. This is because the crux of the contemporary conceptual debate about digitality is moving towards more structural problematisations of the digital condition. Of course, the problem of corporeality in relation to digitality is not being discarded as a whole. This and similar issues have, however, assumed more systemic nuances. It is possible, then, to return to the impasse between continuity and discreteness and to read searches for an incarnated experience of the digital from this standpoint.

For example, a perceptual or experiential continuum is also envisaged by *phenomenological* perspectives on digitality, according to which digital phenomena cannot be explained by their subjective or objective components alone, but rather by the continuity of intentional experience. These views, which range across a variety of disciplines investigating and working with the digital, borrow from the tradition of phenomenology (i.e., the philosophical investigation of the origin and meaning of first-person experience) in order to describe digital practices in terms of their intentionality. Generally speaking, phenomenology observes and describes sensuous and intellectual experiences in order to determine the criteria of existence of abstract entities (proprieties, meanings, concepts, etc.) and to thus legitimate the objectivity of phenomena. Such a phenomenological framework has entered science, technology, and media studies, partly via Hubert Dreyfus's Heideggerian critique of artificial intelligence, and via the influence that Dreyfus's critique has had on cognitive sciences and computing.[15] Phenomenologically oriented approaches to the digital thus focus on a holistic validation of what the ubiquitous computing pioneer Mark Weiser described as a 'calm technology' (namely, informational devices that engage with the full complexity around and within the system by digitally connecting things in the world as seamlessly as possible).[16] In the field of human-computer interaction, this phenomenological holism means that designers focus on the ways in which digital systems are manifest in the environment. In artificial intelligence research, the same phenomenological holism implies an attention to the embeddedness of mental activity, while in new media art it gives a special role to the user as a participant in the construction of the artistic production. Within these approaches, notions such as embodiment and interaction become significant factors in defining the uses of the digital and in evaluating the syntax of human-machine relations. Digitality's acclaimed feature of interactivity is then commonly specified as the systemic coupling of an environment with what Mark B. N. Hansen, for instance, has described as a 'body-in-code'; that is, a body whose embodiment is realised in association with technics.[17] This body-in-code is explicitly a *corps phénoménal*: it is primarily concerned with how it is perceived and acted, a source of intentionality and consciousness, and a ground for the phenomenological disclosure of the world.[18] Such a systemic coupling is, in turn, to be performatively mirrored in the relationship between the participant/user on the one hand and the work/product on the other.

From this phenomenological point of view, interactive and embodied digital structures (whether artistic compositions, commercial products, or industrial applications) are technologies of the context. This is to say that they are considered as always having been constructed within an environment and are addressed in relation to the modes of presentation and of participation with their users that they entail. In this sense, these phenomenological approaches draw partly on the *enactivist* idea that knowledge cannot be passively absorbed but must be actively situated within the agent's system, and that it must also be in contact with the world. The phenomenological continuum of these approaches is then the continuity of phenomenology's notion of 'being-in-the-world'.[19] To put this otherwise, the phenomenological continuum is the meaningful and rich continuity of an intentional relation between the perceiver and the perceived, the actor and the acted out. Phenomenological continuity describes a reflexive link among tools, those who use these tools, and the environment in which they are used. The continuity of such reflexive relations is attributed to the directness or self-presence of situations and objects to our intellectual and perceptual experiencing. Such an experiential and reflexive continuum is, to a great extent, different from Deleuze's continuity, which is not phenomenological, hermeneutical, or psychological, but metaphysical. More precisely, Deleuze's metaphysical continuum is a qualitative field of differentiation, requiring that the conditions and the conditioned of such dynamics of difference are not diverse in kind but in degree, thus entailing the *univocity of being*. Continuity is then predicated on the variation of an infinite multiplicity of elements into the univocal plane of being. The infinite plane of transformation is, from a Deleuzian perspective, life itself. This is neither the life of the self nor any other particular life in the world. Rather, Deleuze talked of 'a life',[20] in the sense of a field of potential realisation that is impersonal, indefinite, and subjectless. 'A life' is never completely specified and never separated from its unactualised conditions.

Having seen the dissimilarity between the phenomenological and the Deleuzian continuum, it can now be made explicit that, although other types of aesthetics of continuity are conceivable, the setting of the impasse between continuity and discreteness introduced above still remains distinctly Deleuzian, precisely as a result of this ontological characterisation. Put simply, I am claiming that the impasse between continuity and discreteness in digital aesthetics is about ontology. My aim is to overcome that impasse. I do not accept the arguably Deleuzian conclusion that an aesthetics of digitality is a contradiction in terms, and I will attempt to show that an aesthetics of the digital is indeed possible. In order to do that, however, I need to move on the ontological level of the debate that the Deleuzian framework so importantly sets out. As a way of summarising what has been claimed so far, the present situation for digital aesthetics can now be rephrased in terms of a contradiction. On the one hand, we are witness to the discretisation of experiences, behaviours, perceptions, actions, and thoughts that the digital has brought forth through the softwarisation of media.[21] The pervasive use of digital technology means that there are few operations and activities today, from reading to buying and talking, that are not entangled, at least to some degree, with informational mechanisms of discretisation. On the other hand, however, we see that aesthetic investigations of the digital might have been successful in addressing the experiential appreciation of digital practices or digital phenomena, yet still arguably break down at a conceptual level when trying to cope with the discreteness of the digital itself. In my view, this is due to the fundamental disparity between ontologies of the discrete and ontologies of continuity. The impasse between continuity and discreteness is then a useful model that allows us to frame this paradoxical situation, and also to tie together different facets and nuances of contemporary digital discretisation under the rubric of the question concerning the possibility of an aesthetics of such discretising technologies.

An *aisthesis of the digital* of Deleuzian inspiration would answer that question in a manner that would afford this possibility. Following Deleuze's ontological characterisation of aisthesis, it is not the body or the subject uniquely but the sensible in general that rises to the role of the recorder or the 'transducer' (to appropriate a Simondonian vocabulary) of experience. In an aisthesis of the digital, this central role of sensibility is also maintained and applied to the digital realm: the sensible becomes key to shaping the arrangement of human-machine relations by bringing the continuous movement of variation into what is static and finite, such as the digital machine. The sensible here might be the human user in her interaction with the machine. However, in a non-anthropocentric fashion, and in a move to surpass the phenomenology of the self, the sensible also includes the material residues of the social, the cultural, and the economic milieux as these entwine with the technological and the informational. In an aisthesis of the digital, the qualitative thus remains superior to the quantitative. The risk, in this respect, is that the specifically discrete and logico-mathematical nature of the digital (in fact, the specific way of systematising reality that is proper to it) is bypassed in favour of the qualities of the situations that digital information deals with. On the aisthetic view, the quantitative abstractions of digital technology must be brought back to the qualitative plane. This qualitative transduction is understood as a necessary conceptual manoeuvre if one is to think the ontological conditions for a digital aisthesis; such a manoeuvre, moreover, also fits with what Nigel Thrift has called 'qualculation'—namely, a new 'calculative sense' in which contemporary modes of calculation (such as digital technology) have acquired a qualitative dimension. [22]

I wish to claim, in the light of these issues, that the impasse between continuity and discreteness, framed in its Deleuzian context, should be translated into a defeat of the relation between the aesthetic and the logical. As a result of this setback, it is the logico-quantitative character of digital technology that is adjusted to be more aesthetic, and this is done by loosening up what is more specific to it: discreteness. This is in part a theoretical operation that is considered to be essential for thinking the digital aesthetically. However, in this respect too, the paradox returns, and one might wonder whether an aisthesis of the digital is really an aesthetics of discreteness; in other words, the difficulty of thinking discreteness and aesthetics together, like the difficulty of thinking a sensibility of such discretisation, remains in place. In my view, we should not accept this defeat of the relation between the aesthetic and the logical. Instead, we should explore the possibility of healing this fracture. In order to understand the circumstances for this possible reconciliation between the aesthetic and the logical, we should interpret the failure of their relation in terms of the incompatibility of two divergent understandings of the structure of the real. Aesthetics, in the etymological sense of aisthesis developed by Deleuze, has to do with perception, sensation, and the thinking that originates from this metaphysical plane of sensibility. From the perspective of aisthesis, in its Deleuzian use, the real is an unstable *flux* of change, micro-variations, modulations, and differentiations to be felt, not cognised. For logic, instead, the real is a fixed *matrix* of discrete points, arranged in chains of premises and consequences. Here, of course, I am using the term 'logic' not in the Deleuzian sense of the absolute differentiation of vitalistically creative movements of thought that are able to account for the production of multiplicities. The defeat of logic is instead the setback of the more traditional rational and rationalist discipline that codifies the inferential principles of valid reasoning into preset norms for prediction and validation. I am also including, in this science of valid reasoning, the formal operativity of the digital device, geared towards problem solving and the fulfilment of specific tasks.

If this *logos* that pushes for a discrete rationing of the world is aesthetically defeated, then this is because, from an aisthetic perspective, the matrix into which formal logic transforms reality affords no room for the production of *novelty*. The formal and symbolic logic of the digital machine is a cognitive abstraction that returns, as output, only what one has put in as an input. Aisthetically, novelty is instead produced in the matter-flow of sensibility. This matter-flow is an energetic transformation of 'pure productivity', [23] which cannot be pinpointed or anchored, and which can 'only be *followed*'. [24] For Deleuze, novelty is the Nietzschean enigma of atemporal genesis, towards which thought points. [25] The production of the new, as the result of an act of creation, is however also 'a fundamentally material *and* aesthetic process', insofar as it concerns the 'construction of sensible aggregates that are themselves creative'.[26] Deleuze's new is, 'in other words, difference', which 'calls forth forces in thought which are not the forces of recognition'.[27] Novelty, according to a Deleuzian aisthetic framework, belongs to continuity, not to discreteness.

Here is yet another problematic node that the Deleuzian setting of the impasse between continuity and discreteness brings to the fore: the digital would seem to be excluded from the production of the new on the basis of its automated repetition of the preprogrammed. Working through possibilities and probabilities, the digital is a way of recognising through prediction. Supposedly no new thought as well as no new being can be produced, because everything is already set up; in the digital machine, there is a lot of iteration and repetition, but no differentiation. For this reason, when seen from a Deleuzian perspective, the digital has no *potentiality*.

SENSATION, THOUGHT, EXPERIENCE

The claim that the digital is devoid of potentiality is part of Brian Massumi's famous thesis about the *superiority of the analogue*.[28] The superiority that Massumi refers to is ontological and should be understood in relation to Deleuze's belief in the metaphysical supremacy of the continuous over the discrete. Massumi's argument refers directly to Deleuze's characterisation of the notion of *virtuality*, so an explanation of this concept is necessary. Objecting to the confinement of the real within the realm of actual representable things, Deleuze made the virtual the transcendental condition of experience. This means that, against Kant, Deleuze purged the transcendental of any reference to the consciousness of a subject and made it a *genetic* (that is, productive) field of conditions of experience. The ontological continuity upon which Deleuze's philosophy and aesthetics are based is that same field of immanent production. The continuum is the transcendental condition of past, present, and future experience. The continuum is the virtual.

Returning now to his claim concerning the superiority of the analogue, Massumi develops this argument by setting out the relationship between virtuality and the perception of a field of continuity within the context of late-capitalist information society. While the word 'virtual' has often been degraded into a synonym for 'unreal', 'artificial', or 'simulated', Massumi stresses that, although the virtual field lacks any reference to the identity of representation, it does not lack reality. Deleuze's virtuality is an unexhausted changing mass of relations in becoming that can never be humanly grasped in their entirety, let alone rendered through digital technologies. As in the well-known topological example of the doughnut that, by expanding and compressing, turns itself into a cup, the virtual has a continuous inside and outside, constantly invented through the affordances of the flow of its immanent action. According to this view, the digital, on the other hand, is always oriented towards what is already coded. It combines and systematises the possible and the probable, because only possibility and probability can be approached quantitatively and codified. Massumi explains processes of quantification and codification as operations that are unable to catch the continuity of life's transformation and that can only approximate the virtual. The analogue is thereby superior by virtue of its capacity to be a pure potentiality in becoming and to connect the digital to the virtual of non-cognitive relationality. Since the digital is 'a numeric way of arraying alternative states so that they can be sequenced into a set of alternative routines',[29] it is excluded from what the neuroscientist Antonio Damasio called 'the feeling of what happens'[30] and removed from any experiential value.

Ironically and by contrast, the promise of new experiences is an attractive attribute of digitality, and, similarly, parameters of novelty are often stressed in digital media studies. In this respect, the discussion of the impasse between continuity and discreteness helps us to bring this rhetoric of novelty to another level of discussion, pertaining to the question of whether the digital is capable of ontological production. From the aisthetic perspective, which I am characterising here as a Deleuze-inspired standpoint, novelty concerns the activity of conception-perception. In other words, it concerns both thinking and feeling as *ontogenetic* activities (i.e., activities that generate being). This point has already been introduced: for Deleuze, aesthetics is not only about feeling, but about thinking too. I can add now that this thought, however, is of a particular kind: it is non-cognitive, apersonal, and irreducible to a single content, a single origin, or a single experience of it. The best way to describe it is to call it *abstract thought* or indeed *virtual thought*.

Deleuze divorced the ontological conditions of the abstract from cognitive functions. For Deleuze, the separation between an ontological and an epistemological plane must be dissolved in order to leave room for 'a new image of the act of thought, its functioning, its genesis in thought itself'.[31] Abstract thought is a type of thinking that does not belong to somebody; it is unbounded, immediate, and indeterminate; and, most importantly, it does not represent anything. Abstract thought is self-positing and self-affirming. This means, against the representational character of Descartes's *cogito* and Kant's faculty of reasoning, that Deleuze's abstract thought is already posited when one emerges as a subject of that thought, and that this subject cannot be identified as the source of such positing. From this Deleuzian standpoint, cognitive functions are secondary to the activity of thinking, understood as an expression of the virtual indeterminacy of the sensible. Suggestively, Deleuze affirmed that the 'theory of thought is like painting: it needs that revolution which took art from representation to abstraction'.[32] The central operation that Deleuze carried out in relation to thought is thus to separate thinking from any specifically mental denotation and make it an immanent expression of the ontological inventiveness of the sensible. Deleuze took the abstract from the exclusive domain of the cognitive and plunged it into the metaphysically productive realm of sensibility. 'Something in the world forces us to think.'[33] This encounter, which triggers thought and which stands as thought's starting condition, is not an encounter with a sensible being or with the result of sense experience as such. Rather, this is the encounter with 'the being *of* the sensible'.[34] In other words, that which can only be sensed as an intensive difference that precedes the categorical unity of the intellect. The abstract is thereby not merely an intellectual judgement and universalising activity of generalisation or *sensus communis*, nor is it a metaphor or an illusion. It is a dimension of ideality or, again, of pure virtuality, which is—to use one of Deleuze's expressions—*abstract yet real*.

Significantly, the Deleuzian aesthetics of what Massumi called the 'thinking-feeling' is about *intensity*,[35] which is the qualitative condition of multiplicities that invent and express being, but which cannot be counted because they are not extended. Deleuze believed that 'it is always by means of an intensity that thought comes to us'.[36] This is the reason why aesthetics is so important for Deleuze: with its focus on sensory knowledge, aesthetics-as-aisthesis can record change beyond measurement, via the intensive force of *affect*. Following a Spinozist conceptual lineage, affect is defined by Deleuze as 'the continuous variation of the force of existing, insofar as this variation is determined by the ideas one has'.[37] Affect is a registration of change, a 'lived transition' or a 'lived passage'. This passage is 'determined by ideas', yet 'in itself it does not consist in an idea' or in their 'intellectual comparison'.[38] For Deleuze, aesthetics can account for thinking outside cognitive structures because affect is already a legitimate modality of what we could call *sensible thought*. Drawing again on Spinoza's metaphysics, Deleuze described affects and ideas as two different modes of thought. While an idea has some defined and characteristic representational features, an affect is a bodily mode of thought that does not resemble or represent anything. According to this Deleuzo-Spinozist framework, affectivity constitutes the most prominent character of experiencing. Experience is addressed here not in the Humean terms of *sense experience* (understood as the traditional empiricist accumulation of clear-cut facts), for the senses, according to Deleuze, are a result of the affective process. Deleuze's experience, however, is neither the *possible experience* of Kant's critical philosophy, insofar as the latter is always pushing outside itself in order to extend the pursuit of knowledge by virtue of the a priori categories of understanding, which make experiencing coherent, structured, and subjected to representation. In contrast, Deleuze talked of *real experience*; that is to say, he addressed experience as the composition of real elements and eventualities that lead to the generation of a certain state of affairs.

Real experience, for Deleuze, is an unmediated and subrepresentational immersion in the plane of immanence of thought and sensation. When one falls into such experience, one feels and thinks without knowing representationally or cognitively. Aesthetics is concerned with this immersion. The conditions of experience are not determined in concepts but in percepts, and aesthetics is the science of sensation that deals with these percepts.[39] Deleuze's aesthetics is thus an access to experience that is never subordinated to representation, but in which both thinking and feeling are operating before and outside the mesh of cognitive organisation. One feels and one thinks, and only then does one understand. Experience is always aesthetic because it is about the affective indeterminacy of thinking-feelings and calls for us to subtract ourselves from the fixed actual singularities of being until one is dispersed into the virtual becoming of the lived.

Such a Deleuzian conception of experience as an access to the virtual distribution of intensities can be related interestingly, and on multiple levels, to aesthetic theories of digital technology. What is often referred to as the *affective turn* in contemporary cultural theory has found occasions for successful development, and much speculative vigour, in digital media theory.[40] In its Spinozist-Deleuzian lineage, the notion of affect can function as an optimal conceptual vehicle for giving ontological credit to inorganic, non-human realities, thus following the Deleuzian injunction to make expressivity and affectivity 'available to things'.[41] Often, this turn to affect has coincided with the revival of metaphysical notions of matter and proposed an approach that does not aim to reduce technology to an effect of the organisation of human practices, but rather sees the technological medium as incessantly reinventing its own material conditions of existence. The affective turn in media theory has thus fruitfully engaged with digitality's abstract modes of processing. The assumption is that, while the digital does not exhaust the virtuality of the real, it is nonetheless entangled with it through the sensibilities and intensities in which it partakes. Although it is definitely materialist, this affective perspective does not, however, reduce matter to a specific corporeal definition, nor does it explain a body through its organs and functions. A body can indeed be anything. A sound, a speed, a virus, a vibration: 'every relationship of forces constitutes a body',[42] and its structure is expressed by the interplay of the affects that it is capable of producing.

From such an affective standpoint, the digital can be interwoven or associated with this material structure as long as it enters into the composition of its relations and distributions of virtual potentials. The affective turn in digital media theory thus focuses on the modes in which this composition is possible and becomes lived in occasions such as those provided by design,[43] literature and poetry,[44] architecture,[45] biomedia and biotechnology,[46] com-

puter simulations,[47] new media and software art,[48] human-computer interfaces,[49] film and screen cultures,[50] sound,[51] movement and dance,[52] and the
technological mediation of time.[53] These arenas and objects of enquiry,
among many others, have been reconsidered through the lenses of what
Timothy Murray has called a 'Digital Deleuze',[54] thanks to interdisciplinary
scholarly debates that have both advocated and advanced the possibility of
such a digital reading of Deleuze's philosophy of affective intensities. On
this view, if digital technology is radically changing the way in which we
perceive and experience, then this is partly because it contributes to the
production of affects and movements of thought, whenever the virtual receives and registers the information, data, and inputs/outputs that the digital
machine produces.

The notion of affect has, therefore, become key to thinking the technological beyond human subjectivity and receptivity. Significantly, the turn to
affect in digital studies has also helped us to think what such a 'non-representational theory' of computational media might be,[55] away from what media
signify or communicate, and more in terms of what they do (that is, in terms
of their affects/effects). This affective turn in media theory streams into
contextual debates about modes of control, consumption, and production in
informational societies and their economies of 'immaterial labour'.[56] These
are modes that are said to exploit the affective because they invest the constitution of subjectivities and collectivities at a non-cognitive and intensive
level. Moving now to a more technological level, the aesthetic-affective attention to the non-representational side of digitality can also be seen to correspond to the cross-disciplinary call to engage with the 'material poiesis of
informatics',[57] which has enabled a vast variety of practice-based research
landscapes and practical applications to establish and flourish. For instance,
tangible and wearable computing, interactive architecture, physical computing, and body-area networking study computer-mediated environments, together with the use of hybrid computational-physical materials, so as to
recreate states of intensity along the spectrum of the scales of sensible variations between the human body, the machine body, and all the infinitesimal
steps in between.

Both in respect to theory and practice, then, the affective turn can be read
as an attempt to engage with the claim as to the superiority of the analogue.
Interestingly, Steve Goodman comments that Massumi's argument about the
superiority of the analogue should not be taken as an 'antidigital phenomenology'. Instead, the rationale behind that provocative assertion is to push for
a rigorous theorisation of 'the enfolded nexus' of the analogue and digital.
The challenge that Massumi's thesis presents to cultural theory and philosophy is thus that of asking 'where the potential for invention lies' in both the
analogue and the digital dimension.[58] In response to this, one can note that
the affective turn in new media theory takes up the difficult task of endowing

digitality with its own actual and virtual dimensions, advancing multiple efforts towards experimenting with an aisthesis of the digital. The inclination of digital aisthesis towards translating the quantitative into the qualitative can, in this respect, also be interpreted as an effort to overcome the fact that digital technologies would not seem to allow for the metaphysical dimension of potential relations in becoming proper to the virtual.

Anna Munster, for instance, talks explicitly of 'aesthesia' to describe her aesthetic approach to information technology.[59] It is useful to linger here on her proposition so as to give a concrete example of the way in which the affective turn in new media theory attempts to respond to Massumi's challenge to find where the potential for creation might be within digitality. In her 2006 book *Materializing New Media: Embodiment in Information Aesthetics*, Munster draws largely from a vocabulary and a theoretical background borrowed from the philosophical work of Deleuze in order to propose an alternative aesthetic genealogy for digital culture. Munster focuses on the intersections between material and incorporeal forces engendered by information technologies. She understands digital code as part of a folding movement that operates through a mutual interplay of immediacies, losses, and complexities, and which lies at the juncture of the human-computer interface. Through the notion of *digital embodiment*, Munster proposes a modality for living and experiencing the body within the digital realm, as organic materiality comes into a relation with the speeds of information.

From the perspective of our present discussion, the most attractive aspect of Munster's argument is the fact that she acknowledges a potentiality proper to digitality. The visceral aesthetics that Munster is pursuing is not the result of direct sense-data perception but travels instead at the level of the body-code and is thus irreducible to spatiotemporal coordinates of specific socio-cultural constructions. For Munster, there is always a 'something' that exceeds experience; this surplus cannot be placed at either the level of materiality or that of coding. Such a body-code perceptual unity forms a whole that is greater than any of its parts. The special configurations between information and materiality necessary for digital embodiment aim to disrupt any pregiven formation, as they arise immanently from the outcomes of interaction itself. Having said this, Munster's argument can, however, be used to exemplify some of the problems that one encounters with that attribution of virtual potentiality to digitality. Whenever Munster describes digitality, she gives it the intensive proprieties that Deleuze assigned to the virtual. An important objection could be raised in connection to this operation: Munster's affective aesthetics of the digital could be seen to bypass what the digital is (that is, discrete), on a technical as much as ontological level, in order to focus instead on what the digital is not (i.e., continuity). The enhanced view of materiality that Munster's argumentation puts forward proposes understanding 'the incorporeal vectors of digital information' as perpetual fluxes of related variables.[60] These sets of variables are said to find the reason for their informational existence thanks to their virtual participation in a non-cognitive status that will not be represented, for it always breaks away from rational synthesis. In effect, Munster *virtualises* the digital, thereby making it a negotiable continuum, the existence of which must be assumed if we are to participate in the experiential 'approximate aesthetics' of proximities that Munster longs for.[61] It is thus also the case that, from this perspective, and despite a certain degree of engagement with digital information, the transcendental condition for the real experience of digitality remains in what the digital is *not*: namely, the continuity of immanent life.

Can the digital be virtual, then? Or can the virtual be digital? In *Moving without a Body: Digital Philosophy and Choreographic Thoughts*, Stamatia Portanova has proposed a 'digital philosophy' of virtuality by focusing on what a 'movement of thought' is and what it could become in the days of ubiquitous digitalisation.[62] Portanova lucidly recognises the difficulty of accounting for both discrete rationalisation and continuous affects. She aims to supersede the intuitive equation between movement and continuity by exposing the former as a 'multiplicity of potential cuts',[63] whether these are bits, objects, or steps. Interestingly, Portanova proposes what could be seen as a discretisation of virtuality. Discreteness is reframed as a tendency inherent to virtuality itself. Such a reconceptualisation of the virtual drifts away from Massumi's characterisation of it as affective continuity and instead enlarges the category of the virtual to encompass 'the unlimited potential that every numerical bit of a program, or every experiential bit of a dance (every gesture and step), has to change and be something else'.[64] From this view, 'the creativity of digital technology derives from the abstract but very peculiar potentiality that stands behind its materiality, namely the idea to cut things (into bits, pixels, points, or dots) and recombine them, ad infinitum'.[65]

Ultimately, it could be argued that abstract or virtual thought is concealed behind the actual functioning of the digital machine that lies at the centre of Portanova's speculation. In her account, the digital has a potentiality because it is itself, as 'a complex and visionary mathematical way to think',[66] a modality of such abstract or virtual thought. In this respect, while Portanova's proposition offers a concrete and serious opportunity to consider the discretisation of the digital as producing Deleuzian movements of thought, it should be observed that such virtual digitality is still fundamentally reliant upon the sensible. In other words, the experiences of the digital that Portanova addresses are the result of the Deleuzian principle of *reciprocal determination*. According to this Deleuzian principle, both actuality and virtuality constitute reality. The two realms remain distinct, with no particular law or norm governing their relationship; yet virtuality and actuality always go together, in the sense that the virtual is always tending towards being actualised, just like the actual is always imbued with a virtual indeterminacy that

will not be fully exhausted. For Deleuze, it is affect that registers this reciprocal determination: the transcendental conditions of experience are virtual
forces or vectors that are recorded and lived through within sensation.

I see both this reciprocal determination and the consequent reliance upon
affect in order to transduce such determination to be a problem. This is
because, in my opinion, taking up the challenge of experimenting with the
specificity of digitality involves attending to its logico-quantitative nature
and thus allowing the digital to have a degree of ontological autonomy from
the qualitative and the affective. Digital machines, as will be discussed later
in the book, organise, measure, and quantify the world by means of formal
discretisation. However, when the virtual is treated as the potentiality of the
digital, this logico-quantitative nature of the digital machine is considered, if
not subordinate to, then at least always codetermined with the being of the
sensible, because it is the logic of sensation (and not formal logic) that
expresses virtuality. In this sense, whenever we think of the aesthetic potential of digitality through virtuality, reciprocal determination stops us from
addressing the irreversible specificity of digitality: that of its ontological
identification with discrete quantities, and with the logical structuring of
these quantities through formal operations of deductive abstraction, which
are not codetermined with or by sensibility.

To the question of whether the digital can be virtual, or whether the
virtual can be digital, I can now respond with a further question: should
either be the case? I agree here with Massumi: the digital is not virtual, and
vice versa. My point, however, is that this disparity does not mean that the
digital is in any way ontologically inferior to the analogue. It simply implies
that the digital is something *other* than virtuality and that its potential should
be found elsewhere. I am not, therefore, denying that perception and sensation add an important qualitative processuality to the quantitative elements in
composition in the digital machine. Of course, digital media are part of
sensibility: the situations that they give rise to mesh with those intensive
modes of sociability, perception, and communication that travel through the
micro-scales of affective variation and, therefore, should also be accounted
for on an expressive register, rather than only on a representational one.
Importantly, those positions that stress the virtualisation of digitality emphasise this expressivity and have exerted a significant impact on current debates
in digital culture. Yet it is my contention that, in addition to that qualitative
processuality, the digital process retains a quantitative and logical character
that needs to be addressed as not being subordinated to, or uniquely codetermined with, sensibility. The impasse between continuity and discreteness in
digital aesthetics requires that we complicate the claim that the conditions of
real experiences are played out upon a plane of sensibility in which the
digital cannot partake without its logical and discrete structures being subsumed by the fluxes of affective continuity.

My critique of the affective turn in digital studies, or of theories of the digital that are based around the Spinozist-Deleuzian notion of affect, is consequently straightforward. I do not want to discard or deny the importance of affect or its significance to aesthetics and experiencing. The problem, however, is that we should look for *an experience of digitality* (which, as we will see later in this book, is not just the experience of the user or programmer, but that of the digital itself) and understand that the conditions of this experience are not uniquely derived from the lived and the living, as are those of affect. For Deleuze, the virtual is a way of talking about the non-representational vectorial structuring of the real. If we want to avoid virtualising the digital, the question then becomes, what kind of structuring do we need in order to engage with the conditions of experience of the digital? My claim is that digitality calls for a type of structuring that is actual, discrete, and logical; however, it is also a structuring that needs to be addressed aesthetically, insofar as it is constitutive of the conditions of experience of digitality itself. This structuring pertains to the abstractive formal operations of *computation*.

NOTES

1. These discontinuous values are abstractions from equally discrete electrical impulses, which have only two possible states, *on* and *off*. The mechanical operations of digital systems are also discrete, and so too are the finite steps of algorithmic procedures. Equally, codes, numbers, bits, scripts, instructions, and rules are composed of finite parts or separate unities.

2. The origin of aesthetics, understood in the modern sense of a proper subject of philosophical study, can be traced back to the German philosopher Alexander Gottlieb Baumgarten, who introduced the term in 1735. Baumgarten's 1750 *Aesthetica* is the first work to employ the name of the new area of philosophical study; it presents aesthetics as the science of sensitive cognition, sensuous knowledge, or sensate thinking (in the original Latin, *cognitio sensitiva*), thus echoing the etymological origin of the term. This etymological lineage is retained in Kant's philosophy. Later in the same century, Kant's *Critique of Judgement* (published in 1790) famously made aesthetics a theory of sensibility, as the form of possible experience on the one hand, and the theory of art as a consideration of real experience on the other. Since Hegel's lectures on aesthetics (published in 1835), however, the discipline has assumed the primary meaning of a philosophy of art. This is a conception that has largely remained in place to this day, as aesthetics is now primarily understood as a body of knowledge about art. See Alexander Gottlieb Baumgarten, *Aesthetica* (Hildesheim: G. Olms, 1961); Georg Wilhelm Friedrich Hegel, *Aesthetics: Lectures on Fine Art*, trans. T. M. Knox, 2 vols. (Oxford: Clarendon Press, 1975); Immanuel Kant, *Critique of Judgement*, trans. James Creed Meredith (Oxford: Clarendon Press, 1978).

3. See Gilles Deleuze, 'Postscript on the Societies of Control', *October* 59 (Winter 1992): 3–7.

4. Gilles Deleuze, *Francis Bacon: The Logic of Sensation*, trans. Daniel W. Smith (London: Continuum, 2005).

5. Daniel W. Smith, 'Deleuze's Theory of Sensation: Overcoming the Kantian Duality', in *Deleuze: A Critical Reader*, ed. Paul Patton (Oxford: Blackwell, 1996), 33.

6. Max Horkheimer and Theodor W. Adorno's analysis of the Enlightenment, for instance, discussed 'formalistic reason' as being directly linked through their mutual calculatory and utilitarian ends, and denounced 'instrumental rationality' as a source of domination and social fragmentation. See *Dialectic of Enlightenment*, trans. John Cumming (New York: Herder and Herder, 1972).

7. Against functional, structural, and teleological understandings of technology, Gilbert Simondon stressed the processes, mutations, instabilities, and materialisations of the technical ensemble. See his *Du Mode d'existence des objets techniques* (Paris: Aubier, 1958). For Martin Heidegger, the poetic is ontologically superior to any other type of discourse or abstraction, and art is key to escape the danger of technological nihilism. See 'The Question Concerning Technology', in *The Question Concerning Technology, and Other Essays*, trans. William Lovitt (New York: Harper and Row, 1977). Before Heidegger, Edmund Husserl defended the intersubjective unity of the 'lifeworld' (*Lebenswelt*) against 'the crisis of European sciences', exemplified by the advance of positivism and its quest for the universality of knowledge in terms of mechanical and objective laws. See *The Crisis of European Sciences and Transcendental Phenomenology*, trans. David Carr (Evanston, IL: Northwestern University Press, 1970).

8. While poststructuralism rejects the equation between rationality and emancipation, as well as the self-sufficiency of structures, postmodernism stresses scepticism, subjectivism, and typically unmechanisable tenets such as irony and playfulness. The post-Marxism of writers such as Antonio Negri sees the digital machines of post-Fordism as part of the matrix of rationalisation of modern information societies and knowledge economies. This rationalisation has entirely encompassed lived social praxis through the ubiquity of 'real subsumption'. However, such rationalisation is also held to afford an emancipatory potential. See Michael Hardt and Antonio Negri, *Empire* (Cambridge, MA: Harvard University Press, 2000).

9. Alain Badiou appeals to the transfinite of Georg Cantor in order to ground the claim that mathematics is ontology, and in order to force thinking into transcending the operative scopes of human knowledge. See *Being and Event*, trans. Oliver Feltham (London: Continuum, 2006).

10. See Gilles Deleuze, *Bergsonism*, trans. Hugh Tomlinson and Barbara Habberjam (New York: Zone, 1991). For Deleuze's take on differential calculus, see his book *The Fold: Leibniz and the Baroque*, trans. Tom Conley (London: Continuum, 2006).

11. That is, its power of activity. See Benedict de Spinoza, *Ethics*, trans. James Gutmann (New York: Hafner, 1949), 128.

12. Henri Bergson, *The Creative Mind: An Introduction to Metaphysics*, trans. Mabelle L. Andison (New York: Citadel, 1997), 135.

13. Brian Massumi, *Parables for the Virtual: Movement, Affect, Sensation* (Durham, NC: Duke University Press, 2002), 28.

14. William Gibson, *Mona Lisa Overdrive* (London: HarperCollins, 1994), 269.

15. See Hubert L. Dreyfus, *What Computers Can't Do: The Limits of Artificial Intelligence* (New York: Harper and Row, 1972). For cognitive science, refer to Julian Kiverstein and Mark Wheeler, *Heidegger and Cognitive Science* (Basingstoke: Palgrave Macmillan, 2012); for computing, see Terry Winograd and Fernando Flores, *Understanding Computers and Cognition: A New Foundation for Design* (Norwood, NJ: Ablex, 1986).

16. Mark Weiser and John Seely Brown, 'The Coming Age of Calm Technology', in *Beyond Calculation: The Next Fifty Years of Computing*, ed. Peter J. Denning and Robert M. Metcalfe (New York: Copernicus, 1997), 75–85.

17. Mark B. N. Hansen, *Bodies in Code: Interfaces with Digital Media* (New York: Routledge, 2006), 20.

18. See Maurice Merleau-Ponty's conception of the lived body, which is explained in his *Phenomenology of Perception*, trans. Colin Smith (London: Routledge and Kegan Paul, 1962).

19. See Martin Heidegger, *Being and Time*, trans. John Macquarrie and Edward Robinson (London: SCM, 1962).

20. Gilles Deleuze, 'Immanence: A Life', in *Pure Immanence: Essays on a Life*, trans. Anne Boyman (New York: Zone, 2001), 25–33.

21. Lev Manovich discusses the process of softwarisation of media in *Software Takes Command* (New York: Bloomsbury Academic, 2013).

22. Nigel Thrift, 'Movement-Space: The Changing Domain of Thinking Resulting from the Development of New Kinds of Spatial Awareness', *Economy and Society* 33, no. 4 (2004): 592, https://doi.org/10.1080/0308514042000285305.

23. Gilles Deleuze and Félix Guattari, *A Thousand Plateaus: Capitalism and Schizophrenia*, trans. Brian Massumi (London: Continuum, 2004), 454.

24. Deleuze and Guattari, *A Thousand Plateaus*, 451.

25. 'As Nietzsche succeeded in making us understand, thought is creation, not will to truth.' Gilles Deleuze and Félix Guattari, *What Is Philosophy?*, trans. Graham Burchell and Hugh Tomlinson (London: Verso, 1994), 54.

26. Simon O'Sullivan and Stephen Zepke, 'Introduction: The Production of the New', in *Deleuze, Guattari, and the Production of the New*, ed. Simon O'Sullivan and Stephen Zepke (London: Continuum, 2008), 3.

27. Gilles Deleuze, *Difference and Repetition*, trans. Paul Patton (London: Continuum, 2004), 172.

28. See Massumi, *Parables for the Virtual*, 133–43.

29. Massumi, *Parables for the Virtual*, 137.

30. Antonio R. Damasio, *The Feeling of What Happens: Body and Emotion in the Making of Consciousness* (London: W. Heinemann, 2000).

31. Gilles Deleuze, 'On Nietzsche and the Image of Thought', in *Desert Islands and Other Texts, 1953–1974*, ed. David Lapoujade, trans. Michael Taormina (Los Angeles: Semiotexte, 2004), 140.

32. Deleuze, *Difference and Repetition*, 346.

33. Deleuze, *Difference and Repetition*, 176.

34. Deleuze, *Difference and Repetition*, 176.

35. Brian Massumi, *Semblance and Event: Activist Philosophy and the Occurent Arts* (Cambridge, MA: MIT Press, 2011), 39.

36. Deleuze, *Difference and Repetition*, 182. It might be interesting to add, as a contextualisation, that in physics an *intensive quantity* is defined as a physical quantity whose value is not dependent on the amount of the substance for which it is measured. While, for example, the mass of an object is an extensive quantity, density is an intensive property of a substance.

37. Gilles Deleuze, 'Cours Vincennes: Spinoza; 24/01/1978' (lecture, University of Paris 8, Vincennes, 24 January 1978), trans. Timothy S. Murphy, http://www.webdeleuze.com/php/texte.php?cle=14&groupe=Spinoza&langue=2.

38. Deleuze, 'Cours Vincennes: Spinoza; 24/01/1978'. In the geometrical portrait of life depicted in Spinoza's *Ethics*, affection/*affectio* regards the condition of the affected body and implies the presence and the action of an affecting body. Affect/*affectus*, on the other hand, concerns the transition—or the movement—from one state to another in the affected body. See Gilles Deleuze, *Spinoza: Practical Philosophy*, trans. Robert Hurley (San Francisco: City Lights, 1988), 48–49.

39. Dorothea Olkowski comments that it is possible to characterise 'every aspect of Deleuze's work as aesthetics or as in some manner grounded in aesthetics'. See her chapter 'Deleuze's Aesthetics of Sensation', in *The Cambridge Companion to Deleuze*, ed. Daniel W. Smith and Henry Somers-Hall (Cambridge: Cambridge University Press, 2012), 265. Pointing back to Kant, but correcting and reforming the Kantian transcendental argument, Deleuze argued that 'aesthetics suffers from a wrenching duality'. On the one hand, 'it designates the theory of sensibility as the form of possible experience', while on the other 'it designates the theory of art as the reflection of real experience'. 'For these two meanings to be tied together,' Deleuze continued, 'the conditions of experience in general must become conditions of real experience; in this case, the work of art would really appear as experimentation.' *The Logic of Sense*, ed. Constantin V. Boundas, trans. Mark Lester with Charles Stivale (London: Continuum, 2004), 297–98. This is also discussed by Steven Shaviro in his 2007 essay 'The "Wrenching Duality" of Aesthetics: Kant, Deleuze, and the "Theory of the Sensible"', which is available online at http://www.shaviro.com/Othertexts/SPEP.pdf. See also Smith, 'Deleuze's Theory of Sensation: Overcoming the Kantian Duality'; Stephen Zagala, 'Aesthetics: A Place I've Never Seen', in *A Shock to Thought: Expression after Deleuze and Guattari*, ed. Brian Massumi (London: Routledge, 2002), 20–43.

40. For an overview of the affective turn in the humanities and social sciences, see Patricia Ticineto Clough and Jean Halle, eds., *The Affective Turn: Theorizing the Social* (Durham, NC: Duke University Press, 2007).

41. Gilles Deleuze, *Cinema 1: The Movement-Image*, trans. Hugh Tomlinson and Barbara Habberjam (London: Continuum, 2005), 99.

42. Gilles Deleuze, *Nietzsche and Philosophy*, trans. Hugh Tomlinson (London: Continuum, 2006), 37.

43. See Betti Marenko, 'Digital Materiality, Morphogenesis and the Intelligence of the Technodigital Object', in *Deleuze and Design*, ed. Betti Marenko and Jamie Brassett (Edinburgh: Edinburgh University Press, 2015), 107–38.

44. For instance, as proposed by Claire Colebrook in *Blake, Deleuzian Aesthetics, and the Digital* (London: Continuum, 2012).

45. See Elizabeth Grosz, *Architecture from the Outside: Essays on Virtual and Real Space* (Cambridge, MA: MIT Press, 2001); Brian Massumi, 'Sensing the Virtual, Building the Insensible', in 'Hypersurface Architecture', ed. Stephen Perrella, special issue, *Architectural Design* 68, nos. 5–6 (May–June 1998): 16–24.

46. See Patricia T. Clough, 'The Affective Turn: Political Economy, Biomedia, and Bodies', in *The Affect Theory Reader*, ed. Melissa Gregg and Gregory J. Seigworth (Durham, NC: Duke University Press, 2010), 207–25; see also Luciana Parisi, *Abstract Sex: Philosophy, Bio-Technology and the Mutations of Desire* (London: Continuum, 2004).

47. Manuel DeLanda engages with this topic in *Philosophy and Simulation: The Emergence of Synthetic Reason* (London: Continuum, 2011).

48. See Anna Munster, *Materializing New Media: Embodiment in Information Aesthetics* (Hanover, NH: Dartmouth College Press, 2006); Timothy Murray, *Digital Baroque: New Media Art and Cinematic Folds* (Minneapolis: University of Minnesota Press, 2008).

49. Refer to, for instance, Mark B. N. Hansen's article 'Affect as Medium, or the "Digital-Facial-Image"', *Journal of Visual Culture* 2, no. 2 (August 2003): 205–28, https://doi.org/10. 1177/14704129030022004.

50. See Patricia Pisters, *The Neuro-Image: A Deleuzian Film-Philosophy of Digital Screen Culture* (Stanford, CA: Stanford University Press, 2012).

51. Sound and digital culture are addressed from an affective standpoint in Steve Goodman's *Sonic Warfare: Sound, Affect, and the Ecology of Fear* (Cambridge, MA: MIT Press, 2010).

52. Refer to Erin Manning's book *Relationscapes: Movement, Art, Philosophy* (Cambridge, MA: MIT Press, 2009).

53. See Timothy Scott Barker, *Time and the Digital: Connecting Technology, Aesthetics, and a Process Philosophy of Time* (Hanover, NH: Dartmouth College Press, 2012).

54. Timothy Murray, 'Like a Prosthesis: Critical Performance à Digital Deleuze', in *Deleuze and Performance*, ed. Laura Cull (Edinburgh: Edinburgh University Press, 2009), 203–20.

55. Nigel Thrift, *Non-Representational Theory: Space, Politics, Affect* (London: Routledge, 2008).

56. Maurizio Lazzarato, 'Immaterial Labour', in *Radical Thought in Italy: A Potential Politics*, ed. Paolo Virno and Michael Hardt, trans. Paul Colilli and Ed Emery (Minneapolis: University of Minnesota Press, 1996), 133–46.

57. Phillip Thurtle and Robert Mitchell, 'Data Made Flesh: The Material Poiesis of Informatics', in *Data Made Flesh: Embodying Information*, ed. Robert Mitchell and Phillip Thurtle (New York: Routledge, 2004), 2.

58. Goodman, *Sonic Warfare*, 118.

59. Anna Munster, *An Aesthesia of Networks: Conjunctive Experience in Art and Technology* (Cambridge, MA: MIT Press, 2013).

60. Munster, *Materializing New Media*, 19.

61. See Anna Munster, 'Digitality: Approximate Aesthetics', in *Life in the Wires: The CTheory Reader*, ed. Arthur Kroker and Marilouise Kroker (Victoria, Canada: NWP/CTheory, 2004), 415–29.

62. Stamatia Portanova, *Moving without a Body: Digital Philosophy and Choreographic Thoughts* (Cambridge, MA: MIT Press, 2013).

63. Portanova, *Moving without a Body*, 3.
64. Portanova, *Moving without a Body*, 9.
65. Portanova, *Moving without a Body*, 8.
66. Portanova, *Moving without a Body*, 15.

Chapter Two

Computation

ABSTRACTION AND ABSTRACTNESS

The computational is not synonymous with the digital. The computational is best described as the problem-solving modus operandi of those digital informational systems that make much of the contemporary world possible. The digital, however, should be understood as a reliable and efficient technology of automating, distributing, and managing the computational method via the representation and processing of data as discontinuous values. Although enhanced, inflated, and stretched out by digitality, computation is not exhausted by the digital devices that it underpins and enables, nor is it confined to a past, present, or future technology.

While the technical understanding of computation is constantly renegotiated,[1] it could be said that, strictly speaking, 'to compute' means 'to calculate'. Throughout history, computation has taken many forms, and digital computers are only its latest, and not its last, incarnation. From the abacus to counting sheep, from the tools used to read the skies to those used to navigate the seas, to compute involves systematising the real through quantitative abstractions. To compute is to organise the world, to measure it, to quantify it, to rationalise it, and to arrange it via logico-quantitative means. Undoubtedly, the twentieth century has witnessed an unmatched acceleration of the capacities and affordances of these systematising operations. The formalisation of the notion of computability, as advanced, for instance, in the seminal independent propositions of Alonzo Church, Emil Post, and Alan Turing, was crucial to this.[2] These propositions stressed the importance of formalising calculation, as well as the importance of founding the notion of computation mathematically. The models of computation that they proposed have also been found to be equivalent, in the sense that what can be computed with one model can be computed with the others too. However, it is Turing's proposition that has been successfully translated, via different but convergent design efforts, into actual finite-state machines such as the electronic digital binary computer. The twentieth-century acceleration of the capacities and affordances of calculative operations has then culminated in the mass-scale commercialisation, distribution, and miniaturisation of these machines, which we have observed in the past seventy years or so.

The computational is a broader category than the digital, but, nonetheless, both are based upon the discrete operations of counting, measuring, and quantifying. This common discrete nature precedes the formal instantiation of computation into a finite-state machine like the computer. This instantiation, however, reflects the affinity of the principles involved: both the computational and the digital rely upon the *discretisation of reality*. The digital is a technique of information processing that represents and manages data in the form of digits, such as, for instance, the zeros and ones of digital binary systems. In the computational, discreteness is similarly expressed via quantifying means, such as models, procedures, representations, symbols, numbers, measures, and formulisations. When we compute—digitally or not—we arrange reality into sets of abstracted relations between these quantifiable entities. Both these entities and these relations can be logically manipulated to give an output in response to an input. The activity of computing is, therefore, much more than the mere crunching of numbers: a computing machine is a 'metamedium',[3] for 'it can represent most other media while augmenting them with many new properties'.[4] These accomplishments rely upon the fundamental discretising nature of computation. A computer can do anything that can be put into the finite and defined terms of executable instructions that are divided into a sequential number of finite steps.

The activity of computation has been equated, via the twentieth-century explorations of the notion of computability, to that of discretising a task into the algorithmic form of a rule-governed activity that can be addressed as a sequential succession of countable, separable, and finite steps. This is how we should read the Turing machine, which Alan Turing proposed as a mental experiment in 1936, and which has long served as the ideal model of the computing device. Turing's computational method will be addressed at length in the second part of this book. Suffice it to say here that the rule-based decisions that characterise Turing's notion of computability are also modes of discretising the real, and so too are the procedural steps that this model employs when addressing problems and tasks, so as to deal with them in algorithmic terms. From a technical perspective, computation is thus a method of manipulating quantifiable entities into a finite sequence of procedures. In this sense, the discretisations of computation recall the discretisations of mathematics and logic, but also go beyond them, for they become a means through which they can be effectively functional (that is, a means through which they can take decisions efficiently and in a limited amount of time).

In this book, I will try to demonstrate that, if we engage with computation's discrete systematisation of the real, we can grasp and also supersede the ontological impasse that characterises contemporary digital aesthetics. Admittedly, this may seem a rather roundabout route to take towards my objective. After all, one could suppose that in order to address digital aesthetics, one should focus on the digital per se. An investigation into the nature of computational procedures, however, is a crucial prerequisite for any such enquiry, inasmuch as the computational method is the functioning principle behind current digital media. Addressing the computational should be seen, therefore, as validating an argument for the *medium specificity* of the aesthetics of the digital. The digital machine is a computing machine, and it is precisely this computational character that gives it its logico-quantitative specificity. In this respect, it is possible to say that a digital aesthetics is, fundamentally, a *computational aesthetics*.[5] Most importantly, however, finding and founding the specificity of the digital in the computational offers a means to advance the prospect of repairing the fracture between logic and aesthetics. Digital media, insofar as they are computational, are technologies with a systematising and rationalising capacity. This should be considered when attempting to account for an aesthetics of such media. Turning attention from the digital to the computational thus provides a way of bringing the systematisations and rationalisations that are proper to the calculative activities of computation back into the aesthetic investigation. The question that needs to be addressed is whether such computational calculative operations have an aesthetic legitimacy in their own right.

It is my contention that computation systematises reality through *abstractive* operations. In my view, these abstractive operations are not a reduction and negation of *abstract* indeterminacy. I am differentiating here between *abstraction* and *abstractness*. Admittedly, in English, the conceptual separation that I am proposing might be confusing, because the terms 'abstraction' and 'abstractness' could be understood as dimensions of the same general concept of the abstract. My point, however, is that they are not. The noun 'abstraction' and its cognate adjective 'abstractive' will be employed here to denote an operation geared towards *determination*. On the other hand, 'abstractness' and the derivative adjective 'abstract' are used to signify an *indeterminate* dimension. Although he did not introduce it himself, I have developed this distinction between the two sets of terms from my reading of Deleuze. For Deleuze, thought is abstract, yet it is not the effect of an abstraction. The abstract, in Deleuze's work, is the ontological condition of the indeterminacy and infinity that characterise the virtuality of life. Thought is thus abstract insofar as it is also free and mobile; it is in fact itself indeterminate and infinite because it is immanent to the virtual dynamism of lived

experience. Thought, in other words, shares the same ontological abstractness as life. Abstraction, in contrast, is for Deleuze an epistemic reduction of
the dynamism of thought's abstract indeterminacy. It condenses the richness
of the lived into merely representational functions of reasoning. These functions are only temporary consolidations of abstract thought, which remains
fluid despite these concretisations. It is by means of abstraction that occasions of thought are isolated from the being of the sensible, and this is, from a
Deleuzian perspective, to the detriment of the virtuality of thinking.

From this Deleuzian standpoint, 'abstraction' is to be understood as a
cognitive stratification oriented towards being: one that is opposed to, and
which also blocks, the ontogenetic deterritorialisations of becoming. Abstraction is a technique of generalisation, universalisation, and measure that
projects us directly into what Deleuze called 'the most necessary and the
most concrete' problem, that of the *image of thought*.[6] To put it as simply as
possible, the image of thought is a set of presuppositions regarding what
thought is, what is possible or legitimate to think about, and in what ways
one might do so. An image of thought is what is assumed at the beginning of
every act of thinking; one needs to have a presupposition of what thinking is
in order to recognise oneself as the originator of such thinking. This might
appear to be a distinctly Cartesian tautology. However, for Deleuze, thought
should think away from such externally posed directives, which dictate the
form that it is to take. For Deleuze, thought is neither natural nor naturally
human. Instead, it is a violent and unnatural encounter: 'something in the
world forces us to think'.[7] Thinking is, then, aesthetic precisely because it is
initiated by a clash with the sensible. After this clash, nothing is ever as it
was. The sensible is a 'shock to thought'.[8] What forces thought to think is the
heavy abstract materiality of this immanent blow. In Deleuze, thought is an
indeterminate and eventual expression of the incalculable transcendental
conditions of lived experience.

I wish to propose here that Deleuze's antipathy towards computers should
be understood in the context of his project of constructing an ontology of
subtractions.[9] Such an ontology was intended to liberate the creative potential of abstract thought from its entrapment within the abstractive methods of
representation. Computers, however, operate upon the basis of such abstractive methods. The concept of abstraction does indeed permeate the theory
and practice of computer science as a tool for representation. The computer
scientist J. Glenn Brookshear notes, 'It is abstraction that allows us to ignore
the internal details of a complex device such as a computer, automobile, or
microwave oven, and use it as a single, comprehensible unit. Moreover, it is
by means of abstraction that such complex systems are designed and manufactured in the first place.'[10] Similarly, the computer scientist Timothy Colburn comments that 'complex virtual worlds . . . are made possible by computer scientists' ability to distance themselves from the mundane and tedious

levels of bits and processors, through tools of abstraction. . . . The computer scientist's world is a world of nothing but abstraction.'[11] To put that otherwise, while using the words of the architect and computer scientist Kostas Terzidis, computational algorithmic structures 'represent abstract patterns that are not necessarily associated with experience or perception'.[12]

These quotations would seem to confirm Deleuze's argument: computing is a discipline participating in 'a race for the universals of communication'.[13] For Deleuze, however, such a 'quest for "universals of communication" ought to make us shudder',[14] insofar as it results in an increasing abstractive infrastructure that stops the generative potential of thought. In Deleuze's work, to think is an ontogenetic act of creation, and any creative activity—whether it be that of art, philosophy, or thought itself—is not 'compatible with circuits of information and communication, ready-made circuits that are compromised from the outset'.[15] According to Deleuze, if computing is compromised from the outset, then this is because everything in computation is preprogrammed into logically determined finite relations that are indifferent to the content and context of lived experience. A computer can return only what you put into it. In this logically determined scenario, abstraction is instrumental to blocking the infinity of thought into the finite order of calculation. To put this otherwise, abstraction is instrumental to the logicist attempt to turn concepts into *functions*. Deleuze's antagonism towards information and communication technologies can thus be read as a passionate defence of the idiosyncrasies of thinking against functionalism, or as a vindication of the non-abstractable (and yet abstract) conditions in which thought comes about. The conditions of thought are transcendental conditions of real experience; as such, they are expressive, not representational. The implicit problem with computational technology for Deleuze, therefore, is that it does not express anything with its abstractive techniques, but rather only represents.

Entering the aesthetics of computation via Deleuze, then, leaves us with a very specific problem: how can we think and talk of computational abstraction after his philosophical critique of representational thought? How can we address the functional abstractive capacities that characterise computation, and indeed how can we consider them in terms of aesthetics, after such a critique? Is what I am attempting a legitimate operation? I believe that the answer to that question is yes: addressing computing via aesthetics is indeed a viable line of investigation. Before expanding on that answer, however, I should contextualise this discussion vis-à-vis the contemporary crisis of formalism in science.

FORMALISM BEYOND REPRESENTATION

The critique of representational thought in contemporary philosophy is comparable to a certain difficulty faced by formal sciences today. In order to examine what I claim to be the crisis of formalism in science, and how this crisis impacts upon contemporary computational culture, we can consider the paradigmatic changes that *computationalism* (also known as the computational theory of mind) is currently undergoing.

Computationalism is close to machine-state functionalism. Viewed as a special case of the representational theory of mind, it holds that cognition is a natural form of computation: minds manipulate mental representations, just like computers process formal symbols. Such a computational view of the mind is a cognitivist by-product of Turing's 1936 formalisation of the notion of computability. Earlier in this chapter, I discussed how the idea of a calculating machine has multiple origins; I also mentioned that the most crucial of these is perhaps the formal elaboration of computation that Turing presented in 1936, and which is epitomised by his eponymous Turing machine. Turing developed this hypothetical device by modelling it on what he hypothesised to be the human mind at work. His presupposition was that a formal model of calculation could be shared both by the computer and the brain.[16] This assumption also lies at the basis of the computationalist view, according to which computational states are program descriptions of actual mental states, and cognitive activities are comparable to the finite operations of computing machines. From this computationalist perspective, thinking is a kind of computation, insofar as it is understood as the activity of receiving inputs, following a step-by-step procedure, and eventually getting a specific output.[17] In the words of Jerry Fodor—one of the most famous advocates of computationalism—such a representational theory of mind might lack a standard formulation, but it is successful in explaining how 'thinking could be both rational and mechanical'.[18]

In the past decades, computationalism has acquired a bad reputation. One of the main criticisms levelled against it is the accusation that it is has detached itself from culture and society, or from embodiment.[19] Another frequent criticism—exemplified, for instance, by the differing positions of Hubert Dreyfus, Steven Horst, Kenneth Sayre, and John Searle[20]—is directed against the computationalist assumption that the calculations of formal logic, together with its symbol manipulations, might be able to justify the entire spectrum of cognition, understanding, and intentionality. Various theoretical and practical factors, such as the failure of 'strong AI' and its agenda of designing a fully intelligent machine, have contributed to the emergence of new perspectives on the computational mind, and on the notion of computation itself. Some of these new perspectives link back to ideas from cybernetics in order to emphasise the emergent, parallel, and networked connections of the brain as the origin of mental phenomena. For instance, connectionism (which arose in the early 1980s) takes neural networks as a central metaphor for the mind, thus underlining the importance of learning rules and of distributed subsymbolic representations arising from the network's activities. Other perspectives have instead argued that the mental is a faculty outside the brain: the active externalism of the philosopher Andy Clark, for example, maintains that organisms are linked with external entities in a two-way interaction, so as to create a coupled system that can be regarded as another cognitive network in itself. Clark then describes the mental cognitive profile of an embodied and situated organism, for which perception and action constitute a meaningful unity.[21] In a similar spirit, but in a different context, the anthropologist of science and technology Lucy Suchman also looks at the situatedness of social behaviour and at the deep asymmetries between a person and a machine. She proposes a theory of situated action, according to which 'every course of action depends in essential ways upon its material and social circumstances'.[22] As a final example, the work of Philip Agre can also be mentioned here. Agre questions representational theories of mind by challenging the mentalism and Cartesianism of traditional artificial intelligence. His aim is to shift the research focus of the AI field 'away from *cognition*—abstract processes in the head—and towards *activity*—concrete undertakings in the world'.[23] For Agre, this activity is not only embodied, but also always embedded into an environment.

Post-computationalist positions are manifold and diverse; the overview proposed above is not, by any means, meant to be exhaustive. What these perspectives have in common, however, is the wish to find what I would call a sensible dimension of thought, with a view towards 'the re-enchantment of the concrete'.[24] For the sake of philosophical speculation, it is possible to read these concurrent (yet often complementary) perspectives from a Deleuzian standpoint. On the one hand, traditional computationalist views participate in the quest for universals of communication that made Deleuze shudder. The attempt to mechanise thought, and to thereby reduce it to automated behaviour, can then be seen to be based on the image of thought's presuppositions that there is a unity of cognitive faculties, and that to think is what makes us human. On the other hand, however, what has happened—and what is still happening—with the new directions in cognitive computing marks a passage from the mechanical towards the famous Deleuzo-Guattarian notion of the machinic. The *machinic phylum*, according to Deleuze and Guattari, is a lineage that 'is materiality, natural or artificial, and both simultaneously; it is matter in movement, in flux, in variation, matter as a conveyor of singularities and traits of expression'.[25] This ontological reworking of the notion of machine is meant to explain the heterogenesis of the real and to demonstrate that all spheres of reality are capable of ontogenetically producing assemblages, in which disconnected organic and non-organic elements conjoin to become a self-creating system. The machines of Deleuze and Guattari are thus far removed from binary machines; they are instead fundamentally analogue, as they must be a little fuzzy in order to absorb and catalyse the matter-flow of the world while also probing spaces of combination and productivity. In other words, these are energetic machines, not formal ones. Moreover, the technological is just one of the many other elements that compose these machines. If 'the machines are social before being technical',[26] then this is because they are always somehow in relation to lived experience, although—and this is a crucial point—their subjectivity is not subordinate to the human but rather parallel to it.

Of course, by introducing these considerations I am not implying that AI scientists follow the ontological principles of Deleuze's philosophy. My point, however, is that today, 'intelligent machines' (if one accepts the conceptual difficulties that come with that expression) are considered to be *social*: the mechanised procedures of computation have entered the world and must now interact with it. According to the *interactive paradigm* in computing, interaction is 'more powerful than algorithms'.[27] The cognitivist 'closed' model of reasoning, founded on the formal abstractions of the Turing machine, has been accused of being incapable of encompassing the complexity of the real world, which always lends itself to the behavioural richness of the living and the lived. In technical terms, rather than algorithms that are capable of carrying out ever more difficult sequential computations, the computational structures that are sought after would be capable of transforming their preprogrammed instructions through their interaction with the real world, thus intervening in their own conditions of production by adapting them to the mutability of empirical situations. For example, in contrast to the Turing model, an interaction machine would extend and couple computation with the environment, thus creating a system that is powered by the ability of the computing device to cooperate with the external world, rather than limiting itself to carrying out ever more difficult sequential operations.

The paradigmatic shift towards interaction is multifaceted. Generally, it responds to the challenges that computing confronts today, such as the vast, quick, and efficient responsiveness that computational systems are required to exhibit in order to handle the sheer volumes of data sets with which they engage. Arguably, the crisis of formalism then rests upon the difficulty of finding regular patterns within ever more multifaceted empirical variation. This is a problem that rationalism has always dealt with: how can an infinite reality, with its uncertainty and mutability, be systematised within a finite procedure? Today, the reduction of complexity to simplicity no longer seems to be a feasible solution, as the ideal of a 'simple rule' is a reduction that neglects the external world of the computing process—a world that must now participate in that process. Today, then, computation must allow user-generated content, robot-to-robot communication, and numerous forms of software programs to inject qualitative and quantitative indeterminacy into the preprogrammed procedure. It is, then, appropriate to ask, how could the formal finitude of logico-mathematical techniques ever cope with that?

Within the picture of computing that I have just outlined, although the functionality of a program is still based upon abstractive formal categorisations, formalism itself has undergone a substantial reconfiguration, resulting from the widespread criticism that has been addressed towards it. This generalised distrust towards the formal constitutes the technoscientific context of my contention that it is possible—and, in fact, necessary—to look again at computational abstraction after the philosophical critique of representational thought. I intend to counter the tendency—a tendency that can be discerned, as I have shown, in both computing and philosophy—of responding to the crisis of formalism by either taking a certain distance from the latter, or by simply embracing that which the formal is *not* (i.e., the empirical). My contention, by contrast, is that computational formalisms should not be discarded but philosophically reassessed. The key to this renewed assessment is to understand computation as a method of abstraction that does not negate or refute abstractness and as a determination that does not negate indeterminacy.

That computation is an abstractive method is evident. By analogy with mathematics, in computer science abstraction is understood as the conceptual practice of reducing and factoring out elements so as to address a few issues at a time. This permits the reasoning and analysis of logical systems. In computer science, abstraction is generally understood as a method that can tell what sort of information one can get from the observed system, what sort of questions are reasonable to ask in this regard, and what sort of answers one might, in principle, be able to get from it. Language abstraction, procedural abstraction, data abstraction: they all specify content, languages, modules, procedures, variables, as well as the consequent operations that can be performed upon them. The abstractive operations of computation are multiple and operate at many scales and different speeds. Some of these abstractions are kept, others discarded; most of them are incessantly organised into sets of relations of objects and of data that are themselves already abstractions.

To prove that computation does not exclude abstractness qua indeterminacy is a little more difficult. This operation involves a fundamental reassessment of what this same indeterminacy might be vis-à-vis computation. I have followed Deleuze up to this point, but I now have to turn in a different direction. For Deleuze, abstract indeterminacy is the infinite becoming of virtuality. To claim, as I do, that computation is a method of abstraction that is open to abstractness entails arguing, against Deleuze, that computation *also* involves becoming, indeterminacy, and infinity. Crucially, however, I propose that such becoming, indeterminacy, and infinity can be found in computation (and that computation, therefore, can be said to be open to the abstract), not despite the discretisations, systematisations, and rationalisations that Deleuze criticised, but because of them. It follows that it is fundamental to my argument to advance a different understanding of what becoming, indeterminacy, and infinity might be vis-à-vis discretisation, systematisation, and rationalisation in computation. In the case of computational systems, they cannot be features of virtual life, as Deleuze understood them to be. Instead, they are specific to the actuality of computation itself. While arguments for an aisthesis of the digital would seem to make computation something that might be abstract (and thus in becoming) by virtue of its participation in the being of the sensible, I propose that the becoming of computation corresponds to actual discretising procedures of quantitative systematisation. Computation can only generate what it has been programmed to generate. Computation, in this sense, is not ontogenetic. Computation has, nonetheless, the potential to engender new reality, insofar it has the potential to actualise itself. This is the becoming that I aim to theorise.

I will do so by suggesting that the indeterminacy and infinity of computation are due to a central and constitutive characteristic of every computational processing: incomputability. The founding paradox of computer science is that it is a field that is defined by what it cannot do, rather than by what it can do. Alan Turing's 1936 foundational paper, 'On Computable Numbers, with an Application to the Entscheidungsproblem', first formalised the notion of computability and demonstrated that some functions cannot be computed. According to Turing's model of computation, to compute is to follow an *effective procedure* (in other words, an algorithm) in order to solve a problem in a finite number of sequential steps. Turing discovered, however, that some problems cannot be solved via algorithmic means, because the steps involved in their processing are not finite but infinite: these problems are incomputable. Incomputability will be discussed in detail later, in chapter 6. However, in order to clarify how I intend to respond to the crisis of formalism, we can simply note here that because the incomputable is this element of undecidability, something in computation remains unknown and, ultimately, beyond representation. This unknown is a decisive element of the actual procedures of computation: it does not belong to life, the living, or the lived, but to computation itself. Although it is beyond symbolic representation, it is still within logos.

Incomputability thus confirms that computational processing is preprogrammed. However, it also shows that the preprogrammed rule always partakes of indeterminacy and infinity. Such indeterminacy and infinity are not encountered at the level of sensation. Instead, they enter the procedure *from within* the logico-formal process itself, during and thanks to the preprogrammed eventuation of the latter. It is, then, not a question of opposing what is lived to what is abstracted by assuming that one would be boundless and the other constrained. Instead, the issue becomes whether it is possible to find, in the abstractive operations of computation themselves, a *computational* infinity that is not to be transduced into the qualities of sensibility, and a *computational* indeterminacy that does not have to simulate the indeterminacies of life.

The crisis of formalism has usually been identified as evidencing that formalism must be challenged and superseded. I challenge formalism too; however, I do not wish to dispose of it. By drawing upon material that has informed the inception of the theory of computability, I aim to develop the view that formal abstraction in computation is not a mere reduction or compression of the complexities of sensibility to the simplicity of preformed representations of intelligibility. Thus, on the one hand I agree with the philosophical critique of representational thought: I too believe that the formal logic employed by computational systems cannot successfully account for the empirically real or for the virtual conditions of lived experience. On the other hand, however, my position also differs from such a critique, for I wish to prove that computation is never really only a reduction and that it never really only represents. Because of formal abstraction, computation is a procedure that is already complex—prior to any coupling with art, matter, or life—insofar as it is ingressed by a quantitative infinity that remains unrepresentable, and which is thereby impractical or useless from the perspective of cognitive computing. In this sense, by engaging with the limits of computational formalism, I challenge the conception of a calculatory preformation and depiction of the real. On that basis, I also refuse to endorse a computational theory of mind that is grounded in the possibility of such preformation and depiction. However, although the impossibility of enclosing procedures of counting into any final systematisation has been traditionally read as an indication of the failure of formal systems, I interpret the limits of formal reasoning not as a fault, a constraint, or a stopping point for computation, but as something that helps us to highlight the actuality of computational formalisms beyond any representational role that they might entail.

I can now return to the question, is it legitimate to consider the abstractive capacities of computation in aesthetic terms, given the philosophical critique of representational thought and the crisis of formalism in science? At this point, I can expand on the positive answer that I have already anticipated and explain that my attempt to establish a computational aesthetics that would not flatten down the logico-quantitative character of computing upon qualitative transductions has to be understood as an effort to justify the abstractive capacities of computation beyond the representational role that computationalism has assigned to them. Radicalising Deleuze's aesthetics of thought is, therefore, a way of offering an alternative to the cognitivism that prevails in the field of computing. However, in contrast to the philosophical critique of representational thought, and in contrast to embodied, enactive, and situated critiques of formalism, I wish to develop an alternative by departing from the same attention to formal abstraction from which computationalism also proceeded.

That is why drawing upon Turing's work is pivotal to my account: I aim to challenge the cognitivist view of computation that developed from his work by proposing another reading of his logico-mathematical results. In doing so, however, I do not assume that formal abstraction can only be understood in the manner that computationalism tends to conceive it. While trying to supersede computationalism, I thus also challenge the philosophical critique of computation, despite the degree to which it accords with my intention to dispose of computationalism. This is because this critique assumes that formal abstraction is what the computational theory of mind made it to be. In the following sections of the book, I will discuss how aesthetics offers us a way of accomplishing such a reconsideration of formal abstraction. This aesthetics will have to be a peculiar one: it will need to be the case that the becoming, indeterminacy, and infinity that it addresses do not break with conceptual structuring but are in fact a part of this structuring. This peculiar aesthetics will thus concern not only sensibility, but intelligibility too. The aesthetic philosophy that can meet these requirements is that of Alfred North Whitehead, which will be addressed in the next chapter.

NOTES

1. See Brian Cantwell Smith, 'The Foundations of Computing', in *Computationalism: New Directions*, ed. Matthias Scheutz (Cambridge, MA: MIT Press, 2002), 23–58.

2. See Alonzo Church, 'An Unsolvable Problem of Elementary Number Theory', *American Journal of Mathematics* 58, no. 2 (April 1936): 345–63, https://doi.org/10.2307/2371045; Emil L. Post, 'Finite Combinatory Processes—Formulation 1', *Journal of Symbolic Logic* 1, no. 3 (September 1936): 103–5, https://doi.org/10.2307/2269031; Alan M. Turing, 'On Computable Numbers, with an Application to the Entscheidungsproblem', *Proceedings of the London Mathematical Society* 42 (1936): 230–65, https://doi.org/10.1112/plms/s2-42.1.230.

3. Alan Kay and Adele Goldberg, 'Personal Dynamic Media', in *The New Media Reader*, ed. Noah Wardrip-Fruin and Nick Montfort (Cambridge, MA: MIT Press, 2003), 394.

4. Lev Manovich, *Software Takes Command* (New York: Bloomsbury Academic, 2013), 102.

5. Arguing for the computational specificity of digital aesthetics, however, does not imply relegating computation to the unfortunate role of an intermediary *substratum*. As I have claimed elsewhere, the 'mediality' of computation should be understood as computation's capacity to be a mechanism for producing modes of being, agency, and thought. See M. Beatrice Fazi and Matthew Fuller, 'Computational Aesthetics', in *A Companion to Digital Art*, ed. Christiane Paul (Chichester: Wiley-Blackwell, 2016), 281–96.

6. Gilles Deleuze, *Difference and Repetition*, trans. Paul Patton (London: Continuum, 2004), xv. The problem of the image of thought recurs throughout Deleuze's work in terms of a critique against recognition and representation as the basis of thinking. Along with *Difference and Repetition*, see *Proust and Signs*, trans. Richard Howard (London: Allen Lane, 1973), and *Nietzsche and Philosophy*, trans. Hugh Tomlinson (London: Continuum, 2006). See also Gilles Deleuze and Félix Guattari's *A Thousand Plateaus: Capitalism and Schizophrenia*, trans. Brian Massumi (London: Continuum, 2004), as well as their book *What Is Philosophy?*, trans. Graham Burchell and Hugh Tomlinson (London: Verso, 1994).

7. Deleuze, *Difference and Repetition*, 176.

8. Brian Massumi, ed., *A Shock to Thought: Expression after Deleuze and Guattari* (London: Routledge, 2002). See also Gilles Deleuze, *Cinema II: The Time-Image*, trans. Hugh Tomlinson and Robert Galeta (London: Bloomsbury Academic, 2013), 161.

9. Peter Hallward also understands Deleuze's philosophy as subtractive, albeit in a manner that differs from my reading. In *Out of This World: Deleuze and the Philosophy of Creation* (London: Verso, 2006), Hallward reads Deleuze's philosophy as deserting actuality, and thus as ultimately guilty of paralysing any possible political action. Although I admire Hallward's flair in systematising Deleuze's thought, I do not endorse his argument here because, in my view, it overlooks the importance that the reciprocal determination between actuality and virtuality holds within Deleuze's ontology. In Deleuze, I would say, the virtual and the actual can only exist as mutually implicated.

10. J. Glenn Brookshear, *Computer Science: An Overview*, 7th ed. (Boston: Addison-Wesley, 2003), 10.

11. Timothy Colburn, 'Methodology of Computer Science', in *The Blackwell Guide to the Philosophy of Computing and Information*, ed. Luciano Floridi (Oxford: Blackwell, 2004), 322.

12. Kostas Terzidis, *Expressive Form: A Conceptual Approach to Computational Design* (London: Spon, 2003), 69.

13. Deleuze and Guattari, *What Is Philosophy?*, 11.

14. Gilles Deleuze, 'Control and Becoming', in *Negotiations, 1972–1990*, trans. Martin Joughin (New York: Columbia University Press, 1995), 175.

15. Gilles Deleuze, 'On the Time-Image', in *Negotiations, 1972–1990*, trans. Martin Joughin (New York: Columbia University Press, 1995), 61.

16. 'We may compare a man in the process of computing a real number to a machine which is only capable of a finite number of conditions.' Turing, 'On Computable Numbers', 231.

17. Gualtiero Piccinini, however, sees computationalism and machine-state functionalism as independent. He defines the latter as a 'metaphysical view', where 'mental states are individuated by their functional relations with mental inputs, outputs, and other mental states'. Objecting to the conflation of functionalism and the computational theory of mind, Piccinini also observes that, while functionalism 'is not committed to the view that the functional relations that individuate mental states are computational', computationalism is instead 'precisely the hypothesis that the functional relations between mental inputs, outputs, and internal states are computational'. See 'Functionalism, Computationalism, and Mental States', *Studies in History and Philosophy of Science Part A* 35, no. 4 (December 2004): 811–12, https://doi.org/10.1016/j.shpsa.2004.02.003.

18. Jerry A. Fodor, *The Mind Doesn't Work That Way: The Scope and Limits of Computational Psychology* (Cambridge, MA: MIT Press, 2000), 19.

19. For a sociocultural critique of computation, see David Golumbia, *The Cultural Logic of Computation* (Cambridge, MA: Harvard University Press, 2009). For a critique of computationalism as a disembodied perspective, see Francisco J. Varela, Evan Thompson, and Eleanor Rosch, *The Embodied Mind: Cognitive Science and Human Experience* (Cambridge, MA: MIT Press, 1991).

20. See Hubert Dreyfus, *What Computers Can't Do: The Limits of Artificial Intelligence* (New York: Harper and Row, 1972); Steven W. Horst, *Symbols, Computation, and Intentionality: A Critique of the Computational Theory of Mind* (Berkeley: University of California Press, 1996); Kenneth M. Sayre, 'Intentionality and Information Processing: An Alternative Model for Cognitive Science', *Behavioral and Brain Sciences* 9, no. 1 (March 1986): 121–38, https://doi.org/10.1017/S0140525X00021750; John R. Searle, 'Minds, Brains, and Programs', *Behavioral and Brain Sciences* 3, no. 3 (September 1980): 417–57, https://doi.org/10.1017/S0140525X00005756.

21. See Andy Clark and David J. Chalmers, 'The Extended Mind', *Analysis* 58, no. 1 (January 1998): 7–19, https://doi.org/10.1093/analys/58.1.7; see also Andy Clark, *Being There: Putting Brain, Body, and World Together Again* (Cambridge, MA: MIT Press, 1997).

22. Lucy A. Suchman, *Plans and Situated Actions: The Problem of Human-Machine Communication* (Cambridge: Cambridge University Press, 1987), 50.

23. Philip E. Agre, *Computation and Human Experience* (Cambridge: Cambridge University Press, 1997), 3–4.

24. Francisco J. Varela, 'The Re-Enchantment of the Concrete: Some Biological Ingredients for a Nouvelle Cognitive Science', in *The Artificial Life Route to Artificial Intelligence: Building Embodied, Situated Agents*, ed. Luc Steels and Rodney Brooks (Hillsdale, NJ: Lawrence Erlbaum, 1995), 11–22.

25. Deleuze and Guattari, *A Thousand Plateaus*, 451.

26. Gilles Deleuze, *Foucault*, trans. Seán Hand (London: Bloomsbury, 2013), 34.

27. Peter Wegner, 'Why Interaction Is More Powerful than Algorithms', *Communications of the ACM* 40, no. 5 (May 1997): 80–91, https://doi.org/10.1145/253769.253801. See also Dina Goldin, Scott A. Smolka, and Peter Wegner, eds., *Interactive Computation: The New Paradigm* (Berlin: Springer, 2006).

Chapter Three

Processes

AN AESTHETICS AT TWO LEVELS:
PHYSICAL AND CONCEPTUAL

Alfred North Whitehead was an English philosopher, but it should be noted that philosophy occupied only the second, American part of his life. Before this, he was, in fact, primarily a mathematician, and quite a famous one too. His *Principia Mathematica*—an influential three-volume work that was co-written with his then-disciple Bertrand Russell and published between 1910 and 1913—was among the most notable attempts to establish the foundations of mathematics in symbolic logic.[1] Despite the objections of mathematician colleagues who may not have been entirely enthused by his metaphysical turn (Bertrand Russell included), Whitehead never really stopped thinking mathematically.[2] He maintained that mathematics is 'the most original creation of the human spirit'[3] and that this science is intimately connected with the reality of order, structure, and quantities. In addition, Whitehead's retention of the status of mathematician is proved by the fact that his metaphysics is a cosmology of quantitative events and processes of abstraction. This is what makes his philosophy a particularly interesting resource for the speculative aims of this book.

Whitehead died in 1947, a year after the ENIAC (one the first electronic general-purpose computers) was announced to the public. His work does not include an account of computing machines. However, the discreteness of the processes that he depicts is very suited to describing digital computation ontologically.[4] Before moving on to assess how Whitehead's philosophy can afford a means of advancing an aesthetic ontology of computation that would focus on the logico-quantitative operations of computing, we should note, following Bruno Latour, that Whitehead had the misfortune of 'provoking too much interest among theologians and too little amongst epistemologists'.[5] I agree with Latour: this is unfortunate, because Whitehead's thinking is far from being an anti-intellectualism or a rejection of scientific knowledge. Whitehead not only engaged with the most challenging scientific theories of his day, such as quantum theory, electromagnetism, and relativity; in addition, his overall *philosophy of actuality* is aimed at constructing a cosmology that could prove significant to these scientific theories and contemporary mathematical concepts. We should thus welcome the fact that, in the past fifteen years or so, the study of Whitehead has been revived by attempts to rehabilitate the onto-epistemological significance of his philosophy. This Whiteheadian revival has often run parallel to a revitalised attention to Henri Bergson, as well as to fresh readings of the radical empiricism of William James, the pragmaticism of Charles Sanders Peirce, and philosophies of expression of Spinozist derivation. The thematic convergences around these directions have resulted in original connections and have offered interesting frameworks through which late capitalist society, together with its art, science, and philosophy, can be deciphered. In addition, these conjunctions have also foregrounded the unavoidable similarities between Whitehead and Deleuze. Deleuze rarely addressed Whitehead in his writings, but he did so more consistently in his teaching.[6] In the past few years, a growing body of scholarly literature has addressed Whitehead's influence on Deleuze ever more explicitly.[7] However, while I acknowledge this literature—and while I also recognise that it is possible to develop a reading of Deleuze and Whitehead that places them in harmony with one another—I will not attempt to propose such a view here. My aim of radicalising Deleuze's aesthetic ontology entails looking for disparities between the two philosophers, and thus for the ways in which Whitehead's philosophy might help us to extend Deleuze's aesthetics of thought in such a way that it would be able to encompass computational processes.

It is possible to claim that Whitehead's metaphysics is, fundamentally, an aesthetics. In this respect, Whitehead's philosophy is very close to that of Deleuze: aesthetics is not based upon the mere sense reception of art, as of anything else, but is instead about determining the ontological conditions for real experience. In *Without Criteria: Kant, Whitehead, Deleuze, and Aesthetics*, Steven Shaviro has insightfully described the 'critical aestheticism' of both Deleuze and Whitehead,[8] stressing their mutual emphasis on feeling as the originary mode of relationship. Shaviro brings Deleuze and Whitehead into conjunction with one another via an innovative reading of Kant's *Critique of Judgement*. He argues that both philosophers have followed what he sees as the third *Critique*'s implicit emphasis on the affective character of experience (a lead that, Shaviro notes, Kant himself did not pursue further). The position that Shaviro advances here is legitimate: an affective reading of Whitehead is possible, and a Whiteheadian aesthetics could be justified upon such a basis. Nonetheless, I wish to address the ontological aesthetics of Whitehead from another perspective. An overlooked and yet profound difference between Deleuze and Whitehead offers the opportunity of establishing a novel ontological approach to the aesthetics of computation. This difference is as follows: Whitehead's aesthetics is not only about the sensible, but about the intelligible too. This means that aesthetics, for Whitehead, is about sensation *and* thought. For Deleuze, too, aesthetics concerns thinking processes. However, in Deleuze's work, thought is aesthetic because it involves a virtual indeterminacy that cannot be grasped intellectually and which can only be felt. For Deleuze, aesthetics is precisely what addresses this sensory knowledge. Whitehead, on the other hand, conceived a conceptual activity that would not rely on virtuality and that would instead be specific to actuality. Whereas for Deleuze thought is virtual, Whitehead described an actual conceptual capacity to make indeterminacy intelligible. Yet, according to Whitehead, it is still aesthetics—and nothing else—that can explain this capacity, because the latter is not cognitive and does not operate through representational reductions. Instead, it is an assimilation that involves a grasping of ideas. What Whitehead's philosophy offers, then, is an aesthetics that operates on two levels: an aesthetics in which non-representational relations are established conceptually as well as physically.

In order to explain this issue further, it will prove useful to outline part of the ontological scaffolding that supports Whitehead's philosophy. In Whitehead's analysis, 'this actual world spreads itself for observation in the guise of the topic of our immediate experience'.[9] The immediacy of this actual world is primarily 'a fact of aesthetic experience', and 'all aesthetic experience', in turn, 'is feeling'.[10] If actuality is given in experience, and experience is feeling, then all actuality is ultimately felt. Shaviro is thus right to stress that a feeling relationship among actualities is, in Whitehead, more basic than any cognitive one. Feeling has a degree of primacy in Whitehead's main work, *Process and Reality*. 'Feeling', however, is a term that should be understood as 'a mere technical word'.[11] Whitehead opted for the term 'prehension' in order to distance himself from any psychological and anthropocentric understanding of what, for him, it meant 'to feel'. 'To prehend' is not 'to cognise', but neither is it 'to perceive'. A prehension should instead be conceived as an 'uncognitive apprehension'[12] —that is, a grasping, a seizing, or the holding of one thing by another thing.

If Whitehead's metaphysics is an aesthetics, and if all experience is aesthetic experience, then this is because, in Whitehead's cosmos, everything that exists prehends everything else. It is important to clarify here that Whitehead distinguished between *conceptual prehensions* and *physical prehensions*. Conceptual prehensions are responses to ideality. To conceptually prehend means to grasp thought in its pure potentiality. A conceptual prehension is a mental operation, but it cannot be localised within the neurocognitive architecture of a mind or of a brain. A conceptual prehension is not a direct cognition, nor is it a recognition or a recollection. Rather, a conceptual prehension is actuality's friction with the ideal. Physical prehensions, on the other hand, are actuality's responses to other actualities. A physical prehension feels what there is, or what there has been, and internalises this feeling into a unity that comes to constitute what there will be. Physical prehensions could be viewed, therefore, as exemplifying the affective tone of reality that Shaviro says is central to Whitehead's aesthetic philosophy. I agree with Shaviro that physical prehensions are 'pulses of emotion'.[13] They are a rhythm to be played out on the bodily level of Deleuzian matter-flows. If we were to remain at this bodily level of prehensive activity, it would be appropriate to view Whitehead's aesthetics as an aisthesis or as sensory knowledge. However, Whitehead's insistence on the concomitant existence of conceptual prehensions also makes it possible to contend that, if Whitehead's aesthetics is an aisthesis, then it is an aisthesis of a very peculiar kind. In Whitehead, a bodily transduction of affective forces is not enough to account for an actuality's relation to the rest of actuality. Everything that exists is in fact 'dipolar'.[14] All actualities in the world—not only humans, but everything that is real, concrete, and indeed actual—have a *physical pole* and a *mental pole*. This means that experience is dipolar too: while being originated by sensible relations, it is nonetheless never completed without a conceptual determination.

Whitehead's aesthetics, therefore, is not just affective. Certainly, the activity that conceptual prehensions perform falls under the category of feeling. I cannot deny that conceptual prehensions are feelings and that—insofar as these feelings are precognitive and impersonal—they exhibit many similarities with the Deleuzo-Spinozist notion of affect. In addition to this, however, it should also be stressed that a conceptual feeling is not an intensive response to change or a response proper to a body that intensively registers such change, as would be the case with Deleuzo-Spinozist affect. On the contrary, a conceptual feeling is the capacity of a mind (or, better, of a conceptual or mental pole) that feels because it selects, evaluates, decides, and orders—that feels, in other words, because it abstracts. Thus, while for Deleuze thinking processes and bodily affects are fundamentally the same (famously, for Deleuze a thought *moves* like a body, and the more one feels, the more one thinks), for Whitehead they are not: he kept the conceptual and the physical planes related, yet also separate. However, one of Whitehead's most striking insights is that this conceptual capacity is still a fundamental part of his aesthetics. Whereas, for Deleuze, a thinking process would have been aesthetic because it is affectively immanent to sensation (and it is in this manner that Deleuze resolved the bipolarity of sensibility and intelligibility, by advocating the superiority of the former via the immanence of the latter), for Whitehead thinking is aesthetic because, although it is a conceptual activity, it is nonetheless prehensive. This conceptual activity goes outside and beyond its cognitive and representational functions, but it is still mental, conceptual, and abstractive.

In my view, if we want to establish an aesthetics of computation that would consider the aesthetic legitimacy of operations of formal abstraction, then it is precisely these Whiteheadian insights that should be investigated. Therefore, while markedly Deleuzian readings of Whitehead generally downplay the extra-affective specificity of conceptual prehensions, I want to place it centre stage and develop its significance as regards the relevance that it might hold for an aesthetic ontology (or an ontological aesthetics) of actual—not virtual—computational processes.

EVENTS: INDETERMINACY

It is necessary to get a little more technical now, for it is only by addressing the peculiarity of Whitehead's understanding of actuality, and how this actuality comes to being through becoming, that it is possible to appreciate the speculative opportunity that Whitehead's philosophy offers to the aesthetic investigation of computation.

The first thing that should be highlighted as regards Whitehead's characterisation of actuality is that, in his philosophy, the actual is always eventual. Quite literally, this means that everything that is actual exists as an *event*. A parallel between Deleuze and Whitehead is often made on the basis that they are both said to be philosophers of the event.[15] According to Deleuze, events are the product of the transformations and interrelations between those intensive forces that constitute the inherent potentialities of the real. Events run through actuality and virtuality 'in terms of changes in degrees of intensity in their relations'.[16] I have already discussed how the notion of intensity is central to Deleuze's philosophy. A Deleuzian event can be described as a change in intensity that marks the reciprocal determination of actuality and virtuality, and thus the occurrence of ontological novelty. The concept of event is also at the heart of Whitehead's philosophical system.[17] Famously, Whitehead rejected the Aristotelian metaphysics of enduring substances and instead favoured an ontology of spatiotemporal atomic processes. For him, events are ubiquitous and constitutive of all there is: with the notion of *actual occasion* (a Whiteheadian expression that is interchangeable with *actual entity*), he described eventuality as a formative condition of reality. Actual occasions are 'the final real things of which the world is made up'.[18] An actual occasion is an atomic occurrence, an episode, something that happens in (and extends through) space and time, but it is also a unit of reality that begins and ends, and which never occurs again exactly as it was.

Of course, the concept of event is also central to other contemporary thinkers.[19] Still, what Deleuze and Whitehead have in common is that they theorised and spoke of events as immanent to, and as productive of, the real. For both writers, events are genetic: events do not happen to things, but things happen, or come to be, in events. Given these similarities, there is, however, also a major distinction between Deleuze's events and those of Whitehead. For Deleuze, an event is virtual. This means that it is indifferent to actualisation, 'since its reality does not depend upon it'.[20] For Whitehead, on the other hand, events are always actual. It is true that, for both philosophers, events are functional in addressing 'the problem of how the eternal and the actual are necessarily combined in the new and are necessary for the new'.[21] Nonetheless, whereas in Deleuze's work an event remains partly unactualised in what he often referred to as the 'chaosmos' or 'plane of consistency' of virtuality, in Whitehead's philosophy events are bits of actuality, or atoms of existence of this world, which must come to full determination. Deleuze's events have no position or temporality, and, as such, they are a pure reserve of multiplicity, with no beginning and no end. By contrast, a Whiteheadian event is a spatiotemporal process that commences and then perishes. It is the result of the production of an actual structure, an actual order, and an actual unification of multiplicity. These considerations allow us to address the relation between indeterminacy and events in both Deleuze and Whitehead. It is my contention that the importance of the notion of the event for both philosophers is an indication of the centrality of indeterminacy to their ontologies. It is only because of indeterminacy that new actuality occurs: one can assume that Deleuze and Whitehead would have agreed with this. They would not have settled, however, on the nature of this indeterminacy, or on the relation that the latter holds with actuality. The ontological dynamic through which new actuality comes about is different in Deleuze and Whitehead, although for both this dynamic is aesthetic. This is another significant point of divergence between Deleuze and Whitehead that can be stressed in order to push Deleuze's aesthetic proposition further than Deleuze himself would permit.

In Deleuze's philosophy, indeterminacy corresponds to *pure difference*— that is, to the virtual totality of unactualised conditions of the real. Indeterminacy is thus virtuality itself: 'a mode of reality implicated in the emergence of new potentials'.[22] In his book on Gilles Deleuze, *Deleuze: The Clamor of Being*, Alain Badiou affirms that it would be 'wrong to conceive of the virtual as a kind of indetermination, as a formless reservoir of possibilities that only actual beings identify'.[23] Badiou's comment might seem to contradict the Deleuzian equivalence between indeterminacy and virtuality that I have just presented, but in fact it does not. Instead, it offers an opportunity to clarify it. In Deleuze's ontology, the mode of reality that corresponds to virtual indeterminacy is not to be mistaken for a probabilism of states of affairs. The indeterminacy of Deleuzian virtual events is metaphysical and should not be confused with the empirical uncertainty of physical phenomena. Deleuze never tired of affirming a crucial distinction between the virtual and the possible. The latter lacks reality; the former does not: its reality is simply not actual. The virtual is not a reservoir of possible options waiting to be merely passed into existence; instead, the virtual is a reserve of very real energies to be exhausted, of forces to be employed, and of potentialities to be actualised. Seen in this light, 'the virtual is change as such'.[24]

Badiou is thus right to stress that Deleuze's virtual is fully determinate, for the virtual does not lack being or existence. What should then be added to my contention is that, in my reading of Deleuze, virtuality corresponds to indeterminacy to the extent that it is the maximally unknown and the maximally unknowable. Its abstractness means that it cannot be preformed or even only presented according to principles of identity and resemblance. In this sense, the potential for ontological production that the virtual stands for is truly contingent because it has 'the capacity to bring forth situations *which were not at all contained in precedent situations*'.[25] It can thus be concluded that, in Deleuze, the indeterminacy of virtuality is an open threshold from which to jump into a lived future that cannot (and will not) be harnessed by any preformation of it. This future, for Deleuze, is expressed in the immeasurability of affective forces that traverse lived experience. One jumps into this future as one falls into 'a life': with a body that feels, that elongates, dislocates, and deterritorialises itself, and which loses all functional structures (and all organs), until it merges with the virtual indeterminate and the virtual unknown. It becomes possible here to fully appreciate the centrality of aesthetics to the metaphysics of events presented by Deleuze. One can, at the same time, also appreciate the opposite (i.e., the importance of the notion of event for the Deleuzian aesthetic enquiry). Both can be understood only if virtual indeterminacy is kept at the centre of Deleuze's ontology. Deleuzian events attest to the ontological superiority of the dynamic activity of becoming in respect to entities and states of being. A Deleuzian event is less a differentiated creature than an act of differentiating creation. It compels a step back from mediation and normalisation in order to channel the virtual, unpresentable composition that is behind everything that exists. This maximal indeterminacy thereby requires modes of insight, intuition, and knowledge that are properly aesthetic, inasmuch as they do not accord with a logic of instrumental truth but with that of unmediated sense and sensation.

Let us now focus on Whitehead's events. For Whitehead, too, events are generative of ontological production. 'The fundamental concepts are activity and process.'[26] In distinction from Deleuze, however, Whitehead holds that processual activity is the most fundamental character of actuality, rather than of virtuality. The creating and the creature are both to be conceived as actual processes. Indeed, they coincide: the creature is a process of self-creation.

Whitehead's self-creating events, then, are not withdrawals from determination or systematisation; they are movements towards it. Indeterminacy is thus also central to Whitehead's ontology, albeit in a way that is quite different from that of Deleuze. In Whitehead, the indeterminacy of events has to be resolved within actuality. This resolution, however, is not a solution but a *decision* that brings about a *completion*. This decision is the way in which an actuality 'adds a determinate condition to the settlement for the future beyond itself'.[27] It can therefore be argued that, in Whitehead too, indeterminacy involves a threshold open towards the future. However, while Deleuze's events prosper on the 'drama beneath every logos',[28] performing the dramatic dynamism of thinking-feelings 'beneath all possible representation',[29] for Whitehead, if there is no logos there is no event, and thus there is no drama either. To put this otherwise, the Deleuzian dynamism of thinking-feelings is characterised by an advocacy of affective indeterminacy, which translates into an argument against mental structuring. In Whitehead's philosophy, by contrast, a systematisation is not a stopping point for thought, but the eventuation of thought itself, insofar as it is the manner in which what we could call the 'contingency of the real' disrupts the stubborn sequentiality of matters of fact and states of affairs.

In order to gain a clearer understanding of this issue, it is useful to return to the prehensive activity that, according to Whitehead, is carried out by all actuality. As I discussed earlier in the chapter, prehensions can either be physical or conceptual. Enough ground has now been covered to elaborate on that dual capacity and to thereby link it to the significance of indeterminacy within the Whiteheadian ontology of events. An actual occasion's physical prehension is a prehension whose datum is another actual occasion: it is the feeling of actuality by another actuality. This is the primary way in which the community of all actual occasions relate to each other. In contrast with the early modern empiricist account of empty factuality that passively impresses itself upon human senses, Whitehead's approach understands actuality as active, in act, and full with the generative potential for novelty and creation. The notion of *real potentiality* is used by Whitehead to describe such a potential for creation; the notion of *creativity* expresses instead the status of actuality's 'underlying activity',[30] or the 'category of the ultimate'.[31] From this perspective, actuality's real potentiality is better understood as the unknown—or as the indeterminacy—that remains 'relative to some actual entity', and which is resolved by actual occasions in order for the latter to be the 'standpoint whereby the actual world is defined'.[32] Actuality is thereby endowed with a very specific potential of creating new actualities (namely, new events) beyond what already exists. Actual occasions from the past have the potential to enter and inform, as data, the constitution of new actual occasions, which in turn have the potential to select the past that will become relevant information for the future. Real potentiality attests to the capacity of actual events to determine themselves out of the indeterminacy that they originate from.

'The notion of potentiality', Whitehead believed, 'is fundamental for the understanding of existence, as soon as the notion of process is admitted.'[33] An actual occasion 'exhibits itself as a process'.[34] However, this becoming-ness is short-term. Every actual occasion begins, determines itself, and per-ishes. The perishing of an actual occasion is consequent to the full determina-tion of the latter: for an actual occasion, 'its birth is its end'.[35] This process from indetermination towards determination indicates how, from this point of view, Whitehead's events are also different from those of Deleuze. De-leuze's events are never complete, inasmuch as they are vectors that express the mutual determination of actuality and virtuality. A Whiteheadian actual occasion, however, must be understood as a drive that always reaches an end. 'There is a becoming of continuity, but no continuity of becoming.'[36] For Whitehead, despite real potentiality being 'the driving force of process',[37] the full determination of an actual occasion is achieved with the ingression into the event of another type of potentiality, which he called 'pure'. Pure potentiality is a general potentiality, which impinges upon actuality thanks to conceptual prehensions. The latter are the 'primary operations amongst those belonging to the mental pole of an actual entity';[38] they are conceptual reac-tions to the physical concatenation of events and prompt 'some possibility as to how actualities *may* be *definite*'.[39] Conceptual prehensions, as I said earli-er, could be described as feelings of ideas. It is crucial to emphasise again that these conceptual feelings are not conscious intellectual feelings; they are the conceptual grasping of a new opportunity. A conceptual prehension cor-responds to the capacity of actuality of 'mentally' grasping (and thus not only of sensing) the unknown. The unknown in question is not the contingen-cy of empirical states of affairs, but the indeterminacy that pertains to the ideality of *eternal objects.*

For Whitehead, actual occasions are the basic particulars of what is real. 'Any entity whose conceptual recognition does not involve a necessary refer-ence to any definite actual entity of the temporal world', on the other hand, 'is called an "eternal object".'[40] As the name implies, eternal objects are entities, not processes. Similarly, they are abstract and eternal, not concrete and time based. This, nonetheless, does not mean that these objects endure or extend indefinitely, but that they have no spatial or temporal parts. The being of eternal objects is thereby not the being of actual occasions: with eternal objects, we are in the realm of ideality, in the territory of the pure potentiality of thought. Abstracted from the actual occasions that they have ingressed, the eternal objects are pure potentials for this *ingression.* Ingression denotes here 'the particular mode in which the potentiality of an eternal object' is realised 'in a particular actual entity, contributing to the definiteness of that actual entity'.[41] An eternal object has the function of determining the actual occasion. However, 'in its ingression into any one actual entity', the eternal object 'retains its potentiality of infinite diversity of modes of ingression, a potential determination rendered determinate in this instance'.[42] Eternal objects should thus be understood as modes of indetermination that are fundamental to the constitution of the actual occasion. They are the pure potentialities that inform the coming into existence of the actual occasion. 'The definite ingression into a particular actual entity', in this sense, 'is not to be conceived as the sheer evocation of that eternal object from "not-being" into "being": it is the evocation of determination out of indetermination.'[43] Actuality needs the ideality of eternal objects: the definiteness and conclusiveness of actuality has to be informed by the indeterminacy and infinity of pure ideality. Different actual occasions can be informed by the same eternal object (e.g., the eternal object 'blue' can be realised in more than one actual occasion), or by different ones. This is because the eternal object is an abstraction: 'blue', for example, is one of the abstract forms determining the actuality of the sky and the ocean alike. When the process of determination is concluded, an actual occasion is fully complete.

Eternal objects are disconnected between each other and unknowable in themselves. Since they are pure potentials and not actualities, their ontological status always entails what is not or what could have been otherwise, as well as what has never been. When 'potentiality becomes reality', it still 'retains its message of alternatives which the actual entity has avoided'.[44] The sky is blue, yet it could have been grey or pink. From this perspective, it becomes evident that, if these eternal objects 'involve in their own natures indecision',[45] this indecision fundamentally pertains to their ingression into the actual occasion. In itself, an eternal object is 'neutral as to the fact of its physical ingression in any particular actual entity of the temporal world'.[46] The eternal object does not choose what to inform or define. Rather, it is chosen by the actual occasion that selects it in conceptual prehensions. For Whitehead, it is worth remembering, '"actuality" is the decision amid "potentiality"'.[47]

In the context of this chapter's comparison between Deleuze and Whitehead, this selective or decisional prerogative of actuality is particularly interesting, because it helps us to understand to what extent the ontological dynamic of determination of indeterminacy, through which new actuality comes about, differs between the two philosophers. For Deleuze, such a dynamic is embedded in the reciprocal determination of actuality and potentiality. 'The actual and the virtual coexist,' he wrote, 'and enter into a tight circuit which we are continually retracing from one to the other.'[48] The virtual is a vector towards actualisation, yet the actual also depends on the virtual insofar as virtuality expresses actuality's transcendental condition. Using Deleuze's terminology, *differenciation* and *differentiation* are the twin ontological movements of reciprocal determination: the first is the actualisation of the virtual, while the second is the continuous flow of combination and division of the virtual field towards new directions and connections.[49] These movements are simultaneous and interdependent. In Deleuze, actuality and potentiality are two distinct fields of reality, yet one cannot exist without the other. In Whitehead, instead, there is no such mutuality between what is actual and what is potential. It is also true that, for Whitehead, the actual is never fully realised without the ingression of pure potentiality, and that this pure potentiality is always inherent to actuality (that is: eternal objects exist *in* events). Many have written about the points of resonance between eternal objects and the virtual;[50] Deleuze himself favoured a parallel between the two, describing eternal objects as pure virtualities that are actualised in prehensions.[51] While I too recognise these similarities, I wish to advance an alternative view on the issue. My claim is that—although the relation between actuality and virtuality, and that between actual occasions and eternal objects, are transformative for both Deleuze and Whitehead—there is also a profound difference between what is involved in one process of determination and what is involved in the other. The relation between the virtual and actual is reciprocal; that between actual occasions and eternal objects is not. In my view, this difference makes the straightforward equivalence between Whitehead's eternal objects and Deleuze's virtuality difficult to sustain.

James Williams has commented that reciprocal determination concerns questions about ontological permanence.[52] He has also emphasised how, for Deleuze, identity pertains to actuality, whereas for Whitehead it is potentiality that has the property of being 'fixed', so to speak. I wish to draw on this line of investigation here, and to argue, by doing so, that—since in the Whiteheadian ontological schema eternal objects are static and permanent entities (indeed, *eternal* and *objects*)—the creative activity that generates the new belongs, according to this schema, to actuality and not to potentiality. Deleuzian actualisation is an irreversible ontological movement, just like the actualisation described by Whitehead. However, for Deleuze, 'purely actual objects do not exist'.[53] Just as lived experience is always extended into the virtual field, so too is reality in general. By contrast, according to what Whitehead called the *ontological principle*, the concrete cannot derive from the abstract, because only the actual is fully real and fully in act.[54] Eternal objects do no generate actual occasions. In turn, actual occasions will not give rise to eternal objects or expand the realm of pure potentiality, and will only engage in self-creation (i.e., self-determination). Certainly, in Whitehead, there is interaction, yet there is no autopoietic or symbiotic relationship between permanence and flux, objects and occasions. Potentiality and actuality are two separate planes. The potentiality of eternal objects is not ontogenetic: eternal objects are 'forms of definiteness';[55] they are ideas or 'pure potentials of the universe',[56] which do not produce anything. Eternal objects are sterile and passive.

It can then be concluded that, with the ontological significance that Deleuze and Whitehead assigned to the notion of event, both philosophers meant to highlight that there is always a potentiality inherent in actuality. While the role that they envisaged for this potentiality, as an ideal element of new existence, might be similar in both Deleuze and Whitehead, its ontological relation with actuality is not.

THE CONDITIONS OF EXPERIENCE

It is a central contention of this book that computation could be addressed as a Whiteheadian actual event: computational processes should be thought of in terms of actual occasions. By investigating the physical and conceptual prehensions of these computational actual occasions, and thus by rethinking both their real and their pure potential, it becomes possible to demonstrate that aesthetics is a relevant mode of enquiry into digital computation. To address computational processes as actual occasions entails committing oneself to an aesthetics that operates on two levels. Computation can, therefore, be addressed in aesthetic terms not solely because it is a physical manipulation of data, or because its quantities could be transduced into affective qualities. Most importantly, according to the view that I am proposing, computation is aesthetic because it involves logico-quantitative operations of formal abstraction. Following Whitehead, these operations need not be considered from a cognitivist or representational perspective. However, they do not need to be understood as codetermined by sensibility either. Drawing on the Whiteheadian ontological schema, the intelligible is consequent to the sensible, yet not inferior to it.

We saw already that any actual occasion has both a physical and a mental pole. Because experience, for Whitehead, is a process of determination of indeterminacy, it too is dipolar: actualities hold relations among each other (via physical prehensions) and with the ideality of eternal objects (via conceptual prehensions). I have also argued that, in contrast to theories of affect, conceptual activity in Whitehead's philosophy is not codetermined by the being of the sensible, but is a genuinely conceptual operation pertaining to forms of intelligibility. Whitehead thus envisaged a conceptual activity that, contrary to Deleuze's thinking-feeling, does not act and feel like a body, but as a mind. Nonetheless, this activity remains aesthetic because it is not a cognitive mediation or representation but a prehensive grasping of thought. It is exactly these characteristics of Whitehead's ontological repertoire that I wish to use to radicalise Deleuze's aestheticisation of thinking processes. Deleuze's aesthetics requires these thinking processes to be an expression of sensibility, albeit of the metaphysical kind. Whitehead's aesthetics, by contrast, does not locate the strictly mental and conceptual character of thought upon the plane of sensibility.

By looking through the lenses of a Whiteheadian ontology, and by considering computation as a Whiteheadian actual event, the fracture between aisthesis and logos appears to be repairable. The two are not antithetical fields any longer. Whitehead understood aesthetics and logic as 'the two extremes of the dilemma of the finite mentality in its partial penetration of the infinite'. Remarkably, he believed that 'the analogy between aesthetics and logic is one of the undeveloped topics of philosophy'. This analogy lies in the fact that aesthetics and logic 'are both concerned with the enjoyment of a composition, as derived from the interconnections of its factors'. In both aesthetics and logic, 'importance arises from the vivid grasp of the interdependence of the one and the many'.[57] These comments are most interesting, for they attest to the relevance of a Whiteheadian framework to an authentic reconciliation between aisthesis and logos. In the context of computational practices and theories, this reconciliation is significant, because it shows that there is no need for computational formalism to be made more aesthetic via the injection of empirical variation. Computational logos is *already* aesthetic: aesthetics concerns the conditions of reality (in fact, of real experience, as Deleuze would have it), and these conditions—for computation as for everything else—are not only about the sensible, but about the intelligible too. Via Whitehead, logico-quantitative operations can then be understood as crucial to the constitution of computation's real experience. Drawing from Deleuze, I understand aesthetics as an enquiry into the conditions of real experience. With Whitehead, however, I can now enlarge this enquiry to consider what these conditions are for computational systems, inasmuch as conceptual operations, in his theory of experience, are instances of these conditions. This Whiteheadian contribution is a very helpful means of elaborating this book's core contention that formal abstraction, in computation, is not a representational depiction of experience, but rather the manner in which the very experience of computation comes about. This, as already anticipated, should be understood not as 'our' experience of computation, but that of computation itself. Nevertheless, in order to develop these claims, the importance that abstraction holds in Whitehead's philosophy should be explained further.

Whitehead's analysis of practices and of methods of abstraction is very sharp, and evidences the fact that his philosophy is the product of a mathematical mind. Being a mathematician, Whitehead was not afraid of abstractions. He claimed that 'the first man who noticed the analogy between a group of seven fishes and a group of seven days made a notable advance in the history of thought'.[58] Precisely because he was a mathematician, however, Whitehead also understood that 'the intolerant use of abstractions is the major vice of the intellect'.[59] The proliferation and misuse of mathematical abstractions in science has given rise to an apparatus of generalities that are, for Whitehead, guilty of reducing and diminishing experience, to say the least. Whitehead was very critical of what he called the 'scientific materialism' of his time. The problem with scientific materialism is that it downgrades immediate experience to a collection of empty or bare factualities in need of interpretation, as though every mental valuation of such factualities could only be external to the actual constitution of the factualities themselves. The depth of Whitehead's 'speculative reform or emendation of our very culture of abstraction' is epitomised in his refusal to assign to abstractions the status of mind-dependent representations of a mind-independent world.[60] This refusal is among the reasons why Whitehead rejected the early modern British empiricist tradition that informed scientific materialism; a tradition that is epitomised by the philosopher David Hume, and according to which perceived facts are associated with the impressions and ideas that a perceiving subject, external to these facts, has elaborated from them. With his critique of the 'brute fact' of scientific materialism,[61] Whitehead highlighted the risk that, if we analyse experience away into nothing, we could end up mistaking 'our abstraction for concrete realities'.[62] For Whitehead, any analysis of concrete experience must always return to this concreteness. As a mathematician, he understood the importance of generalisations for knowledge and understanding. However, as he was also a *radical empiricist*, he believed equally that 'the true method of discovery' takes off 'from the ground of particular observation', that it then 'makes a flight in the thin air of imaginative generalization' and eventually 'lands for renewed observation rendered acute by rational interpretation'.[63]

I am touching on Whitehead's speculative scheme of philosophy here. *Speculative philosophy*, in his view, is a movement towards abstraction, which attempts to grasp the concreteness of experience. While Whitehead appreciated that one 'cannot think without abstractions',[64] I would claim that he also believed that one cannot experience without abstractions either. This is another striking disparity between Deleuze and Whitehead. For Deleuze, an abstractive matrix is what separates thought from lived experience; for Whitehead, by contrast, an abstractive matrix is the essential vehicle for past actuality and ideality alike to become constitutive of experience. This means that it is essential to *any experience*. From this perspective, the task of the speculative philosopher is that of constructing a philosophical system that would account for the correspondingly systemic character of experience. Experience, according to Whitehead, always implies the construction of patterns of relatedness. Whereas, for Deleuze, abstraction is something that breaks, disrupts, and harnesses relations, for Whitehead, abstraction is what makes these patterns of relations possible in the first place.

This abstractive matrix described by Whitehead is not a representation of sensible or intelligible relations. However, it is not a Deleuzian *diagrammatics* either. Just like Deleuze's diagram, the abstractive matrix of Whitehead

'constructs a real that is yet to come'.[65] Like the diagram, this matrix attends
to the genesis of new actuality. Nonetheless, in a manner that departs from
Deleuze's diagram, Whitehead's matrix abstracts *extensively*, not intensively.
In order to appreciate the strength of Whitehead's proposition of a genetic
(i.e., productive of novelty) matrix of abstraction, and the significance that
this proposition holds in relation to the aesthetics (i.e., in relation to the
investigation into the condition of real experience) of computation, the difference between Deleuze's use of the notion of intensity and Whitehead's
concept of extension should be introduced briefly. This discussion is not
intended to remove the notion of intensity from Whitehead's ontology. Arguably, Whitehead envisaged a place for it in his philosophy.[66] This is predomi-
nantly evidenced by the fact that, for Whitehead, time is as important as
space. However, in contrast to the views held by Deleuze (and, before him,
Bergson), for Whitehead time is not a transcendental continuity that grounds
being and becoming. Time, like space, is held to be delimited by actual
occasions. Time is always discretised by actuality because it exists only in
discrete processes of actualisation. Time, in other words, is the outcome of
actualisation, just as space is: it is not a Kantian a priori intuition, but neither
is it a Deleuzo-Bergsonian transcendental field. While it is important to
acknowledge Whitehead's *epochal theory of time*, I will not address this
aspect of Whitehead's philosophy further here because it is not strictly pertinent to what I wish to consider. Instead, my focus is as follows: Whitehead's
abstractive matrix is not necessarily a structure of lived experience; in fact, it
is a structure of experience at large. Experience, in turn, is a process of self-
actualisation of discrete and finite processes that, as such, are to be understood in the quantitative terms of actual spatiotemporalities, rather than in the
qualitative terms of the durational dimensions of virtual life.

Deleuze's notion of intensity explains the importance of sensation for real
experience. Yet intensity is never given in itself: it can only be grasped as
resolved by the qualities to which it gives rise in actual things. 'Intensity is
simultaneously the imperceptible and that which can be only sensed.'[67] Like
Whitehead, Deleuze expanded the possibility of real experience well beyond
the human. However, since in the Deleuzian framework the virtual is the
transcendental condition of experience, and since this condition can only be
experienced via affectivity, experience itself ultimately remains under the
rubric of the existential. By contrast, for Whitehead experience is not necessarily to be lived, because it is not grounded upon a virtuality that is to be
transduced by the sensible, and is instead an actual process that *extends* in
space and time. Such extension is the general structure that actual entities
have in common. This structure is general, but it is also very complex,
because it conveys the 'system of relatedness of all possibilities'.[68] Experience, for Whitehead, is the determination of indeterminacy. This determination is an operation of unifying data, both actual and eternal, in the creation

of atomic yet processual entities such as the actual occasion, which dies once it is born and enters the composition of another actual occasion. While Deleuze's intensive experience is a subtraction from determination, Whitehead's experience is extensive, because it is an addition of 'drops' of reality: it is a real structure of atomic events in which a part (i.e., the actual occasion) always extends over other parts (i.e., other occasions).

Whitehead, however, also envisaged a type of ontological continuity in order to explain the relatedness of events. Still, unlike a Deleuzian flow of uninterrupted transformation, Whitehead's *extensive continuum* is atomised by the actual occasions themselves.[69] This continuum is not an intensive whole but an extensive sum of part over part. The connection between things is a relation established through succession, thanks to the activity of actual occasions that extend over one another. Having clarified this, it becomes evident why Whitehead, unlike Deleuze, could not endorse Leibniz's concept of the *infinitesimal*. Deleuze found that the differential point of view of Leibniz's infinitesimal calculus was suitable to his own development of an expressionist philosophy of difference, in which the becoming of intensive forces folds and unfolds *ad infinitum*. Deleuze's infinitesimal continuity of becoming increases by intensive multiplication and never ruptures. Whitehead's extensive continuum, on the other hand, is a 'potentiality for division',[70] in which disjunction is a starting point, not the end product. In other words, discreteness is the only way in which continuity can exist. Whitehead's dismissal of Leibniz's infinitesimal thus also explains the rationale behind his correction of Zeno's famous paradoxes about the illusion of motion. According to the pre-Socratic philosopher Zeno of Elea, an arrow never hits a target because its movement can be split in half, and that half can be split into two other halves, and so on. For Whitehead, the error of the Eleatic paradoxes consisted in presupposing a continuity that is then split into smaller and smaller entities. This presupposition invites infinite regression; it also assumes that becoming belongs to a continuous whole. Whitehead claimed, instead, that it is not the whole that becomes, but the part. That is to say, becoming belongs to the actual occasion.

It was necessary to explain these issues at length to show that Whitehead's ontology can afford a means of surpassing the aesthetic impasse between the ontological categories of discontinuity and continuity. Specifically, Whitehead might help us to conceive an aesthetics of digital computation because aesthetics, according to Whitehead, is an investigation into the becoming of discreteness (or, indeed, into discrete becoming). To address *computational actual occasions*, then, implies looking for the ways in which the discrete part becomes. This investigation gives rise to some striking speculative propositions: that togetherness is a disjunctive diversity, for instance, and that the intimate connectedness of all computational things requires a potential that is to be received not only with a body, but with a mind too.

Drawing on Whitehead's eventual actuality, one is ultimately exempted from virtualising the digital insofar as, in Whitehead, becoming is not a virtual movement but an actual one. This actuality, nonetheless, is not a mere succession of facts, for it is always ingressed by the ideality of eternal objects. In Whitehead's aesthetics, the discrete part does not fragment experience: instead, the discrete part is rather the sole object and subject of experience, for it is what determines indeterminacy, and is thus what truly becomes.

NOTES

1. See Alfred North Whitehead and Bertrand Russell, *Principia Mathematica*, 2nd ed., 3 vols. (Cambridge: Cambridge University Press, 1925).

2. 'In England, Whitehead was regarded only as a mathematician, and it was left to America to discover him as a philosopher. He and I disagreed in philosophy, so that collaboration was no longer possible. . . . His philosophy was very obscure, and there was much in it that I never succeeded in understanding. . . . He was impressed by the aspect of unity in the universe, and considered that it is only through this aspect that scientific inferences can be justified. My temperament led me in the opposite direction, but I doubt whether pure reason could have decided which of us was more nearly in the right.' Bertrand Russell, *Autobiography* (London: Allen and Unwin, 1978), 129–30.

3. Alfred North Whitehead, *Science and the Modern World* (New York: Free Press, 1967), 19. For an assessment of the relation between Whitehead's philosophy and his mathematical work, refer to Robert Palter, 'The Place of Mathematics in Whitehead's Philosophy', *Journal of Philosophy* 58, no. 19 (September 1961): 565–76, https://doi.org/10.2307/2023192. See also David Harrah, 'The Influence of Logic and Mathematics on Whitehead', *Journal of the History of Ideas* 20, no. 3 (June–September 1959): 420–30, https://doi.org/10.2307/2708119.

4. This has, for instance, been demonstrated by Luciana Parisi's study of algorithmic architecture; see *Contagious Architecture: Computation, Aesthetics, and Space* (Cambridge, MA: MIT Press, 2013). Interestingly, an early exploration of Whitehead's philosophy vis-à-vis computing is offered by Granville C. Henry in *Forms of Concrescence: Alfred North Whitehead's Philosophy and Computer Programming Structures* (London: Associated University Presses, 1993). However, Henry aims to explain Whitehead's philosophy by means of computer programs rather than the opposite. Stamatia Portanova, in *Moving without a Body: Digital Philosophy and Choreographic Thoughts* (Cambridge, MA: MIT Press, 2013), addresses Whitehead in relation to the aesthetics of the digital; as already mentioned in chapter 1, her proposition advances a virtualisation of discrete processes that I will not pursue here. Another author who explicitly considers Whitehead in relation to aesthetics and computational media is Timothy Scott Barker. In *Time and the Digital: Connecting Technology, Aesthetics, and a Process Philosophy of Time* (Hanover, NH: Dartmouth College Press, 2012), Barker focuses on the parallels between Whitehead and Deleuze in relation to experiences and conceptualisations of time generated by human interaction with digital technology. Mark B. N. Hansen's *Feed-Forward: On the Future of Twenty-First-Century Media* (Chicago: University of Chicago Press, 2015) also focuses on the encounter between human experience and digital media. In order to address such an encounter, Hansen proposes a meeting ground between Husserlian phenomenology and Whitehead's radical empiricism. This orientation towards phenomenology has led Hansen to stress Whitehead's views on experience in the phenomenological terms of a 'living through'.

5. Bruno Latour, 'What Is Given in Experience?', *Boundary 2* 32, no. 1 (Spring 2005): 222, https://doi.org/10.1215/01903659-32-1-223.

6. The most extensive treatment of Whitehead that Gilles Deleuze gave in written form can be found in chapter 6 of *The Fold: Leibniz and the Baroque*, trans. Tom Conley (London: Continuum, 2006).

7. See, for instance, Éric Alliez, *The Signature of the World: What Is Deleuze and Guattari's Philosophy?*, trans. Eliot Ross Albert and Alberto Toscano (London: Continuum, 2004); Michael Halewood, 'On Whitehead and Deleuze: The Process of Materiality', *Configurations* 13, no. 1 (Winter 2005): 57–67, https://doi.org/10.1353/con.2007.0009; Brian Massumi, *Semblance and Event: Activist Philosophy and the Occurent Arts* (Cambridge, MA: MIT Press, 2011); Keith Robinson, 'The "New Whitehead": An Ontology of the "Virtual" in Whitehead's Metaphysics', in *Gilles Deleuze: The Intensive Reduction*, ed. Constantin V. Boundas (London: Continuum, 2009), 45–81; Steven Shaviro, *Without Criteria: Kant, Whitehead, Deleuze, and Aesthetics* (Cambridge, MA: MIT Press, 2009); Isabelle Stengers, 'Thinking with Deleuze and Whitehead: A Double Test', in *Deleuze, Whitehead, Bergson: Rhizomatic Connections*, ed. Keith Robinson (Basingstoke: Palgrave Macmillan, 2009), 28–44; Isabelle Stengers, *Thinking with Whitehead: A Free and Wild Creation of Concepts* (Cambridge, MA: Harvard University Press, 2011); Arnaud Villani, 'Deleuze et Whitehead', *Revue de métaphysique et de morale* 101, no. 2 (April–June 1996): 245–65; James Williams, 'A. N. Whitehead', in *Deleuze's Philosophical Lineage*, ed. Graham Jones and Jon Roffe (Edinburgh: Edinburgh University Press, 2009); James Williams, *Encounters and Influences: The Transversal Thought of Gilles Deleuze* (Manchester: Clinamen, 2005).

8. Shaviro, *Without Criteria*, xiv.

9. Alfred North Whitehead, *Process and Reality: An Essay in Cosmology* (New York: Free Press, 1978), 4.

10. Alfred North Whitehead, *Religion in the Making* (Cambridge: Cambridge University Press, 2011), 101.

11. Whitehead, *Process and Reality*, 164.

12. Whitehead, *Science and the Modern World*, 69.

13. Shaviro, *Without Criteria*, 47.

14. Whitehead, *Process and Reality*, 45.

15. See Williams, 'A. N. Whitehead'. See also André Cloots, 'Whitehead and Deleuze: Thinking the Event', in *Deleuze, Whitehead, Bergson: Rhizomatic Connections*, ed. Keith Robinson (Basingstoke: Palgrave Macmillan, 2009), 61–76. Deleuze himself acknowledged the centrality of the notion of event in both his and Whitehead's philosophy. See *The Fold*, 86–93.

16. James Williams, 'If Not Here, Then Where? On the Location and Individuation of Events in Badiou and Deleuze', *Deleuze Studies* 3, no.1 (June 2009): 105, https://doi.org/10.3366/E1750224109000506.

17. While in *Science and the Modern World* the term 'event' is used in a manner that gives it distinctive prehensive characteristics, in the later work *Process and Reality* Whitehead seemed to prefer to use the expression 'actual occasion', and employed 'event' more generally, when denoting a nexus of actual occasions.

18. Whitehead, *Process and Reality*, 18.

19. See Alain Badiou, *Being and Event*, trans. Oliver Feltham (London: Continuum, 2006); Jacques Derrida, 'A Certain Impossible Possibility of Saying the Event', in *The Late Derrida*, ed. W. J. T. Mitchell and Arnold I. Davidson, trans. Gila Walker (Chicago: University of Chicago Press, 2007), 223–43; Martin Heidegger, *Contributions to Philosophy (Of the Event)*, trans. Richard Rojcewicz and Daniela Vallega-Neu (Bloomington: Indiana University Press, 2012); Jean-François Lyotard, *The Differend: Phrases in Dispute*, trans. Georges Van Den Abbeele (Minneapolis: University of Minnesota Press, 1988).

20. Deleuze and Guattari, *What Is Philosophy?*, trans. Graham Burchell and Hugh Tomlinson (London: Verso, 1994), 156.

21. Williams, 'A. N. Whitehead', 290.

22. Brian Massumi, 'Sensing the Virtual, Building the Insensible', in 'Hypersurface Architecture', ed. Stephen Perrella, special issue (profile 133), *Architectural Design* 68, nos. 5–6 (May–June 1998): 16.

23. Alain Badiou, *Deleuze: The Clamor of Being*, trans. Louise Burchill (Minneapolis: University of Minnesota Press, 2000), 50.

24. Massumi, 'Sensing the Virtual, Building the Insensible', 16.

25. Quentin Meillassoux, 'Potentiality and Virtuality', *Collapse: Philosophical Research and Development* 2 (March 2007), 72. Meillassoux eloquently explains the difference between

potentiality and virtuality, albeit in the context of his own—different—argument. He also offers an interesting parallel between virtuality and contingency, as well as a fundamental distinction between contingency and chance. However, while Meillassoux assigns to chance the status of potentiality, in the argument advanced in this chapter I claim that chance is not about potentiality and that it instead concerns possibility. Meillassoux's philosophy will be discussed again in chapter 6.

26. Alfred North Whitehead, *Modes of Thought* (New York: Free Press, 1968), 140.

27. Whitehead, *Process and Reality*, 150.

28. Gilles Deleuze, 'The Method of Dramatization', in *Desert Islands and Other Texts, 1953–1974*, ed. David Lapoujade, trans. Michael Taormina (Los Angeles: Semiotexte, 2004), 103.

29. Deleuze, 'The Method of Dramatization', 98.

30. Whitehead, *Science and the Modern World*, 107.

31. Whitehead, *Process and Reality*, 21.

32. Whitehead, *Process and Reality*, 65.

33. Whitehead, *Modes of Thought*, 99.

34. Whitehead, *Science and the Modern World*, 175.

35. Whitehead, *Process and Reality*, 80.

36. Whitehead, *Process and Reality*, 35.

37. Whitehead, *Modes of Thought*, 100.

38. Whitehead, *Process and Reality*, 240.

39. Whitehead, *Process and Reality*, 33.

40. Whitehead, *Process and Reality*, 44.

41. Whitehead, *Process and Reality*, 23.

42. Whitehead, *Process and Reality*, 149.

43. Whitehead, *Process and Reality*, 149.

44. Whitehead, *Process and Reality*, 149.

45. Whitehead, *Process and Reality*, 29.

46. Whitehead, *Process and Reality*, 44.

47. Whitehead, *Process and Reality*, 43.

48. Gilles Deleuze and Claire Parnet, *Dialogues II*, trans. Hugh Tomlinson, Barbara Habberjam, and Eliot Ross Albert (London: Continuum, 2006), 114.

49. See Gilles Deleuze, *Bergsonism*, trans. Hugh Tomlinson and Barbara Habberjam (New York: Zone, 1991); Gilles Deleuze, *Difference and Repetition*, trans. Paul Patton (London: Continuum, 2004).

50. This parallel has been made, for instance, by Tim Clark, 'A Whiteheadian Chaosmos? Process Philosophy from a Deleuzian Perspective', in *Process and Difference: Between Cosmological and Poststructuralist Postmodernisms*, ed. Catherine Keller and Anne Daniell (Albany: State University of New York Press, 2002), 191–207. See also Robinson, 'The "New Whitehead"'; Shaviro, *Without Criteria*; Massumi, *Semblance and Event*.

51. See Deleuze, *The Fold*, 90.

52. See Williams, *Encounters and Influences*, 77–100.

53. Deleuze and Parnet, *Dialogues II*, 112.

54. Whitehead's ontological principle states that what is real is actual and that the reasons for anything that happens must be found in actuality: 'no actual entity, then no reason'. *Process and Reality*, 19.

55. Whitehead, *Process and Reality*, 158.

56. Whitehead, *Process and Reality*, 149.

57. Whitehead, *Modes of Thought*, 60–61.

58. Whitehead, *Science and the Modern World*, 20.

59. Whitehead, *Science and the Modern World*, 18.

60. Alberto Toscano, 'The Culture of Abstraction', *Theory, Culture & Society* 25, no. 4 (July 2008): 58, https://doi.org/10.1177/0263276408091983.

61. Whitehead, *Science and the Modern World*, 8.

62. Whitehead, *Science and the Modern World*, 55. This error is what Whitehead called the 'fallacy of misplaced concreteness'. I will address this fallacy in greater detail in the third part of this book.

63. Whitehead, *Process and Reality*, 5. Whitehead explicitly acknowledged his intellectual affinity with William James and his philosophy of 'pure experience'. See, for instance, *Process and Reality*, xii. I too recognise the explicit debt that Whitehead's empiricism owes to that of James. However, I will not dwell on this connection, for I understand the work of William James as still being focused on the lived dimension of experience. See his *Essays in Radical Empiricism* (Cambridge, MA: Harvard University Press, 1976).

64. Whitehead, *Science and the Modern World*, 59.

65. Gilles Deleuze and Félix Guattari, *A Thousand Plateaus: Capitalism and Schizophrenia*, trans. Brian Massumi (London: Continuum, 2004), 157.

66. Intensity takes centre stage in the reading of Whitehead proposed by Judith A. Jones. In a manner that differs from the approach taken in this book, Jones argues that continuity, not discreteness, is of primary ontological importance in Whitehead's philosophy. See *Intensity: An Essay in Whiteheadian Ontology* (Nashville, TN: Vanderbilt University Press, 1998).

67. Deleuze, *Difference and Repetition*, 290.

68. Whitehead, *Science and the Modern World*, 162.

69. Whitehead, *Process and Reality*, 67.

70. Whitehead, *Process and Reality*, 67.

Part 2

Abstraction

Chapter Four

Computational Idealism

BEAUTY AND TRUTH

'"Beauty is truth, truth beauty,"—that is all Ye know on earth, and all ye need to know.'[1] It is probably safe to assert that when, in the second decade of the nineteenth century, the Romantic poet John Keats wrote these famous closing lines to 'Ode on a Grecian Urn', he knew nothing of computation. His aim was, perhaps, to reflect on the relationship between art and life, and on the possibilities and constraints of the artistic medium. Likewise, it can also be supposed that when the free-software programmer and media artist Jaromil crafted a single-line piece of code in 2002—a code that looked, amusingly, like a short string of ASCII smilies, but which was nonetheless able to bring down a whole Unix-like system—he was not paying homage to the neoclassical ideals celebrated by British Romanticism. Jaromil was less concerned with the orderly world of antiquity than with the very present and uncomfortable disarray of an operating system that crashes when a large quantity of programs are run simultaneously, eating up all its memory and exhausting processor time. His *ASCII Shell Fork Bomb* is a command-line script that does exactly this. By launching two or more copies of itself upon start-up, the piece of code initiates a chain reaction in which the number of launches multiplies itself exponentially. The machine halts, incapable of coming to terms with the recursive spawning of processes. Rebooting is the only means of restoring normal functionality.[2]

There is an undeniable historical, conceptual, and programmatic distance between the two instances. The correspondence that I am suggesting is not meant to create any interpretative parallel between Keats and Jaromil. Rather, Keats's statement can be viewed as an exemplification of the long-standing intellectual belief that beauty and truth are uniform and interdependent.

This identity of beauty and truth echoes all the way from the numerology of Pythagoras to the golden ratio of the Renaissance. It resonates in contemporary classes on computational logic and arrives at the cursor in a terminal prompt, where the fork bomb is inputted. It is my contention that the equivalence between beauty and truth also lies at the core of certain approaches to computational aesthetics. Within the context of computation, this equivalence exceeds the limits of meditations about classical virtues (such as the Hellenism of Keats), but it also maintains the classical age's concern with the supremacy of simplicity over complexity, of order over chaos, and of unity over parts. This classical uniformity of beauty and truth in computational aesthetics lies at the basis of what I call *computational idealism*. The term 'idealism' is to be taken here in its metaphysical sense. It indicates the principle according to which abstract laws are more fundamental to reality than the phenomena that we are presented with through perception and sensation.[3] What I am depicting as an idealism of computation is a technocultural view that would maintain that computational structures are *ideal forms*, insofar as they are immutable entities, independent from matter as well as from contingency. From this perspective, aesthetic significance corresponds to a mathematical conception of beauty, articulated as the ultimate value or a cipher of computational being per se.[4] The latter, in turn, is truthful insofar as it presents, through algorithmic inference, a means to an ideal of eternal and abstract formality that is essentially indifferent to change. Beauty and truth are thus not conjoined through the ethical (as would be argued by a classical aesthetics concerned with moral worth),[5] or via correlationalist representation (which a transcendental interpretation of idealism would see as lying at the core of the relationship between form and matter).[6] On the contrary, computational idealism holds that an equivalence between beauty and truth can be found via *logical proof*: computational structures are truthful insofar as they are logically consistent; this consistency is beautiful because it adheres to the axiomatic character of computation.[7] This equivalence of the beautiful and the truthful is thus based on *deduction*. In other words, my claim is that logical validity not only grounds the operative workings of computer science (that is, determinism is what defines a computing machine), but also grounds some attempts to create an aesthetically pleasing formality within computational laws.

Like the Platonic solids of ancient tradition, beautiful and truthful computational structures are assumed to be permanent, closed, and reliant only on their internal conditions of necessity.[8] They are taken to be a priori (in other words, to come both ontologically and epistemologically before experience) and to need no real-world evidence in order to exist. The ideal beauty of the closed system is evident in the example of Jaromil's fork bomb. Inherently self-referential, the fork bomb draws a full circle from input to output and to input again, while showing no interest in flirting with the gaze of any beholder. To appropriate Friedrich Kittler's famous remark on the role of software, this code seems to 'have been explicitly contrived to evade perception'.[9] While fork bombs and similar coding tricks are common in hacking culture, Florian Cramer comments that 'Jaromil manages to condense them to a most terse, poetic syntax, arguably the most elegant fork bomb ever written'.[10] The elegance that Cramer attributes to the script is achieved via syntactical density and through compression of notation and execution. From this point of view, Jaromil's piece complies with Donald Knuth's definition of elegance in computer science, which takes such elegance to be conditional upon the coder's proficiency in the 'art of computer programming', as much as upon quantitative concision and logical consistency.[11] Examples of the popularity and persistence of similar understandings of computational elegance can be found by looking at the plethora of programming manuals and textbooks that invoke the cleanliness (and therefore goodliness) of 'beautiful code', and in those first-person accounts given by software developers who emphasise personal efforts towards minimising inscription whilst maximising functionality.[12]

The reading of the aesthetic significance of the fork bomb that I propose here, however, is intended to go beyond an intellectual appreciation of the digital mastery of the artist or the programmer. My aim is to focus on the fork bomb as a *closed formal system* in order to read—and to thereby criticise—its script as an instance of the idealised conformity between logical truth and aesthetic beauty described above. I am aware that Jaromil emphasises the fork bomb's status as an experiment on the cracks and gaps of the digital domain and that he employs it to comment on the creative potential which he sees as intrinsic to the vulnerability of digital systems.[13] Thus, from Jaromil's perspective, the *ASCII Shell Fork Bomb* would seem to be less an inhabitant of the ivory towers of computational formalism than of the playgrounds of glitch and error. In a specific media art context, Jaromil's fork bomb can be understood as a sort of computational ready-made: as something that explicates the autopositing and self-affirming force of art, as something that stands between the recreational and the radical, and as something that is a bit odd, but which, through artistic appropriation and popular misuse, is capable of reassigning the meanings and consequences of media systems. Yet, having clarified this, I would like to stress that, while I acknowledge these interpretations of Jaromil's work, I will not be addressing the fork bomb here as a glitchy product of imperfect computation. This is because I am interested in viewing it in entirely the opposite manner. In other words, I am interested in pursuing the sense in which Jaromil's script is neither an anomaly nor a bug, but rather a small program that does exactly what it is supposed to do. In this sense, I am heading in an interpretative direction that differs from the ways in which the script has been talked about by its own creator and others.[14] I believe that the work's exponential disruptiveness is not dependent upon the messiness of a machine running amok, but that the fork bomb can be disruptive purely because of the formal consistency of the script's logical formulation. The pace of the fork bomb is relentless, inexorable, inescapable. Marching towards the physical limits of the machine (such as memory and processing capacity), this piece of code is dangerous not just for the actual damages or the end-user discomfort that it can produce by halting the functionality of the operating system. The fork bomb seduces and scares as a result of the effectiveness of its method, and because of the intrinsic correctness of its proof. No less autarchic than it is anarchic, Jaromil's *ASCII Shell Fork Bomb* does not care for external agents and cares even less for the empirical. Given the necessary conditions, it works independently of empirical phenomena and users. There is no evolution, no generation, and no dynamism—only the internal repetition of its conditions of logical necessity.

The idealism of computational forms—and I take Jaromil's fork bomb to be an example, however involuntary it may be, of that idealism—might not be explicitly acknowledged in everyday computing practices. However, this concept is relevant and useful, because it can help us to expose a certain way of looking at abstraction and experience in computation. In the classicist aesthetics of computation, the relation between abstraction and experience is based on the *transcendence* of the former over the latter. This is because, in its classicist and idealistic orientation, computational structures are a priori forms. The abstract (expressed via logico-mathematical formalisation) is assumed to bear a transcendent relation to the empirical, regulating it through its unilateral and unidirectional power of imposing itself upon the perceptual and the physical. The connection between classical aesthetic endeavours and idealist metaphysics can now be stated more explicitly. Computational idealism reiterates the Platonic top-down approach of the intelligible informing the sensible. Aesthetically, this idealism of computational forms lends itself to a focus on classicist aesthetic features such as elegance, simplicity, symmetry, and harmony. Such qualities purportedly lead towards the unity and order of deductive abstractive methods. Epistemologically, computational idealism becomes a rationalist affair: it maintains deduction as its fundamental mechanisms of invention and discovery, and it endorses the prospect of advancing, one day, an all-inclusive account of the workings of nature and mind. Moving from epistemology to ontology, the abstract is considered to be metaphysically superior. Computational logos is intelligible, not sensible; it is thus metaphysical, because it is beyond the physical (metà tà physiká), and has perseity in virtue of the self-referentiality of its formal structures. Finally, from a cultural perspective, computation, when it is assumed to be both beautiful and truthful, comes to ground the all-too-human faith in a computing machine that can do no wrong, as well as the technosocial construction of an image of infallible and impenetrable algorithmic rationality.

This idealisation of computational forms can be seen as a powerful account of the transcendent relation. between 'what is here' (what constitutes a natural reality, known through sensation and empirical knowledge) and 'what is there' (a sort of Platonic *hyperuranion*: a most fundamental, archetypal kind of reality, where abstractions of all possible scales and degrees are already defined).[15] These abstract determinations are not Deleuzian potentialities of virtual indeterminacy to be expressed immanently in the actual. In the framework of computational idealism, the abstract is instead the ideality of the intelligible realm of logico-mathematical rules of organisation of this actual. This abstract does not partake in the construction of experience: it directs it transcendentally. In this respect, the explicative and regulative force of computational idealism's forms is appealing, almost irresistible. From a philosophical perspective, it is based on the presupposition that the intelligible dimension of eternal ideality might offer a means of regulating the phenomenal and the material, and that this normative character might be expressed through the transcendent nature of the realm of logico-mathematical formulation in respect to its sensible instantiations. This transcendence is the target of my critique of the aesthetics of computational idealism. In order to develop that critique, however, I will need to start by looking at the onto-epistemological principle that turns the ideal dimension of beautiful computation into the idealisation of a closed formula. I call this principle *Universal Computation*.

UNIVERSAL COMPUTATION

In Douglas Adams's comic sci-fi novel *The Hitchhiker's Guide to the Galaxy*, a race of hyperintelligent, pan-dimensional beings have devoted a lot of time and money into building a giant supercomputer named Deep Thought in order to finally reveal the 'Ultimate Answer' to the 'Ultimate Question of Life, the Universe, and Everything'.[16] In Adams's story, it takes Deep Thought seven and a half million years to run the program, at the end of which the result is finally revealed: '42'. This is the 'Ultimate Answer'. Unfortunately, the alien creatures quickly come to realise that the 'Ultimate Question' itself remains unknown.

Adams's famous joke provides a good fictional and parodic example of *metacomputation*: an approach that, in its broadest and most accessible articulation, calls for a comprehensive science of calculation through which one would be able to grasp the fundamentals of reality itself.[17] This dream of a universal science of reasoning, which is classical in origin, is one of the main ideas of Western civilisation.[18] One of its most relevant champions is the Baroque philosopher and polymath Gottfried Wilhelm Leibniz, who envisioned a complete discipline (called *mathesis universalis*) through which one would have been able to design a compendium of all human knowledge.[19] Modern attempts to automate thought, proposed by mathematical logic, can be seen as continuous with such rationalist experiments in metareasoning. The lowest common denominator between these instances is found in the importance attributed to the employment of problem-solving strategies that, by specifying the rules of the game, expect that we can also know what we can achieve by playing it. In what follows, I will argue, on the one hand, that metacomputation epistemologically justifies a computational aesthetics of beautiful and truthful forms; on the other, I will contend that it also underpins this aesthetics ontologically. The deterministic possibility of giving an 'Ultimate Answer to the Ultimate Question of Life, the Universe, and Everything', to use the words of Douglas Adams, is worked out exactly on this onto-epistemological premise. The fact that the 'Ultimate Question' itself remains unknown, however, betrays the nagging suspicion that computation is never as straightforward as one might imagine.

Hereafter, I will refer to the onto-epistemological duality of the metacomputational approach as *Universal Computation*. The phrase is used for two reasons. The first is that it evokes the universal Turing machine (UTM). The expression 'Universal Computation' transversally refers to the specific method of computation envisaged by the mathematician Alan Turing—a method that is said to have defined our current conception of mechanical calculation.[20] This technique is to be understood, in Turing's original development, less as an actual computing technology than as a formalisation of what it means 'to compute'. It should be seen as an automatic principle of deductive inference, which is considered universal insofar as it is capable of computing anything that can, in principle, be computed. The postulation of a universal method of computation is one of Turing's most far-reaching achievements; one that justifies the view that he first conceived the principle behind modern digital computers. Universality is a foundational concept in computer science. Among the most fundamental facts about modern automatic computing machines is their capacity to simulate any calculation that can be carried out by any other automatic computing machine.[21] This simulation is possible precisely because of the universal, general-purpose character of these devices. Turing's insight into the theory of computation will be treated in greater detail later, in chapter 6. For now, it is enough to stress that the UTM's general-purposiveness can be seen to characterise conceptually the metacomputational approach discussed above.

The principle of Universal Computation pushes a metacomputational agenda, which in turn pursues a comprehensive science of valid reasoning. According to this perspective, the concept of Universal Computation is strong and powerful and is able to explain (1) how computing machines are supposed to work, and (2) how such functionality implies a horizon of total operativity. In order to defend the latter claim, my second motivation for using the phrase 'Universal Computation' must now be introduced. This reason concerns the specific onto-epistemological role that abstraction assumes in Universal Computation. Informally, to compute is to systematise, to rationalise, and to order the real via logico-quantitative means; formally, via Turing, it means to quantify and to extrapolate, through a method, a finite rule that aims at the 'effective calculability' of this quantification.[22] In accordance with these informal and formal definitions, a metacomputational theory of reasoning searches for an ordering technique to structure the diversities of life. It expresses a will to produce and master the whole organisation of the thinkable and the arguable in the hope that something like deductive calculation can successfully account for reality. The general-purposiveness of this epistemic endeavour makes claims of comprehensiveness plausible and viable. Universal Computation is, in this respect, the abstractive technique proper to deductive reasoning: to compute is to systematise deductively, by finite sequences of quantities organised according to rules of inference, and such a concatenation is possible thanks to its general validity and purposiveness, which are themselves based upon deductive abstraction.

Metacomputational abstraction, however, is not only about knowing; it is also about *being*. Therefore, my second reason for employing the phrase 'Universal Computation' is that, by stressing the universality of the computational method, I can make the case for the onto-epistemological status of metacomputational abstraction in computation. Drawing on the contention that epistemology constructs metaphysics (and vice versa), I believe that the functional determinism of Universal Computation also underpins a specifically metaphysical position. According to the metacomputational view, the epistemological techniques of deductive abstraction subtend ontological transcendence. The abstract, in this sense, has a proper ontological status. In the metaphysics of Universal Computation, computational forms are above the empirical: software rises above hardware, and its formalisms rise above its particular executable instantiations. Questions about metacomputational ontology are, therefore, questions about transcendent entities—namely, entities that are not determined by others, which exist by virtue of logical necessity, and which are the foundation and principle of empirical things. While, epistemologically speaking, the quality of metacomputational universality has thus originated from deduction, from an ontological view metacomputation is universal because it is based on transcendence. Distinctively Platonic positions could again be seen to be the direct reference point here, insofar as they postulate a realist yet transcendent ontology of the universal. I am thus proposing the view according to which *mathesis universalis*, reconsidered and repurposed via twentieth-century attempts at formalising a definition of computability, is underpinned by a transcendent metaphysics similar to that of Platonic philosophy. The question now, therefore, is this: what are the consequences of thinking Universal Computation as an onto-epistemological principle, according to which computation is held to be separate from empirical phenomena, and yet is also held to possess the power of accounting for what there is to know and be? And what does this tell us about its aesthetics?

SIMPLICITY

When confronting the non-relation between abstraction and experience in computation, one faces a twofold idealism. On the one hand, there is the idealist canon of computational perfection. This perfection concerns elegant logico-mathematical formalisations that would not be disturbed or corrupted by anything empirical. Such a position underpins a classicist type of idealism, for it recalls the transcendent metaphysical systems of the classical age. This classicism is expressed through the aesthetic equivalence of beauty and truth, which is in turn based on the non-sensorial character of deductive formulation. However, there is more to the idealisation of computation than classicist nostalgia. Formal abstraction's transcendent relation to experience also underpins a distinct form of idealism that is specific to the computational operation. This is still an idealism of the a priori form, but it possesses an instrumental character that is proper to the general-purposiveness of computability, as exemplified by the UTM. This is what could be called the 'functionalist' idealism of a machine that can operate anywhere and on anything. As in the influential and widespread theory of mind known as *functionalism*, what is important here is not the material substratum upon which an operation is instantiated but rather its being a universal function with multiple realisations.[23] So, while on the one hand the aesthetic ideal of a beautiful and truthful computation revisits a conception of harmonic and regulative intelligibility that was already present in Plato, on the other hand it can be argued that, with the universal Turing machine, this classicist idealism becomes *operative* via the automation of functional rules. Both facets of computational idealism (the classicist and the functionally operative) imply onto-epistemological transcendence. This double development is implicitly endorsed and extended by computational practices whenever they pursue an aesthetic canon of logico-mathematical beauty, according to which the real can be subsumed under the principles of rational construction.

In order to clarify this point, a pivotal concept in computational aesthetics needs to be discussed: *simplicity*. The ideal of a simple computational form pertains to the metacomputational quest for a rational systematisation, a quest that is, as we saw, both classicist and functionally universalist. The work of the designer, artist, and technologist John Maeda can be used as an example here. 'Simplicity' is certainly the key word in Maeda's commercial and academic work. He never tires of advocating what he calls 'the laws of simplicity', which he claims to be just as applicable to digital design as to business and life in general.[24] The efforts of the Aesthetics + Computation Group (hereafter, ACG), directed by Maeda at the Massachusetts Institute of Technology's Media Lab, can be viewed as shared expressions of this quest for the simple in computation. In its seven years of activity (from 1996 to 2003), the ACG aimed to advance the study and production of digital architectures, focusing on the procedural composition of computational spaces and shapes.[25] Within the environment of the MIT Media Lab, simplicity was the tacit but persistent measure of all computational things, and the measure of success of any 'design by numbers'.[26]

Maeda also made simplicity an organisational principle in his personal use of this measure. This standard of order took on the role of the fundamental idea behind computing itself. His artwork *AI Infinity* (1994) can help us to develop this claim. In this work, the shape of the symbol of infinity (∞) is drawn via the looping of an intrinsic and essential element of graphic design: the line. However, I would suggest that we should sidestep the visible outcome of the artwork in order to consider Maeda's implied emphasis on the processes of computation.[27] From this perspective, the line-thin loops outlined by the computer are the perceptible visualisation of the ideal of a formulation (the algorithmic instructions) imposed on the concrete (the actual computing machines). There are two primary aspects of simplicity at work here. On the one hand, the simple is equivalent to the lean, the agile, and the sustainable. This is the conception of simplicity that is most often identified by the community of designers and technologists that Maeda would seem to be openly addressing his efforts towards. On the other hand, however, *AI Infinity*'s procedural nature articulates computation as an independent method of transcendent formulation, and as a technique according to which instructions and set conditions (in other words, the a priori maintained by the algorithmic setting of the work) precede the physical act of drawing. In this view, a simple computational form is much more than a pretty visible shape. Instead, this is the simplicity proper to metaphysical 'first principles'. The simple, therefore, involves the deductive character of computational media: it builds on the ideal of an algorithmic formality through which deduction is expressed, and, in doing so, it withdraws itself from any unnecessary empirical clutter that the latter might stumble upon. It is this aspect of computational simplicity that interests me most, as it can be said to encapsulate the idealist and universal dimensions of the metacomputational enterprise.

I am aware that I could be said to be reading between the (thousands of) lines of Maeda's advocacy of the concept of simplicity. The subtext that I am inferring from it presents simplicity as the rationale of computer science and also as that of much computational art. This rationale is best understood in terms of the independence of computational proofs, which are universal in nature (as they have general validity and comprehensive applicability in order to be reliable) and idealist in spirit (because they assign to the programmatic rule—i.e., the algorithm behind the visualisation—the effective causality of the phenomenal level of the artwork). Ultimately, these simple computational forms bring us back to a consideration of the twofold character of idealism in computation. *AI Infinity* would seem to declare: empirical phenomena cannot be understood in themselves; however, it is possible to have a rule that encompasses an ideal of beauty as a simple self-referential structure, and which can—when instantiated into the machine's operability—bring such an ideal into the realm of the given, where the physical and the empirical dwell. The simple in computation is thus seen as valid and effective for two reasons: on the one hand, it is independent from the empirical; on the other, it is meant to provide a universal solution for a particular problem. To conclude this point, simplicity stands here as the epitome of a logico-mathematical formulation: the raison d'être of computation itself.

Some evidence capable of supporting this reading of *AI Infinity* can be found in Maeda's decision to exhibit the work as a print. To reach a perceptual level of sensuous reception, the artist has to hijack the computational recursion with the introduction of an external stimulus (namely, the print input). The thousands of interconnected loops created by the algorithm only confront the empirical when the artist stops the computational process in order to print its visual result. However, let us not focus on the subjective fruition of the work in its observation and appreciation by a spectator (which the print format would imply as the final recipient of the piece). Instead, let us consider the non-sensory aspect of computational abstraction that is not explicitly addressed in this example, but which is nonetheless presupposed by it. Maeda's decision to exhibit the work as a print would seem to imply that one can experience the artwork only when it is brought into the sensible realm of the caused and the given. This assumption would appear to confirm the claim according to which abstraction is understood as the method of the transcendent production of both the ideality and the universality of computation. The simple computational forms employed by Maeda are thus not perceptual but conceptual, because their computational simplicity transcends sense experience and appeals to a higher realm of intelligibility. When staring at *AI Infinity*, one is looking at the metacomputational construction of a total determinism: partly because of the image's symbolism, but most importantly because the work presents the totality of a simple operation that closes the circle of both its ideation and actuation. To understand universality according to simplicity, therefore, means to address it in terms of a question of *metacomputational closure*—a closure that is resolved within intelligibility, not sensibility. This resolution between ideation and actuation within intelligibility is the ultimate horizon of a universal science of computation. The idealisation of computational forms is oriented towards just such a determinist conclusion.

NOTES

1. John Keats, 'Ode on a Grecian Urn', in *Complete Poems* (Cambridge, MA: Belknap, 1982), 282–83.

2. For the *ASCII Shell Fork Bomb* script, see Jaromil, ':(){:|:&};: - Ou de la Bohème Digitale', *Jaromil's Musings* (blog), 2002, https://jaromil.dyne.org/journal/forkbomb.html.

3. There are many kinds of idealist approaches. Looking at the history of thought, one can distinguish between a British school of idealism and a German one, as well as between epistemological idealism (which focuses on knowledge and on the mind dependency of reality) and ontological idealism (which is concerned with metaphysical questions, and which maintains that everything is in some respect spiritual or immaterial). In this chapter, my use of the term 'idealism' refers to a classical and specifically Platonic tradition, according to which the realm of the sensible is separated from (and inferior to) the realm of the intelligible. This latter is autonomous from, and also the cause of, the former. One final qualification: my understanding and elaboration of Platonic idealism draws from Giovanni Reale's interpretation of the Platonic system. See *Per una nuova interpretazione di Platone*, 21st ed. (Milan: Vita e Pensiero, 2003).

4. In what is one of the most popular modern defences of the aesthetic value of mathematics, G. H. Hardy writes that 'beauty is the first test: there is no permanent place in the world for ugly mathematics'. *A Mathematician's Apology* (Cambridge: Cambridge University Press, 2009), 85. Similar comments about the aesthetic nature of mathematics are countless. An interesting collection of texts addressing the past and present consequences of this relationship can be found in Nathalie Sinclair, David Pimm, and William Higginson, eds., *Mathematics and the Aesthetic: New Approaches to an Ancient Affinity* (New York: Springer, 2006).

5. For the ancient Greeks, the idea of beauty was indivisible from notions of the good, the virtuous, the excellent, and the divine. These qualities constituted the basis of a good life. For the classical conception of beauty, see Umberto Eco's *On Beauty: A History of a Western Idea*, trans. Alastair McEwen (London: MacLehose, 2010), 37–51. For a more specifically Platonic understanding of beauty, see Drew A. Hyland, *Plato and the Question of Beauty* (Bloomington: Indiana University Press, 2008).

6. This comment refers to Immanuel Kant and his transcendental idealism, which takes ideal forms to be part of human structural methods of reasoning. See *Critique of Pure Reason*, trans. John Miller Dow Meiklejohn (Mineola, NY: Dover, 2003).

7. The general notion of logical proof denotes a sequence of formal statements according to which conclusions are consequences of their premises. It is thus impossible for the premises to be true and their conclusions false. An account of the relation between mathematical proof and beauty can be found in Doris Schattschneider, 'Beauty and Truth in Mathematics', in *Mathematics and the Aesthetic: New Approaches to an Ancient Affinity*, ed. Nathalie Sinclair, David Pimm, and William Higginson (New York: Springer, 2006), 41–57.

8. Plato envisaged five solids (the tetrahedron, the cube, the octahedron, the dodecahedron, and the icosahedron) to be the fundamental archetypes of the beautiful and to represent the natural elements. See Michele Emmer, 'Art and Mathematics: The Platonic Solids', in *The Visual Mind: Art and Mathematics*, ed. Michele Emmer (Cambridge, MA: MIT Press, 1993), 215–20.

9. Friedrich A. Kittler, 'There Is No Software', in *Literature, Media, Information Systems: Essays*, ed. John Johnston (Amsterdam: Gordon and Breach, 1997), 148. It should be added that, as a short piece of written code, Jaromil's fork bomb has been printed and exhibited many times; it has been reproduced on T-shirts and has even been the subject of tattoos. This phenomenal level of the work is not the focus of my analysis; my aim is in fact to address Jaromil's fork bomb for its non-sensory formal character, which makes it akin to an ideal computational form.

10. Florian Cramer, 'Entering the Machine and Leaving It Again: Poetics of Software in Contemporary Art', 2006, http://www.gwei.org/pages/press/press/Florian_Cramer/fullversion.html.

11. Donald E. Knuth, *The Art of Computer Programming*, vol. 1, *Fundamental Algorithms* (Upper Saddle River, NJ: Addison-Wesley, 1997). See also *Literate Programming* (Stanford, CA: Center for the Study of Language and Information, 1992). My understanding of the

relevance of the concept of elegance for computational culture is informed by Matthew Fuller's characterisation of the elegant programming of Knuth as a self-referent discipline. See Fuller's text 'Elegance', in *Software Studies: A Lexicon*, ed. Matthew Fuller (Cambridge, MA: MIT Press, 2008), 87–92.

12. See, for instance, Andy Oram and Greg Wilson, eds., *Beautiful Code: Leading Programmers Explain How They Think* (Sebastopol, CA: O'Reilly, 2007); Robert C. Martin, *Clean Code: A Handbook of Agile Software Craftsmanship*. (Indianapolis: Prentice Hall, 2009); Peter Seibel, *Coders at Work: Reflections on the Craft of Programming* (New York: Apress, 2009). On a broader technoscientific scale, comparable qualitative appraisals based on the quantitative standards of the shortest possible encryption are produced in the sciences, especially theoretical physics.

13. See Jaromil, ':(){:|:&};: - Ou de la Bohème Digitale', and also Jaromil, '*ASCII Shell Forkbomb*', *Jaromil's Musings* (blog), 2002, https://jaromil.dyne.org/journal/forkbomb_art. html.

14. See, for instance, Tatiana Bazzichelli, *Networking: The Net as Artwork*, trans. Maria Anna Calamia and Helen Pringle (Aarhus: Digital Aesthetics Research Centre Aarhus University, 2009), 192; Alexander R. Galloway and Eugene Thacker, *The Exploit: A Theory of Networks* (Minneapolis: University of Minnesota Press, 2007), 176; Charlie Gere, *Community without Community in Digital Culture* (Basingstoke: Palgrave Macmillan, 2012), 140; Jussi Parikka, *Digital Contagions: A Media Archaeology of Computer Viruses* (New York: Peter Lang, 2007), 179.

15. See Plato, *Phaedo*, trans. David Gallop (Oxford: Oxford University Press, 2009).

16. Douglas Adams, *The Hitchhiker's Guide to the Galaxy* (London: Pan, 1979), 130.

17. Technically, 'metacomputing' refers to those activities employing computational tools for the study and improvement of computational systems. In this book, I turn the expression 'metacomputation' into a philosophical concept, meant to denote the intellectual quest for a universal science of reasoning that has been known historically as *mathesis universalis*. In my use, metacomputation can thus be understood as the project of calculating and systematising, via rational means, all reality, and as the onto-epistemological principle through which this has been attempted (which I will be referring to as 'Universal Computation'). I will also be using the expression in parallel with the notion of metamathematics (see chapter 6). In both cases, the prefix *meta-* implies the exponential growth of the mathematical and computational framework.

18. For instance, Plato argued for all mathematical sciences to be brought together into one comprehensive view of the world. See *The Republic*, trans. R. E. Allen (New Haven, CT: Yale University Press, 2006). The Cartesian dualism between thought and extension can be seen as carrying the same ancient burden of wanting to maintain the distinction between the sensible and the intelligible by finding a method to separate spatially extended things from how we think about them. See René Descartes, *Meditations on First Philosophy, with Selections from the Objections and Replies*, ed. and trans. John Cottingham (Cambridge: Cambridge University Press, 1986).

19. See Gottfried Wilhelm Leibniz, 'Mathesis Universalis. Praefatio', in *Mathematische Schriften*, vol. 7, *Die Mathematischen Abhandlungen* (Hildesheim: G. Olms, 1971), 49–52.

20. The universal Turing machine was not the only early twentieth-century attempt at formulating a comprehensive method of calculation. Although they were both unaware of each other's contribution, in 1936 Alan Turing and Alonzo Church were 'doing the same things in a different way'. Alan M. Turing, quoted in Andrew Hodges, 'Alan Turing and the Turing Machine', in *The Universal Turing Machine: A Half-Century Survey*, ed. Rolf Herken (Oxford: Oxford University Press, 1988), 5. Both Church and Turing were indeed working on definitions of computability and reached equivalent conclusions, albeit via dissimilar means, regarding functions whose values are effectively calculable. An account of the professional relationship between the two men, along with the similarities and differences between their reciprocal contributions, is given in Andrew Hodges, *Alan Turing: The Enigma* (London: Vintage, 1992), 111–59. See also Church's 1984 interview with William Aspray, quoted in David Leavitt's *The Man Who Knew Too Much: Alan Turing and the Invention of the Computer* (London: Phoenix, 2006), 113–14.

21. 'There are two fundamental concepts at the heart of computer science. One is the *algorithm* or *program*: a sequence of instructions, written in some general but precise language, that carries out some calculation or solves some problem. The other is the *universal computer*: a programmable device that can carry out any algorithm we give to it.' Cristopher Moore and Stephan Mertens, *The Nature of Computation* (Oxford: Oxford University Press, 2011), 224.

22. Alan M. Turing, 'On Computable Numbers, with an Application to the Entscheidungs-problem', *Proceedings of the London Mathematical Society* 42 (1936): 231, https://doi.org/10.1112/plms/s2-42.1.230.

23. In the 1960s, functionalism responded to the demise of the mind-body identity theory by advancing the view that causal roles and relations between mental states should be described in terms of functions and not identified at the material level of the brain, or of a physical medium such as neurons. According to the functionalist view, what matters is not the internal constitution of a mental state, but the way in which this mental state works, or the role that it plays in relation to other parts of the same (mental) system. The philosopher Hilary Putnam has famously claimed that 'we could be made of Swiss cheese and it wouldn't matter'. See his 'Philosophy and Our Mental Life', in *Philosophical Papers*, vol. 2, *Mind, Language and Reality* (Cambridge: Cambridge University Press, 1975), 291. It is interesting to note, however, that since the late 1980s Putnam has rejected his own earlier views on machine-state functionalism. See *Representation and Reality* (Cambridge, MA: MIT Press, 1988); Oron Shagrir, 'The Rise and Fall of Computational Functionalism', in *Hilary Putnam*, ed. Yemima Ben-Menahem (Cambridge: Cambridge University Press, 2005), 220–50.

24. See John Maeda, *The Laws of Simplicity: Design, Technology, Business, Life* (Cambridge, MA: MIT Press, 2006).

25. Maeda has commented on the work of the ACG in the book *Creative Code: Aesthetics + Computation* (London: Thames and Hudson, 2004). See also Stephen Wilson, *Information Arts: Intersections of Art, Science, and Technology* (Cambridge, MA: MIT Press, 2003), 319–20.

26. John Maeda, *Design by Numbers* (Cambridge, MA: MIT Press, 1999).

27. References to the series of works to which *AI Infinity* belongs can be found in John Maeda's book *Maeda@Media* (London: Thames and Hudson, 2000), 28–31.

Chapter Five

Axiomatics

FORMULAE

Closure is a crucial feature of Universal Computation. This closed character is also central to idealist conceptions of aesthetics in computation, according to which there is a correspondence between aesthetic value (beauty) and logico-mathematical validity (truth). An idealist computational aesthetics of deductive forms employs techniques of formalisation in order to close the system, figuratively speaking, thereby attempting to give logical and mathematical structures an onto-epistemological primacy and operative universality over the empirical. Of course, the closure in question is a metaphorical property. The history of computing is populated with closed or open constructs. A closed/open dichotomy involves, for instance, parallels with physical instantiations of calculating machines (e.g., the openness or closure of an electric circuit), with information theory's transmission of communication over a channel, or with the feedback models of cybernetics. The metaphorical closure that I am interested in investigating, however, is a more hypothetical and speculative aspect of computational idealism, denoting the conclusive character of transcendence and apriority in computational aesthetics and in computational culture at large. On the one hand, this closure stands as a sort of metaphysical barrier. The transcendent bounces the empirical back, opposing obstacles to any attempt, made by the mutable, to cross over the barricade and merge with the transcendent. This is the gatekeeping of computational idealism in its twofold classicist and functionally operative character. On the other hand, however, the mechanisms of logical deduction are also figuratively closed. A striving for conclusion is an internal feature of deductive systems, which are closed to experience because they are separate from it.

Undeniably, computational systems are *formal axiomatic systems*. This means that they involve a starting point that is self-evident and which defines the inferential steps that can be taken from it towards a result via the manipulation of a list of finite instructions. The classical or traditional theory of computation—that is, Turing's—is established and operates in parallel with the axiomatic nature of logico-mathematical abstraction. The latter is a way of reasoning that privileges deductive legitimacy over induction, and which holds that if premises are assumed to be true, then so too are the conclusions that one can deduce from them, with no need for empirical justification.[1] The mechanical automation of the axiomatic method facilitates the possibility for computer science to be systemically closed. In both a computer program and an axiomatic system, everything is closed because everything is inferentially connected with everything else. Nothing is presented without being defined; nothing is affirmed without being proven. Axioms can indeed be considered to be computer programs.[2] Such conformity between the axiomatic and the computational can be established at many levels, but it is most clearly evidenced in their common deductive coherence. Non-contradiction is an absolute requirement for the axiomatic method and for computation. It is the consistency of self-evident propositions that locks and closes the deductive systemic which axioms and computer programs both construct and depend upon.

In chapter 4, I claimed that Universal Computation should be understood as a twentieth-century reformulation of *mathesis universalis*. This affirmation can now be developed further by stressing that both Universal Computation and *mathesis universalis* rely on the axiomatic method for the automation and universalisation of procedures of valid reasoning. Adams's fictional supercomputer Deep Thought, Leibniz's *calculus ratiocinator*, Boole's propositional calculus, Frege's *Begriffsschrift*, even the ordinary laptop that I typed this text on: they could all be seen to serve the agenda of a logos that aims to assign, through chains of sequential operations, an inferential and procedural form to the real. The axiomatic method is the powerful fuel that makes these 'engines of logic' (as the mathematician Martin Davis would call them) spin faster and better.[3] If effective calculation is defined, via Turing, as an automatic, finite, and mechanical procedure, then the axiomatic method is the mechanism that guarantees the universal applicability of automation through the finite means of deductive demonstration.

Computational axiomatics is very common today; one could say that it is present at each touch of our fingertips upon the new computational devices that have proliferated within our societies. Yet computational axiomatics is not at all popular. Critical questions about axiomatic methodologies do not, however, pertain only to logic, mathematics, or computing, but they also extend to views of society and culture, as well as to accounts of subjectivity, agency, and reason. The axiomatic, when seen in this light, transfers its deductive and determinist structure from the mathematical and technological to the societal, the economic, and the political. It is from this perspective that Deleuze and Guattari, for example, characterised axiomatics as the programmatic way in which contemporary capitalism operates and organises itself.[4] Deleuze and Guattari developed a social articulation of capitalist axiomatics from their understanding of the modes of invention proper to *royal* or *major* sciences. In their view, the axiomatic nature of major sciences is antagonistic to (and repressive of) the problematic pole of *nomadic* or *minor* sciences. For Deleuze and Guattari, the *problem*—namely, the method of formalisation that corresponds to that minor or nomadic pole—opposes the extensive and algebraic methods of axiomatics, as it privileges a topological, qualitative, and projective modality of systematisation.

Of course, this Deleuzo-Guattarian account is not the only conceptualisation of axiomatics that one can find in cultural theory or philosophy. It could be said that, in keeping with its Frankfurt School origins, critical theory as a whole has also turned its back on the axiom, in favour of other figures of the systematisation of being and knowing—figures that are not held to be quite as suspect as is axiomatics, which has been tainted by its supposed association with exploitation, domination, and instrumentalisation. Likewise, it can be remarked that the philosophical critique of computation (which was discussed in the first part of this book) should also be understood as a critique of the mechanised operations of the axiomatisation of thought. This observation returns us to the aesthetic impasse between continuity and discreteness: for axiomatics, when addressed from what might be termed an aisthetic point of view, can be seen as a stopping point that blocks the continuity of life and sensation. Thus, according to this perspective, if computation cannot generate true novelty and can only produce an output in accordance with whatever has been provided as input, then this is due to its axiomatic nature: axioms are self-evident truths that confirm what is already known.

Axiomatisation, or the act of transforming a theory into a system of axioms, offers optimal deductive presentation, inasmuch as it eliminates references to content and does not resort to direct observation. 'By presenting a deductive theory in axiomatic form', writes the philosopher of mathematics Robert Blanché, 'we aim to eliminate the concrete and intuitive meanings on which it was originally built so as to exhibit clearly its abstract logical structure.'[5] The axiomatic method's disinterest towards the empirical is best attained through the use of symbols, which encapsulate abstract forms into mechanisms of exact thought. *Symbolisation* is a distinctive feature of axiomatisation. It is also a central feature of computer programming, in which complex statements are reverted into higher principles and into an alphabet of symbols, a grammar, and rules of inference. In computer science (just as in mathematics and logic), axiomatisation is thus conjoined to techniques of *formalisation*.[6] Formal languages, rules of transformations, and axioms are the defining elements of a formal system, elements that find one-to-one correspondence in digital computing machines. The isomorphism between the computational and the formal provides additional evidence of the closed character of deductive forms. Formalism itself, as a philosophical, historical, and mathematical enterprise, is in the business of conclusion; it constructs conclusive systems through the combination and manipulation of expressions that are closed because they are derived from the premises of the system itself.

Obviously, one must acknowledge the existence of many variations of formalism and of many different approaches to formal systems. To put it very generally, formalism considers mathematics to be meaningless and akin to a game of rule-governed syntactic manipulations, with no commitment to the reality of mathematical objects, regardless of whether the latter are considered as residing outside the mind or as cognitive constructs. It follows from this broad definition that there is an essential dissimilarity between strictly formalist ontologies and the Platonist metaphysics of a priori entities that computational idealism, as I argued in chapter 4, would endorse. The former would imply a nominalist attitude; the latter, by contrast, a realist approach. While such an ontological divergence cannot be denied, it is worth remembering here that I am not interested in discussing formalism as a well-formed arrangement of characters. Likewise, my focus is not on the notational development of formal languages in computation. Instead, I want to address formalisation in connection to the abstract conception of modern mathematics, according to which the discipline develops into a repository of *formulae*. Deductive abstraction then becomes *formulisation*: partly a tool to uncover the a priori principles of valid thought, and partly an instrument to enumerate these principles via the mechanisation of reasoning through symbols and formal languages.

Having developed the argument that computational structures are formal axiomatic systems, I will now assert the following: Universal Computation can explain ontological and epistemological production precisely insofar as it takes the latter to respond only to the pure operational rule or, in other words, to the *formula*. From an epistemological view, metacomputational formulae are universal and transcendent functions of knowledge of the actual; from a metaphysical perspective, they convey being without origin and without change. Formulae describe calculations that are final, predictable, and unavoidable. A formula can be thought of as a principle of proportion and measure from ancient tradition, according to which self-contained rules are 'cuts' towards a higher order of things. In its operative relevance, a formula is a recipe, a blueprint, and a universally applicable procedure: it is a metacomputational organisation of the real via the instrumental paradigm into which formalism transforms abstraction. From this idealist perspective, empirical phenomena cannot be understood in themselves; one needs an abstract rule to make sense of them. If that is the case, then the role of the closed formula is to preform the idea that will come to regulate the sensible. The primary relevance of axiomatic formulisation for a computational aesthetics of deductive forms is evident here. Computational idealism values methods of abstraction according to axiomatic standards of reasoning. Ideal computational forms find in the formal systems of computation a transcendent retreat from the empirical, as well as the possibility of being beautiful insofar as they are truthful (and vice versa). An aesthetics geared towards classicist questions such as beauty, elegance, simplicity, and harmony is thus an aesthetics of the idealisation of a closed formulation of what can be intelligible.

But there is more: computational idealism pursues what I call an *aesthetics of necessity*. Computational abstraction, understood as a logico-mathematical formulisation of the intelligible, abides by the laws of necessary truths of deduction. The term 'necessary' is commonly used to denote that which could not be otherwise, that which responds to the principle of non-contradiction, and that which one cannot subtract from. Necessity is a property of the self-referential and self-predicative formulisations of computational axiomatics. It is the logical condition of computable structures, which are necessary insofar as they are conclusive and a priori. In the case of the aesthetics of computational idealism, however, necessity also pertains to the ontological status of the computational forms, which are necessary inasmuch as they are unchanged by anything incidental or circumstantial.

It is possible to link this back to Leibniz and to his *mathesis universalis*. Leibniz's formulation of a *principle of sufficient reason* is well known; it states that everything has a cause, or that everything has a reason for being what it is rather than something else.[7] For Leibniz, the principle of sufficient reason is the primary and fundamental justification of actuality and possibility, as it accounts for the *ratio existendi* of the real. Sufficient reason does not express only a mere necessity: it implies the necessity of total determinism. That is to say, if the reason for something is known, then this reason is sufficient to determine it both logically and ontologically. It is exactly because the principle of sufficient reason has both an ontological and logical validity that it is also possible, I believe, to look at Leibniz's project for a *mathesis universalis* from the perspective of his argument for the sufficient rationality of the real. It can in fact be argued that *mathesis universalis* trusts the preprogramming of reality that is implicit in the principle of sufficient reason, for that principle entails that whatever occurs is indeed, in Leibniz's words, 'certain and determined beforehand'.[8] From this perspective of total determinism, Universal Computation (understood as a contemporary expression of *mathesis universalis*) is based on the same logical and ontological sufficient rationality. If the ultimate laws of valid reasoning can be found, and the real can indeed be computed, then this is, on the one hand, because anything that is rationally true is deduced from its premises and, on the other, because everything is already calculated or preprogrammed. Universal Computation, on this view, needs nothing beyond itself.

In computational idealism, the sufficient reason of the a priori forms is an absolute order of the existence of things and of unconditional systems of thought and being. The conformity between the logical and aesthetic is established not at the level of the sensible but on the plane of the intelligible. The aesthetic value of the abstract is in turn conveyed via the regulative character of the analytic rule, and enters the work of artists and practitioners in the terms of a commitment to a non-sensuous conception of the aesthetically worthy. In computational idealism, total determinism is thus a channel for the expression of those aesthetic qualities (such as elegance or beauty) that are attributed to the ideal form.

ALGORITHMS OF NECESSITY

The algorithm is perhaps the best encapsulation of necessity in computational axiomatic systems. As a well-defined list of instructions for solving a problem, the algorithm is in equal parts a concept, a method, and a result fundamental to computer science. Algorithms are series of rules used for calculation, data manipulation, and, commonly, to formalise processes performing some sequence of operations. A problem is broken down into subsequent steps, which are rationally addressable because they are defined in finite and unambiguous terms. These sequential steps are necessary. One state inferentially follows from the other and builds on its predecessor to construct the chains of logical inference that found the formalisation of the notion of calculability itself. Algorithmic necessity thus has something of the glacial objectivity of the mathematical formula. Here, however, problem solving is an automated process, according to which a procedure is as universal as it needs to be in order to have general operability, and inasmuch as it dodges the vagueness and ambivalence of the empirical. Algorithms are 'independent from programming languages and independent of the machines that execute the programs composed from these algorithms'.[9] In this sense, they are the epitome of the ideal as opposed to the empirical: avoiding any assumption about the equipment to be used to solve the problem, they are the more abstract layer of computing.

While algorithmics (i.e., the analysis and development of algorithms) might rightfully be considered to lie at the core of computing, the concept of algorithm is a methodological paradigm that precedes and exceeds computer science. Algorithms do not pertain uniquely to computing machines but are broader idealisations of procedural abstraction. The transcendent and a priori character of these regulative abstractions renders them a prime medium of logico-mathematical deduction. Consequently, algorithms are the optimal axiomatic infrastructure for defining and implementing problems that can be addressed mechanically and, therefore, problems that can be computed. In this sense, the axiomatic organisation that algorithmic procedures capture is a sort of base level or ground for the computational form, and it is upon that ground that the metacomputational project of the automation of formal reasoning is to be erected. Universal Computation takes advantage of the automated strengths of computational axiomatics, sublimated into the algorithmic form. The algorithm is the 'padlock', so to speak, that secures the abstractive techniques that endow logical and mathematical structures with onto-epistemological primacy and operative universality.

In the context of an aesthetics of necessity, the prospect of constructing something that might be considered to be aesthetically pleasing in terms of this supposed connection between beauty and logical validity is as daunting as it is exhilarating. One must rely on the legitimacy of deduction and on the sophistication of rigorous formulation, and one must also ultimately have faith that metacomputational ends will always meet and that the circle will always close. The result is a sense of aesthetic value that is at odds with sensuous reception, lived experience, and participation, but which requires the trained intellectual eye of the mathematician, the philosopher, and the programmer to be grasped fully. An aesthetics of algorithmic necessity would thus seem to move within the same parameters of what Paul Fishwick named 'aesthetic computing',[10] according to which artists are vehicles of selection for beautiful computational patterns to enter the realm of aesthetic fruition, and whose informed and educated programming choices enable the aesthetic to emerge and to become the object of judgement.

An example of such aesthetics of algorithmic necessity can be found by looking briefly into the work of a group of artists that go by the name of Algorists. While the term 'algorist' was generally employed to identify people that use algorithms to resolve mathematical problems, in an art context the expression is borrowed to give a name to artists employing algorithms as the driving force of their artistic production. Working independently since the 1960s and gaining a loose group status only in the 1990s, artists such as Jean-Pierre Hébert, Roman Verostko, Charles Csuri, Manfred Mohr, Harold Cohen, Vera Molnár, Herbert W. Franke, Frieder Nake, and Helaman Ferguson, among others, use algorithmic procedures 'for generating forms that are accessible only through extensive computing'.[11] Elaborating on previous artistic stances such as conceptualism, abstract expressionism, and late modernist experimentations with kinetic and programmed art, these early pioneers of electronic art write algorithms and then allow the computational procedure to create the artistic composition. The results, which engage with heterogeneous media such as paper, sand, and metal, include automatic penplotter drawings, spontaneous brushstrokes, sculptural compositions, and experiments with materials and colour behaviour.

The work of the Algorists is particularly interesting, for one can interpret it as implying a refusal to conform to the imperatives of instrumental thinking, according to which the ideal of a method is downgraded into its mere utility. For the Algorists, computational procedures are not plain tools through which to 'draw something' digitally (as one would do with a computer-aided design program). Algorists make the a priori computational form the driving force of their art practice. It could be objected here that a sensible or perceptual outcome is what Algorists are ultimately looking for. This is a valid observation. The figurative level that Algorist art ultimately pursues has generally no semantics or denotative connotations, but still results in a visual composition. Despite the orientation of the Algorists towards a final visual outcome, my point here is that their work can be taken to exemplify the transcendent connotation assumed by algorithmic necessity in the context of rule-based axiomatic activity. Stephen Wilson indicates that Algorist art 'aspires towards universals—either spiritual or probing the essential geometry of the universe'.[12] We can develop that comment further and affirm that the Algorists engage with algorithmic formations in their metacomputational valence of universal forms of intelligibility. In their work, rule-based procedures give us a sensible outcome, insofar as these procedures preside over Universal Computation's abstract legislation of the empirically real. The Algorists perfect a sequential procedure that anticipates and produces the concrete. 'In its purest form such art does not *re-present* other reality. Rather it *is* the reality.'[13] Algorist art thus shows axiomatic forms as fulfilling the idealist schemata according to which a simple rule (an algorithm or an axiom) maintains its transcendent and a priori regulative superiority over the particular concrete instantiation. The procedural abstraction of the algorithm encloses a double principle of formality: the 'search for a pure visual form' is conditional to the axiomatic closure of a reality-producing transcendent formulation.[14] The link between the empirical and the formal is therefore established via a rapport of dependency between the intelligible construction of preprogrammed algorithmic functions and a sensible result (which the artist can exhibit and possibly sell). This 'drawing with the mind' (to paraphrase here the title of an exhibition by Jean-Pierre Hébert, held at the Santa Barbara Contemporary Arts Forum in 2008) requires a significant degree of controlled abstraction from the artist. In fact, it involves 'imaging the unseen' through deductive formalisation.[15] What Verostko has called a 'mind-hand' arranges worlds of a priori forms, while the sensuous dimension of the artwork is deduced from such underlying ideal structure.[16]

In conclusion, one might find, in the work of the Algorists, an exemplification of the transcendence of computational idealism, and of the ways in which such metaphysical transcendence is substantiated in the manner in which logico-mathematical intelligibility (a formula) informs the physical (a plotter and an ink line drawn on paper, for instance). The software that the

Algorists develop must be coupled with the appropriate hardware and with suitable algorithmic implementations. Nevertheless, the logico-mathematical idea precedes any contingent realisation. The algorithmic mechanisms of the Algorists do not simulate any gestural bodily practice but affirm themselves as a unique source of new sensuous possibilities. Such opportunities are always preformed—in fact, calculated—at the level of the intelligible. The non-sensorial necessity of a formula, understood as an a priori calculation of consequences, is thus the foundation and principle of the sensible.

CONTINGENT BUT NOT EMPIRICAL

At this point in the present discussion about algorithmic axiomatics, one could legitimately ask, is it right to consider algorithms solely in terms of the necessity of a closed metacomputational system? Do not algorithms, and therefore computational axiomatics, exhibit a non-necessary dimension too? It is interesting to note here that even though the opposite of necessity is, strictly speaking, non-necessity, the concept of contingency often assumes, according to popular use, the role of the necessary's counterpart. Something that is said to be contingent is described as such because it does not appear to be justified by anything, and yet nothing contradicts it either. From this perspective, something is commonly called 'contingent' when it might or might not happen, when it can or cannot be. One can affirm or negate contingency: while necessity is a priori, contingency is understood to be a posteriori. On this view, asking whether an algorithm has some levels of contingency would then imply questions as to whether an algorithm, despite being a universal technique of valid reasoning, would or should also be part of a course of actions that are neither indispensable nor impossible. Were we to follow this line of argumentation, we would be led to wonder whether algorithmic structures—these quintessential constructions of mathematical purity and logical detachment—could be part of sensibility, which lacks the crystalline nature of the formula, and which instead embraces the opacity of empirical explanation. The answer here would be yes: an algorithm could be said to participate in three key levels of empirical explanation. I will call the first *application*, the second *implementation*, and the third *performance*. It is worth considering each of them in a little more detail in order to better understand the complexities of the relation between necessity and contingency in computation.

Application: Practical applications of algorithmic procedures are pervasive and extensive. Algorithms are not just remarkable ways of accounting for the intelligible; they fix numerous applied problems in the realm of sensibility too. I am, of course, stating the obvious here: algorithms lie at the core of most contemporary technologies, and the algorithmic method's problem-solving abilities are optimally suited for computer-aided logistics, trade, finance, travel, and medicine, to name but a few of the industries whose advances would not be possible in the absence of algorithmics.

An algorithm is a general concept that can be applied to many specific situations. A good example is the Viterbi algorithm, a procedure meant to find the most likely sequence of states that could have given rise to a certain event. Andrew Viterbi proposed the algorithm in 1967 and used it for decoding convolutionally encoded data transmitted over a noisy channel.[17] Today, the method is fundamental to wireless communication systems, and it is also applied in areas such as voice recognition, magnetic recording, and DNA sequencing analysis. Another example that shows how an algorithm can be functional in a number of real-world situations is the Simplex method, formulated in 1947 by George Dantzig as a general strategy for dealing with linear programming.[18] Dantzig's iterative procedure builds on the geometrical abstractions of multidimensional space. It treats a problem as if it was a geometrical shape, the number of dimensions of which is equal to the number of variables of the problem, and the boundaries of which are determined by the restrictions of the problem itself. Applications of the Simplex method are ubiquitous; the uses of this procedure are, in fact, so abundant that it has gained the title of 'the algorithm that runs the world'.[19]

From the perspective of their application, the contingent mutability of algorithms is bound to the concrete variability of real-world situations and is thus dependant on the specificity of a particular task (e.g., how do we encrypt an online banking transaction? What procedure would give us a lossless compression of data? How is it possible to index a document to match a query?). Some procedural abstractions are better for certain undertakings than others. In these cases, a contingent dimension might be seen to lie in the instance of a problem, in what might or might not happen, and in the efficiency of a practical application that can be measured and valued according to its behaviour in various circumstances.

Implementation: Real-world computing machines need to be fed the correct bits of instructions in order to operate. The artificial formalism between an input and an output that an algorithm ideally captures has to be brought to effective functionality through some practices of symbolic expression (e.g., programming languages, scripts, codes). It is thus critical to distinguish between an algorithm and a piece of code. An algorithm is an idea that may or may not get embodied into the real code, pseudo-code, or even the natural language of computer programming. If the algorithm is the a priori intelligible, then codes and programs are the means of implementing such intelligibility a posteriori, so as to give it a concrete computer application. Perhaps it is useful to pursue here the parallel proposed by the computational theorist

J. Glenn Brookshear, who likens the algorithm to a story and computer programs to the many books that narrate such a story.[20] Similarly, by looking at sorting algorithms, one can get a better sense of this distinction between an algorithm and its implementations. Searching and sorting are some of the most studied problems in computing. Their solution involves devising an effective procedure that would arrange the elements of a certain group, class, or list in a certain order using minimal resources and time. Quicksort, merge-sort, heapsort, introsort, insertion sort, bubble sort—these are some of the sorting algorithms currently used in the industry. Each of them provides a different abstract method that specifies what steps should be taken to solve the problem. In this sense, the quicksort algorithm is independent of the particular programming language used in its incarnation. For instance, it could be written in C, or in Python. It is through solid practices of implementation, and thanks to the infrastructure of concrete data, that quicksort finds its place at the fulcrum of operating systems, database engines, and file formats.

To implement implies bringing the highly abstracted into the regime of communication. Contingency-as-implementation is then bound to the changeable outcomes of such communicative endeavours. It results partially from the contextual work of the programmer: from the hours spent in front of the screen perfecting a function and detailing data structures. For the most part, however, contingency is, on this view, a status that is inherent to the material nature of signs and utterances that instantiate the intelligible rule into an arrangement of communicational situations.

Performance: Finally, there is the contingent flexibility of performance. As Adrian Mackenzie argues, 'algorithms carry, fold, frame and redistribute actions into different environments'.[21] In this respect, algorithmic agency can be considered as taking place at two stages. The first stage is machine execution. Here, agency lies in the processuality of a program that is run. Through execution, passive collections of instructions become active agents. Algorithmic agency is then contingently variable (or indeed non-necessary) because it is circumstantial to the compromises that take place between various software or hardware components, among secondary storage and main memory, and amid synchronisation, multitasking, and time-sharing. So, in this view, the concept of contingency concerns the situations that are coming into existence via the performative selection of characters and factors that happens in a certain way, but which could have been arbitrarily otherwise.

In moving to the second stage of algorithmic performance, let us now consider how algorithmic actions have effects on society, economy, culture, politics, etc. We have already seen that algorithms are applied to concrete problems; I am now making a slightly different point about the material agency of a rule which, when executed, influences multiple conditions of being and compound modes of knowing and doing. In this sense, algorithmic performance is contingent, or not bounded to preprogramming, since it participates in world-making processes. To put it otherwise, algorithmic performance might be considered to be contingent because it is entangled with the mundane of collective life and governance, consumption, and creativity, while continually negotiating meanings and goals with other abstractions such as culture and society. The field of software studies is the interdisciplinary research area that, in the past decade, has best acknowledged such material performativity of algorithmic agency, affirming that this latter should become the subject of cultural analysis in its own right.[22] In this sense, the focus has shifted from the uses and experiences that humans might have of computational artefacts to the liveness of those algorithmic operations informing causal relations and spatiotemporal coordinates.

From the perspective of the approaches that consider the algorithmic contingency of application, embodiment, and performance, computational idealism is partly an intellectualist exercise in classicist metaphysics and partly a reactionary manoeuvre in cultural theory. Crucially, it is a position fundamentally devoid of any actual significance for those communities of hackers, programmers, media artists, and media practitioners at large who mediate the sociocultural politics of everyday life through the computational. In other words, from this perspective, an aesthetics of deductive abstraction fails at providing an accurate account of computational culture on a technical level, as well as on an ethnographic one. In this respect, focusing on computational contingency in terms of the application, implementation, and performance of its algorithmic structures is a valuable operation. By articulating logico-mathematical formality as just one factor among others, these heterogeneous assessments of what is algorithmically variable and mutable oppose the intrinsic elitism of the aesthetics of necessity, according to which an equivalence between truth and beauty could and should be perpetuated through educated choices and cultivated taste. By contrast, perspectives on algorithmic applications, implementations, and performances spread outside the mathematical black box to construct a full-fledged account of computational acts as they are rooted in diverse sets of material relations. These perspectives look at scripts and codes as 'words made flesh'[23] and search for all of those instances in which 'software takes command'.[24] In doing so, they also exhibit a will to analyse the computational inasmuch as the latter is actual 'stuff' that operates in the world: stuff that is in fact a 'contingent product of the world and a relational producer of the world'.[25] Computation, then, is understood as pertaining to networks of means of production, user appropriations, and deployments of automated agency. Such an understanding helps to rephrase the agenda of media theory in terms of the concreteness of computation, thus moving beyond McLuhanite characterisations of media as man's extensions. Finally, discourses on and around algorithmic mutability are particularly significant in relation to my proposed critique of Universal Computation. While the promotion of algorithmic applications, implementations, and performances remains relatively marginal in comparison to more conventional idealist ontologies of computing machines, such perspectives show significant explanatory powers in relation to how ontogenesis might belong to computation too. These perspectives, in other words, negotiate empirical states of being and categories of knowing, and, in doing so, they hijack systems of representational thought geared towards metacomputational universalisation. This opposition to the metacomputational is often implicit. Nevertheless, it remains a fundamental critical contribution, which can be gathered from the focus on algorithmic application, implementation, and performance.

Stressing the contingency of algorithmic applications, implementations, and performances is therefore important, and it is particularly so in relation to the non-metacomputational argument that I am proposing in this book. This is because stressing that contingency involves emphasising the actuality of computation (as opposed to its supposed virtuality). Some conceptual problems might arise, however, if—in the process of refocusing our attention from algorithmic necessity to algorithmic contingency—we understand the latter uniquely in terms of empirical mutability, and we thus lose sight of the internal dynamism that axiomatic computation holds within itself. This is because, although approaches that focus on the algorithmic contingency of applications, implementations, and performances object to metacomputation, they do not fully confute it. Considering computation in terms of the application, implementation, and performance of its formal structures does not, in fact, entirely break with the golden ratio of 'beauty equals truth'. The core of the issue is that these perspectives only partially alter computational idealism's transcendent onto-epistemological framework. Certainly, abstractive formalisms are acknowledged as crucial objects of study. Much attention is devoted to the conceptual nature of the computational medium—an attention that, as mentioned above, has in recent years put forth interesting material ontologies of computation. Nevertheless, such efforts to reconceptualise the actuality of algorithms can also be said to often flatten down the contingent dimension of these algorithms' material reality onto the empirical variability of technosocial and technocultural assemblages. The contingent is thus taken to be synonymous with the empirical (and vice versa). This is problematic, as the actuality of contingent computation is consequently addressed primarily in terms of the empirical analysis of the social, the cultural, and the economic manifestations of the computational.

This sociocultural analysis is obviously an important contribution, yet one can note that Universal Computation already established the equivalence between the empirical and the contingent and that this equivalence was consequently reinforced by the aesthetics of computational idealism. The meta-computational equation for the proportion upon which computational ideal-ism's transcendence is established is as follows:

$$\text{Necessity : Ideal} = \text{Contingency : Empirical}$$

In the perspectives discussed above concerning the contingency of algorith-mic application, implementation, and performance, the first part of the equa-tion is obscured, while the second is highlighted through the lenses of the sociocultural:

$$\text{~~Necessity : Ideal~~} = \text{Contingency : Empirical}$$

The original metacomputational proportion, however, still remains, for what one is confronted with here is a partial ontological shifting. Of course, I do not intend to assign this fault generally and indiscriminately to what is in-stead a multifaceted mode of investigation. However, my point is that this renewed focus on empirical contingency effectively infiltrates, in particular, the sociocultural approaches to the analysis of computation. Moreover, it is also to be found in different arenas where computation's flexibility is played out. For example, in computer science and computability theory, the criti-cism of strictly deductive models of computation has resulted in direct at-tempts to formulate more empirically oriented definitions of what it means to compute.

Some of these alternative understandings of computational procedurality will be addressed in the third part of this book. However, in what remains of this second part, I want to stay focused on deduction. Our eyes are staring firmly at the axiomatic and formal character of computation. I am proposing that we should take computational systems for what they are: formal axio-matic structures. However, I am also proposing to think about computational axiomatics in a different manner, and through a different understanding of contingent computation: an understanding that would focus on its formal dimension, rather than on its empirical aspects. In this respect, it is important to stress that I am reluctant to accept computational idealism and its conse-quent aesthetics of deductive necessity. This is not because idealist ap-proaches do not aim to encompass an empirically contingent plane of algo-rithmic applications, implementations, and performances, but rather because they do not consider computation's internal logical indeterminacy and even-tuality. Computational idealism and the metacomputational view fail to rec-ognise that the axiomatic, deductive, and self-sufficient computational struc-tures to which they pertain can be understood as actual events that always already encompass indeterminacy at the formal level.

In order to fully unfold this argument, one must consider the origin of the theory of computation itself and look back at the period in the history of computing when axiomatic reasoning and logico-mathematical deduction were first coupled with procedures of mechanical computation. In the next chapter, I will place Turing's logical formalisation of the notion of computability within the larger debate about the limits of formal reasoning. By looking at these limits, it becomes possible to unfold the potential of the axiomatic in computation and thus to identify fully the internal fallacy of an idealist aesthetics geared towards the non-relation between abstraction and experience.

NOTES

1. The axiomatic method originated twenty-four centuries ago in the work of the Greek mathematician Euclid. Euclidean geometry is considered to be the paradigmatic model for deductive theories, and the 'geometric method' is another name for the traditional axiomatic method. The meaning and scope of the axiomatic method have, however, been significantly broadened by the discovery of non-Euclidean geometries in the nineteenth century. In ancient mathematics, axioms are the basic, fundamental, evident propositions of a theory. They could be grasped intuitively, and from them any other proposition could be derived through demonstration. By contrast, according to the modern formal approach, logical consistency and non-contradiction are the main characteristics of the axiomatic method, and no place is left for the ancient intuitive character of evident propositions.

2. This is discussed in Gregory Chaitin, *Meta Maths: The Quest for Omega* (London: Atlantic, 2005), 65.

3. Martin Davis, *Engines of Logic: Mathematicians and the Origin of the Computer* (New York: Norton, 2000).

4. See Gilles Deleuze and Félix Guattari, *A Thousand Plateaus: Capitalism and Schizophrenia*, trans. Brian Massumi (London: Continuum, 2004).

5. Robert Blanché, *Axiomatics*, trans. G. B. Kleene (London: Routledge and Kegan Paul, 1966), 45.

6. See Blanché, *Axiomatics*, 50–51.

7. Gottfried Wilhelm Leibniz, *The Monadology, and Other Philosophical Writings*, trans. Robert Latta (Oxford: Oxford University Press, 1925), 235.

8. Gottfried Wilhelm Leibniz, *Theodicy*, ed. Austin Farrer, trans. E. M. Huggard (London: Routledge and Kegan Paul, 1952), 151.

9. Andrew Goffey, 'Algorithm', in *Software Studies: A Lexicon*, ed. Matthew Fuller (Cambridge, MA: MIT Press, 2008), 15.

10. Paul A. Fishwick, 'An Introduction to Aesthetic Computing', in *Aesthetic Computing*, ed. Paul A. Fishwick (Cambridge, MA: MIT Press, 2006), 3–27.

11. Roman Verostko, 'Algorithmic Fine Art: Composing a Visual Arts Score', in *Explorations in Art and Technology: Intersection and Correspondence*, ed. Linda Candy and Ernest Edmonds (London: Springer, 2002), 131.

12. Stephen Wilson, *Information Arts: Intersections of Art, Science, and Technology* (Cambridge, MA: MIT Press, 2003), 317.

13. Verostko, 'Algorithmic Fine Art', 131.

14. Verostko, 'Algorithmic Fine Art', 135.

15. Roman Verostko, 'Imaging the Unseen: A Statement on My Pursuit as an Artist', 2004, http://www.verostko.com/archive/statements/statement04.html.

16. Roman Verostko, 'Epigenetic Art Revisited: Software as Genotype', in *Code: The Language of Our Time; Ars Electronica 2003*, ed. Gerfried Stocker and Christine Schöpf (Ostfildern-Ruit: Hatje Cantz, 2003), 156.

17. See Andrew Viterbi, 'Error Bounds for Convolutional Codes and an Asymptotically Optimum Decoding Algorithm', *IEEE Transactions on Information Theory* 13, no. 2 (April 1967): 260–69, https://doi.org/10.1109/TIT.1967.1054010.

18. See George B. Dantzig, 'Programming in a Linear Structure', in *The Basic George B. Dantzig*, ed. Richard W. Cottle (Stanford, CA: Stanford University Press, 2003), 23.

19. Richard Elwes, 'The Algorithm that Runs the World', *New Scientist*, 11 August 2012, 33.

20. See J. Glenn Brookshear's *Computer Science: An Overview*, 7th ed. (Boston: Addison-Wesley, 2003), 158.

21. Adrian Mackenzie, *Cutting Code: Software and Sociality* (New York: Peter Lang, 2006), 43.

22. See Matthew Fuller, 'Introduction: The Stuff of Software', in *Software Studies: A Lexicon*, ed. Matthew Fuller (Cambridge, MA: MIT Press, 2008), 1–13.

23. Florian Cramer, *Words Made Flesh: Code, Culture, Imagination* (Rotterdam: Media Design Research, Piet Zwart Institute, 2005), https://www.netzliteratur.net/cramer/wordsmadefleshpdf.pdf.

24. Lev Manovich, *Software Takes Command* (New York: Bloomsbury Academic, 2013).

25. Rob Kitchin and Martin Dodge, *Code/Space: Software and Everyday Life* (Cambridge, MA: MIT Press, 2011), 43.

Chapter Six

Limits and Potential

In 1936, the *Proceedings of the London Mathematical Society* published a paper authored by a young Cambridge fellow named Alan Turing. The essay, which was titled 'On Computable Numbers, with an Application to the Entscheidungsproblem', is considered today to be a momentous achievement, as it stripped what was then the purely mental activity of computation down to its basics and thereby proved what hypothetical computing machines could or could never achieve before actual general-purpose computers were built. [1]

Turing originally wrote the paper in an attempt to engage with some of the programmatic questions posed by the most influential mathematician of his time, David Hilbert. Between the end of the nineteenth and the beginning of the twentieth century, a succession of foundational crises had given rise to the requirement that mathematical concepts should be rigorously determined in order to elude logical traps. In the early 1920s, Hilbert proposed a specific research project—known as 'Hilbert's programme'—which was famously summarised in three key points: consistency, completeness, and decidability. [2] Hilbert believed that the increasing abstract character of mathematical reasoning called for the systematisation of all mathematics into the axiomatic form and for a general, *metamathematical* proof able to secure the provability of such a formalisation. [3] However, in 1931 the logician Kurt Gödel showed that there were inherent problems with Hilbert's absolute proofs. [4] Hilbert's programme, Gödel argued, could not be carried out because consistency and completeness cannot both be accomplished within the same formal system. Gödel's *incompleteness theorems* famously demonstrated that there exist statements which, when viewed from the outside, are certainly true, although their provability cannot be deduced inside the formal system in question. Gödel's proof concerned the problematic reality of *undecidable propositions*, whose existence can be expressed but whose decidability cannot be demonstrated through the finite axiomatic means of the formal system itself. Gödel's response to Hilbert—who, legend has it, was 'somewhat angry' after receiving the bad news[5]—'presented mathematicians with the astounding and melancholy conclusion that the axiomatic method has certain inherent limitations'.[6] It incontrovertibly ruled out the ability to derive all true formulae from axioms. Consequently, it precluded the possibility that any final systematisation can be accomplished, or that any assurance can be given regarding the absence of internal contradictions in the foundations of mathematics.

Studying and writing in the immediate aftermath of the incompleteness bombshell, Alan Turing approached Hilbert's foundational demands by directly addressing the need for a conclusive definition of 'method'. His paper addressed the *Entscheidungsproblem* (German for 'decision problem')— namely, Hilbert's challenge concerning the discovery of a general symbolic process capable of delivering either 'true' or 'false' as output, and of doing so in conformity with the actual truth or falsehood of the formula itself.[7] Turing proved that such an algorithm does not exist by devising a thought experiment (today known as the *Turing machine*) that was so compelling that it also indirectly proved that it would be impossible to reduce all deductive reasoning to mechanical calculation. Whereas Gödel addressed the theoretical consistency and completeness of formal rules for the description of logic and mathematics, Turing investigated the possibility of finding a mechanical, finite-step, and formally expressed process that would set the standard for deductive procedures. In doing so, he framed a mathematical impasse in the figurative terms of machines executing instructions.[8] Arguably, his genius consisted in casting the problem in terms of computability. 'The real question at issue', Turing wrote, 'is "What are the possible processes which can be carried out in computing a number?"'[9]

In attempting to answer this question, Turing's 1936 paper provided a formal method of computation, laid out through his hypothetical computing machine. The Turing machine should be understood as an abstract symbol-manipulating machine, similar to a finite automaton but with unrestrained memory. The device is composed of an infinite tape, which holds the information that the device is to process. This tape is divided into cells, each of which may contain only one symbol from a finite alphabet (for instance, 0s and 1s). Such symbols are written and read by a head that moves left or right on the tape, one cell at a time. The machine operates sequentially: it finds itself in one of a finite number of states at any point during the computation, and its next move is determined by the input/symbol from the tape as well as by a set of designed behavioural rules. In order to carry out its operations, the machine needs to 'know' only two variables: its present state and what cell on the tape it is pointing to. If the machine needs to store information, it can do so by writing it in a standard format on the tape itself, for the number of available cells is limitless.

The Turing machine is extremely simple: its activity consists in writing or erasing a determinate symbol, moving the head one square to the left or right, and changing to a new state. Yet the Turing machine is also profoundly complex, and it is so precisely by virtue of its generality. Each table of behaviour (i.e., the set of rules controlling the movement of the head) could be considered to be a different Turing machine in its own right. However, one machine (which is said to be *universal*) can be envisaged that could perform, given the proper inputs and the proper configuration, any task that any individual Turing machine could carry out. In other words, anything computable through a definite set of instructions that can be composed as a series of symbols can also be computed by the universal Turing machine (hereafter, UTM). The problems that a UTM can resolve, therefore, are all those that are executable by an algorithmic process or by an effective method of computation.

Returning now to Hilbert's *Entscheidungsproblem*, Turing proved that there is no algorithm (that is, no *effective method*) that can decide, in advance of its calculation, whether a statement is true or false. He did so by demonstrating that there are some tasks that cannot be accomplished by his universal computing machines. These problems are said to be *incomputable functions* with no solution. Turing thus showed that there are limits to what can be computed because there are functions that can be said to be algorithmically irresolvable, thus invalidating the decision problem. This conclusion, however, also provided a mathematical model for an all-purpose computing machine, formalised a very concrete notion of definite procedure, and put forth the definition for a whole new category of numbers (the computable numbers).

THE AUTONOMY OF FORMAL AXIOMATIC SYSTEMS

Gödel and Turing offered solid explorations of the decidability of formal axiomatic systems. Their discoveries are paradoxical but extremely powerful. Gödel showed the incompleteness of the axiomatic method by constructing a deductive system that demonstrates its own improvability. Equally, Turing showed that the formal notion of computation rests upon the conclusion that there are numbers and functions that cannot be computed. The impact of Gödel's and Turing's breakthroughs had the force of a collision: it took mathematical logic by storm, while ushering in new philosophical, scientific, and technological challenges. Hereafter, I will argue that Gödel's and Turing's discoveries also carry unavoidable consequences for the ontological investigation of computational aesthetics, insofar as incompleteness and in-computability severely undermine Universal Computation and, by extension, the aesthetics of beautiful and truthful forms founded upon that metacomputational approach. I will claim that, by engaging with the incomplete and the incomputable, I can put forth a *non-metacomputational* understanding of formal axiomatic systems. I will build my argument against computational idealism on that non-metacomputational basis. My argument is meant to expand my earlier claim that computation is a method of *abstraction* that is open to the *abstract*. It will do so by showing that computation is always exposed to indeterminacy. This indeterminacy is not that of life or lived experience, but is instead a mode of indetermination that is inherent to the logico-mathematical character of the computational system. Addressing this logical and formal indeterminacy will serve to highlight another sense of contingency in computation: one that is not dependent on empirical mutability, but which instead works through computational processes of formal discretisation. This, then, is my proposed strategy: the notions of incompleteness and incomputability will be employed here not to undermine axiomatic formal systems, but rather to enhance the possibility of an open-ended—or, indeed, of a contingent—understanding of them. The central point of this approach is the assertion that incompleteness and incomputability call for another level of investigation of axiomatics. Because this level of enquiry considers the non-metacomputational reality of computational processing, it has the capacity to uncover the internal fallacies of the aesthetics of beautiful and truthful computation on the one hand, and a potentiality that is specific to computation itself on the other.

The first step in this speculative direction involves bringing the debate about the limits of axiomatics to an implicit, yet extreme, consequence: the affirmation of the *autonomy* of formal axiomatic systems from the empirical. Let us look at this question more closely. Gödel's incompleteness theorems have drawn a great deal of attention from mathematicians and non-mathematicians alike, together with the consequential uses and misuses that such popularity often entails. According to one of the most common misconceptions, Gödel would be a sort of postmodern champion of relativism. Indeed, Jean-François Lyotard (perhaps the most prominent theorist of the 'postmodern condition') saluted Gödel as an ally in the postmodern 'reformulation of the question of the legitimation of knowledge'.[10] Employed in this manner, Gödel's work on the limits of formal reasoning has helped to invalidate scientific objectivity, while also moving beyond quests for certainty and signification.[11] The congeniality between Gödel's incompleteness theorems and postmodern relativism is, however, only apparent, and is as much the result of a misinterpretation of Gödel's mathematical work as it is a misconception of its profoundly philosophical connotations. Postmodern cultural theorists who hope to use incompleteness as the final nail in the coffin of metaphysics should, therefore, be careful. From the perspective of his philosophy of mathematics, Gödel was a die-hard Platonist. This means that he believed in the objective reality of mathematical entities and concepts. His work on the foundation of mathematics was committed to a rationalist ontology of unchangeable and mind-independent mathematical entities, and it was permeated by the desire to expand such *conceptual realism* from mathematics to metaphysics. [12] To say that Gödel's incompleteness theorems commend the dismissal of reason, then, is to twist the actual technical results of Gödel's 1931 proof. Moreover, arguing for a relativist reading of the incompleteness theorems also means overlooking his entire anti-empiricist perspective.

Turing's philosophical position, on the other hand, is much more implicit, and thus difficult to reconstruct from the scarce body of publications that he left upon his premature death. His biographer, Andrew Hodges, comments that the 1936 paper 'On Computable Numbers' appeals to 'operations that could actually be done by real things or people in the physical world'. [13] In other words, the paper addresses the concreteness of calculative procedures. This is surely true. However, it is also possible to argue that computation, via Turing's groundbreaking work, is formalised into a process of producing and collecting abstracted entities, and of showing how a conclusion necessarily follows from a set of premises. This computational activity of pinning down chains of abstractive reasoning into a fixed formal structure can thus be seen as something that has to do with the necessary and the a priori. It holds up the demand for the self-evidence of first principles, albeit (and this is a crucial distinction) within the constraints, limits, and confinements of the system in question. In this sense, one could read Turing's effective method of calculation as an exploration of the possibility of predicating deductive thought uniquely on its extra-empirical terms. To conclude this point, both Gödel and Turing never intended to abandon the ship of deductive reasoning, or sought to imply that that ship was sinking. Incompleteness and incomputability do not suggest an arbitrary 'anything goes' attitude or indicate that deductive abstraction is inescapably mistaken. On the contrary, they prove that logico-mathematical reasoning cannot be contained within a finite formulation.

The impossibility of enclosing logico-mathematical procedures into any final systematisation is one of the most important consequences that can be drawn from Gödel's conception of incompleteness and Turing's account of incomputability. Yet, although this impossibility has been traditionally read as evidence of the failure of axiomatic systems, I would contend that Gödel's and Turing's breakthroughs attest to the fact that axiomatics does not correspond to empirical individuations; I would also argue that this has direct consequences for the metacomputational principle of Universal Computation on the one hand, and for the aesthetics of computational idealism on the other. Hilbert hoped for a twentieth century where 'there is no *ignorabimus*'. [14] His metamathematical initiative moved within the assumption of metacomputation; it accorded with the conviction that a complete circle of logical necessity can be drawn from premises to conclusions, and that it is possible to fulfil this circle in a finite number of steps. The spectacular demise of Hilbert's programme, as caused by the logical genius of Gödel and Turing, showed, however, that these steps are not finite, and that the inferential circle cannot be closed. This discovery confounds any attempt to pursue a comprehensively valid deductive science of reasoning. Moreover, it also entails the independence of axiomatics from the metacomputational project that would attempt such a pursuit.

This independence is one of the most urgent effects of the incomplete and of the incomputable for computational aesthetics. Incompleteness and incomputability show that computational forms are not metacomputational formulae. The axiomatic method is supposed to frame such forms into strictly deductive and reductive formalisations. However, incompleteness and incomputability demonstrate that such a method cannot account for the transcendent relation between the ideal and the empirical: a transcendent relation that Universal Computation had aimed to authenticate by appealing to deductive operations that would close the circle of their ideation and actuation via simplification. Ultimately, Universal Computation falls short of providing an entirely workable account of the exactness and certitude of its axioms because the transcendent ontology to which it appeals fails to map a completely deductive path from abstract objects to concrete entities. The equivalence of beauty and truth that grounds the computational idealism of certain computational practices is predicated instead on the possibility of walking that deductively regulative path from start to finish. I argued in chapter 5 that a closed formal systemic grounds computational idealism's equivalence between logical truth and aesthetic beauty. That this inferential route is less a closed circle than a 'strange loop' is something that Gödel and Turing demonstrated more than eighty years ago.[15] This demonstration does not amount to saying that beauty and truth do not exist. Rather, it shows that there cannot be a golden ratio that will provide us with the exact proportion of their relation. Deductive abstraction is not a formula upon which logico-mathematical models of simplicity, elegance, harmony, and the like can be built. Moreover, axioms are not instruments that precede and explicate reality. Via Gödel and Turing, we understand that there cannot be a complete deduction of everything: axioms cannot even explain themselves.

Commenting on the self-referential paradoxicality of Gödel's 1931 results, the philosopher Rebecca Goldstein emphasises that, 'according to Gödel's own Platonist understanding of his proof, [its paradoxical nature] shows us that our minds, in knowing mathematics, are escaping the limitations of man-made systems, grasping the independent truths of abstract reality'.[16] Following Goldstein's assertion, one can ask, what do these independent truths of abstract reality involve? In my opinion, they show that such a reality is beyond the plane of metacomputational organisation and representation. Perhaps most telling of all is the fact that both Gödel's proof of incompleteness and Turing's computational limits can be understood to have rephrased the difficulty faced by man-made formal encodings and procedures in attempting to mirror exactly the empirical world. On the one hand, the instrumental prospect of a final axiomatic systematisation cannot be matched by any particular concrete instance. On the other hand, the transcendent relation between the purely intelligible and the given, manifest, and sensible reality is also proven to be largely impractical, if not biased, when attempted via symbolic reductions. This mismatch between the ideal and the empirical shatters the fundamental premise of *mathesis universalis* (namely, the assumption that a transcendent ontology of ideal formality can attain a conclusive systematisation of the real by means of deductive calculation). In this sense, Gödel and Turing profoundly upset the transcendentally closed depiction of formal axiomatic systems advanced by computational idealism. More precisely, they preclude the possibility that axiomatic formulation could be the method through which the metacomputation of the real is fulfilled. With Gödel and Turing, one discovers that formal axiomatic structures are not returning the transcendent blueprint to preform and regulate the sensible through deductive and logically necessary representational forms of intelligibility. Rather, one discovers that formal axiomatic structures always tend towards their own infinity. Incompleteness means that more axioms can be added to the formal system; incomputability means that more digits and steps can be added to computation. I will expand on these considerations in the following sections of this chapter. First, however, I must specify the ways in which Gödel could be said to allow for an *open-ended axiomatics*. This specification is essential: in reassessing computational axiomatics, I intend to endorse such open-endedness while at the same time using Gödel to go beyond Gödel, so to speak.

Gödel's commitment to the independent truths of abstract reality involves an ontological commitment to the extra-empirical reality of the logico-mathematical a priori, along with the epistemic prospect of its conceptual comprehension. It is well known that Gödel advocated rational intuition as the privileged access to mathematical certainty, stressing that his work in mathematical logic does not determine 'any bounds for the powers of human reason, but rather for the potentialities of pure formalism in mathematics'.[17] For Gödel, the axiomatic route is still the paradigmatic way towards valid reasoning. In his opinion, however, only the human faculty of mathematical insight can lead us along that road, by way of a mixture of intuition and deduction. Axioms, Gödel wrote, 'force themselves upon us as being true'.[18] Mathematical reasoning partakes of conceptual imagination and ingenuity and cannot possibly be limited to a rule-following activity. Against formalist games of symbolic manipulation, Gödel urged that the task of securing the certainty of mathematics could be performed 'by cultivating (deepening) knowledge of the abstract concepts themselves which lead to the setting up of these mechanical systems'.[19] It should come as no surprise, then, that Gödel's advocacy of rational intuition led him, later in his life, to turn his philosophical attention towards Edmund Husserl's eidetic phenomenology. Gödel recognised an intellectual kinship between himself and Husserl—an affinity that is evidenced in Husserl's emphasis on categorial intuition and on the possibility of 'uncovering what is given to us from inside'.[20] Gödel's rebuttal of computational theories of mind should thus be read in the light of his advocacy of rational intuition. Mathematical thinking, according to Gödel, is not translatable into computational terms. Similarly, truth-discovery processes are not programmable into rule-bound machine formulations: 'Leibniz's program of the "calculemus" cannot be carried through'.[21]

Gödel's rational intuition is not a special kind of sense perception but rather the latter's 'a priori analogue'.[22] In his renowned paper on Cantor's continuum problem, Gödel defined intuition as the source of new axioms in set theory: as 'something like a perception', which can access and accommodate even those abstract entities (the objects of transfinite set theory, in the paper in question) that show a certain 'remoteness from sense experience'.[23] While for Hilbert intuition had to appeal to concrete things and could be replaced by finite symbol manipulations, for Gödel intuition was the 'sudden illumination' through which one grasps the essence, the form, or the idea of abstract mathematical objects.[24] Certainly, there is a degree of similarity between Gödel's account of rational intuition and a possible interpretation and exposition of Whitehead's conceptual prehensions. Nonetheless, it is important to stress here that such an affinity is casual and that the two are profoundly different. First of all, if one follows Gödel's philosophical inclinations towards rational intuition, the possibility of a relation between experience and abstraction is shown to be dependent on human insight. In addition to this evident level of anthropocentrism (which is inherent to Gödel's view, but alien to that of Whitehead), the other key disparity between Gödel's rational intuition and Whitehead's conceptual prehensions is this: the former presupposes a subject of perception that is external to its perceived object, while the latter does not. In Gödel's rational intuition, the perceived object might not be an empirical phenomenon, and might in fact be an idea or the essence of a mathematical entity; yet it is possible to argue that this object remains phenomenal insofar as it is given to the consciousness of a subject that is already predefined. This is a tricky situation. Figuratively speaking, although, thanks to Gödel, metacomputational transcendence has left the stage through the main door, a transcendental subject has now made its arrival through a side entrance. Gödel's intuition can be understood as a rational yet still existential insight into the logico-mathematical a priori, as it reveals an a priori that is given to human intuition as a kind of non-sensory datum. There is a gap between the ideal and the empirical. This fracture has scared off man-made symbolic mechanisms by showing them to be superfluous and always incapable of accounting for the inexhaustibility of logico-mathematical thought. Nevertheless, according to the Gödelian epistemological framework, a metaphorical eye of the mind can gaze past this metaphysical breach. In some cases, it can even manage to contemplate what is beyond that rupture. This intuitive sight is subjectively experiential, for Gödel's open-ended orientation of the axiomatic method takes place from a subjectivist view. Formal rules and procedures cannot justify axiomatics; only this subjectivist point of view can do so by glimpsing the reality of mathematical objects.

It follows from these comments that, while Gödel's work on incompleteness has helped us to argue for the autonomy of formal axiomatic systems, Gödel's very own philosophical endorsement of rational intuition can only take us so far in the elaboration of such an autonomy vis-à-vis automated systems. Gödel's existential perspective, therefore, is not one that I wish to adopt. From this point onwards, I will focus on Turing's conception on incomputability because the incomputable adds an important non-existential aspect to the open-endedness of axiomatics that I intend to pursue. Gödel's axiomatics gives itself to human intuition as an experientially personal construction; Turing's axiomatics, however, opens inwardly and impersonally, towards itself. Of course, I am not claiming that Turing's results are superior to Gödel's. Undeniably, any accurate reading of Turing's incomputability has to take Gödel's account of incompleteness as its starting point. Equally, the emphasis that has been placed here on the open-ended character of axiomatics is my own, not Gödel's or Turing's. I am attempting to build a non-metacomputational argument on that open-endedness, and to thereby advance my own claims. Incompleteness and incomputability, then, are the conceptual means through which I can put forth the non-metacomputational stance that I have proposed. As quoted above, Gödel explicitly stated that his work on the foundations of mathematics was not intended to undermine the power of human reason, but rather to show the potentialities of pure formalism in mathematics.[25] Simply put, incomputability allows us to look into the limits of formalism that Gödel envisaged, and to do so vis-à-vis its utmost mechanisation (i.e., via the computational automation of formal procedures). I am not, therefore, making a claim against intuition per se, nor is it my intention to dismiss the transcendental value of such insight for human experience. Axiomatics might as well be accessible to human reason. What I wish to stress, however, is that formal axiomatic systems are exposed to their own indeterminacy before any empirically or existentially based attempt to access them. But how does Turing's incomputability point towards this direction? The answer, I would argue, is through the infinite.

THE DISCRETISATION OF INFINITY

From a mathematical point of view, Turing's 1936 work was intended to engage with the existence of numbers that cannot be computed. This was (and still is) an actual problem in mathematics, confronting one of the most uncomfortable yet exciting concepts of the discipline: *infinity*. At the core of Turing's investigation on computability there is a transversally posed but crucially metaphysical problem: how is it possible to define the infinite in finite terms? The infinity in question is that of real numbers: a class of values representing quantities along a continuum, like points in a line, whose digits are infinite and thus uncountable. The finite steps, conversely, are those of the deterministic method used by Turing to cope with the dilemma itself. Turing divided the machine's functionality into small operations, whose complete purpose and conclusion were ruled by their own configuration and whose actions were set out by an equally finite table of behaviour. A Turing machine program is itself a description of an effective method of calculability, facing the possibility of encountering real numbers that cannot be computed with any desired certainty via an enumerable (and hence countable) set of instructions. The impossibility of processing the vast majority of real numbers through a mechanical procedure couples infinity and decidability in a binding logical argument: it is impossible for any Turing machine to prove if any other similar device would be able to write (which means, to calculate) the infinite digits of a real number on its blank tape.

At first, this conclusion would only seem to be relevant within the lecture hall of a mathematics department or at the repair bench of the local computer shop. However, incomputability haunts economists as much as it does biologists, physicists, and pretty much anybody who has ever switched on a computing device. It is because of incomputability that, to this day, there does not exist a 100 percent bug-free computer program. The correctness of a piece of software cannot be finally determined because of the inherent limits of algorithmic methods of testing, which check a computer program by executing the tested code in a finite-step, line-by-line manner. The infinite possibilities of endless loops in a program are beyond the finiteness of the time-constrained procedure constructed to infer its fallaciousness. We just do not know until we execute or run the program itself. We just do not know, for instance, if a program will halt until we run that program, and we cannot tell which inputs will lead to an output. This condition can also be said to pertain to the reasons for the contemporary software industry's tendency to neglect its capacity for generalisation in favour of more specific, limited solutions that are viable only within certain contexts and parameters. In concrete terms, rather than engaging in creating software that provides a universal answer for a certain requirement, the industry finds it more relevant to provide the market with very specific products, whose finite algorithmic determinacy is thus easier to be tested or proven. Constraints, restrictions, bounds, and iterations are added to the software, along with the pseudo-consolatory interface option for the end user to terminate a process that shows no hope of halting.

These and equivalent programming practices are useful examples for the conceptual point that I am making here. They appear to ban or relegate the relevance of infinity to the very peripheral role of an inconvenience: something of a theoretical annoyance in the solution of a problem via closed axiomatic means, and thus a distraction to be estranged from the counting of zeros and ones. Computer science is often quite pragmatically indifferent to Cantor's paradise (namely Georg Cantor's thesis about the existence of actual infinity, hailed by David Hilbert as the final conceptual locus of mathematics). Such a 'heavenly' status is not a shared destiny for the numbers crunched in and out by computing machines. Computational 'virtues'—to keep the eschatological metaphor—are rather defined in terms of the capacity to break down infinitely many data into enumerable finite sets of processes, eliding anything that will not fit a univocal correspondence between proof and execution. Of course, this agnosticism in computability theory is so much more than mere *horror infiniti*. The questions that it raises cannot be dismissed as a clever tactic to avoid the headaches of mathematical counting or to bypass digressions concerning the final systematisation of logical sciences. From this perspective, it can be said that computing machines are constructed upon the twentieth-century discovery of the logical deadlock between finitude and infinity. But what happened to formalism once it had been demonstrated that there are limits beyond which the deduction of abstract systems necessarily confronts (and even generates) undecidability? How is the axiomatic method complicated and challenged by incomputability, and yet also envisaged as the artificial and fully automated process that stands at the very cusp of the domain of instrumental rationality?

My hypothesis is as follows: Turing's theory of computation appears to be grounded on formalisation, understood as a method of *discretisation*. According to a functional view of the computing machine, computers might be made of any kind of stuff; their only requirement, following the Turing machine model, is that this stuff is deterministically sufficient to move the machine from finite state A to finite state B. From this functional perspective, *formalisation-as-discretisation* finds its highest realisation in the computing machine, where discrete outputs rigorously follow from a set of previously defined and equally discrete rules. The investigation into the laws of computational formalisation can then be seen as a practice of the strict adherence to, or dependence upon, discrete entities. What is formalised inside the computing machine? The operational answer would be that we formalise a procedure that works by dividing the infinite into finite parts. The main advantage of binary codes corresponding to concrete electrical switches is only the most blatant example that comes to mind. Discretisation thus stood as computation's principle of formalisation long before digitalisation. It is perhaps in virtue of such considerations that one must resist the sociocultural rhetoric about the revolutionary character of digitality as regards the representation of information. From the perspective that I suggest, discretisation is the methodological status of deductive thinking, and also the proper business of logical sciences. While formalisation meshes with the theory of computation as an ideal of mechanisation and prediction, the digital, in turn, works as the facilitator of such a conversion by providing and applying the technical reductions necessary for the automation, compression, and optimisation of quantitative processing.

But there is more to formalisation-as-discretisation. One could object that many, if not the majority of formalising systems of thought, can be seen to confront the question of how to relate the discreteness of their intelligible symbols and rules with the sensible continuity of the empirical reality that is to be encrypted. While I agree with this objection, my own point here as regards computational formalism is slightly different. It pertains to computation's validation of the discretising formalism of its systems, via the logical discovery that rules of deduction are limited and yet useful. These limitations and this usefulness are established through the conceptual and mechanical discretisation of logico-mathematical infinity. Arguably, this emphasis on infinity echoes Gödel's confidence in the inexhaustibility of mathematical thought. Such a resonance is appropriate, for this is in fact the case. Nonetheless, with Turing's incomputability we are witness to something especially surprising: it is the mechanical rule itself that, in its own operations of discretisation, generates the inexhaustibility of computational processing. In this sense, incomputability brings Gödel's results beyond the thought of Gödel himself, given the logician's scepticism towards computational mechanisations of reasoning. Of course, the question of infinity was already implicit in Gödel's incompleteness, according to which (and here I am simplifying Gödel's proof a great deal) more and more axioms can be added to the formal system. With incomputability, however, not only is the very existence of axiomatics freed from a metacomputational systematisation, but so too is the regulative and procedural character of the axiomatic method. This latter becomes non-metacomputational because it is opened up to infinity. Turing's notion of computability is founded upon a quantification of logico-mathematical infinity. Such quantification, however, cannot be fenced within a horizon of totality, for between input and output there is an infinity of quantities. At the core of Turing's model of computation there is a revolutionary ontological proposition, with important epistemological implications: computation is made up of quantities, yet these quantities cannot be fully counted. These quantities are not metacomputational measures and amounts. On the contrary, they express the quantitative character of a function that is determinable but not decidable, and which is not, therefore, computable.

Here, however, an important qualification needs to be added: computational formalisms work. In fact, they work very well. The foundational crisis over the superstructure of mathematics might have permanently undermined logicism by demonstrating that there are consequences that cannot be said to follow necessarily from initial assumptions. At the same time, though, the establishment of a theory of computation urgently reproblematised the relation between the ideal and the empirical via the paradox that there are things that can be described finitely, but which cannot be computed. While doubts about rigorous criteria for a satisfactory foundation of mathematics have profoundly threatened the possibility of reducing mathematics to logic, and of arriving at a unified framework for different scientific fields, Hilbert's critical proposal for a 'word game' method of formalisation is kept alive and well by the investigation of the computational relation between rules for deductive abstraction and calculability. In the shadow of the failure of Hilbert's quest for metamathematical proofs, his formalist study of mathematics as a mechanical and context-independent symbolic manipulation seems to have found, in the theory of computation, both its own declaration of intents and the examination of its possibilities and limitations.

At first glance, formalisation-as-discretisation would seem to provide a justification for computational idealism. To some extent, Turing was looking for the metacomputational formula. He actually managed to offer a model for a general-purpose, discrete-state machine by which to attempt universal calculations. However, the greatness of Turing's 1936 work lies in showing that the comprehensive character and regulative scope that Universal Computation would ascribe to deductive general-purposiveness is not attainable. Turing's account of the incomputable is a by-product of formalisation-as-discretisation. Yet this by-product confirms Gödel's results: Hilbert's programme is unrealisable, for a final systematisation of axiomatics cannot be accomplished. Nevertheless, despite this conclusion, it is the operative character of computational formalisation that finds its functional justification in Turing's establishment of the notions of computability and incomputability. The axiomatic processes of computation work fine. Crucially, however, they do so as long as they do not exceed the limits of the formal structure upon which the deductive system itself is modelled. Thus, while Turing's account of incomputability confirms that Universal Computation works in terms of the operability of an effective method of calculation, it also disproves the transcendent premises on which the metacomputational approach of Universal Computation is established and developed.

Both Turing's operational justification for pursuing a universal method of computation on the one hand, and his proving the usefulness of formal axiomatic systems for such an endeavour on the other, invalidate Universal Computation's assumption that computational axiomatics can make the formal system a transcendent blueprint for the empirical. In consequence, such

justification and usefulness also invalidate the assumption that a closed systemic of deductive abstraction can give computation an onto-epistemological
primacy and operative universality over phenomena. Turing's method of
computation was looking for the universality of a procedure. By addressing
this universality, however, Turing found that while one can devise a method
of calculation that would be able to compute anything that can be computed,
it is impossible to guarantee that this very method would always fulfil a
circle of closed deduction. This latter was the very supposition at the core of
the ontology and epistemology of Universal Computation, which is thus, via
Turing, invalidated. The fact that, within a computational formal axiomatic
system, there are things that cannot and will not be calculated opens up,
therefore, the possibility for computation to be something other than a *mathesis universalis*, and for the formal axiomatic structures, which computation
employs, to be less self-contained than such a *mathesis universalis* would
assume them to be.

FROM TOTAL DETERMINISM TO A
PROCESS OF DETERMINATION

We saw how the incomputable expresses the indeterminacy that is inherent
to computation's actual operations of formalisation-as-discretisation. What
needs to be discussed next is how the status of this indeterminacy *is not*
equivalent to that of Deleuzian virtuality. Deleuze's virtual is abstract because it is unbounded, unmediated, and never fully attained: it corresponds to
the ontogenetic capacities of the being of the sensible. Such an ontological
inventiveness is conveyed through intensities that cannot be measured or
represented. The virtual cannot be computed, inasmuch as it is an unknown
that is only to be felt. In this respect, it is interesting to note that Turing's
incomputability cannot be successfully measured or represented either. By
definition, the incomputable cannot be computed. Yet, while the infinity of
the virtual is intensive and therefore outside counting, the infinity of the
incomputable is extensive and can thus be understood as *the infinity of counting* itself.

This difference should suffice to indicate the disparity between virtuality
and incomputability, and that the virtual and the incomputable suggest two
different orders of indeterminacy. However, another striking dissimilarity
between Turing's notion of incomputability and Deleuze's virtuality lies in
the fact that the indeterminacy of Turing's incomputable is not a qualitative
dimension that can be lived and experienced by a body, but rather a quantitative dimension that needs to be grasped with a mind. This is because the
indeterminacy of the incomputable is algorithmic and thus logical, not physical. For Deleuze, indeterminacy is the virtual totality of the unactualised

conditions of the real, and this virtual whole impacts upon experience in the affective terms of the shock to thought exerted by the being of the sensible. Deleuze's advocacy of such an affective indeterminacy involves a critical stance against mental structuring and against logos. In the context of the present discussion, highlighting Deleuze's aversion to rational organisation allows us to stress that Turing's incomputable is not the affective indeterminacy of the virtual, for incomputability is not outside logos but *within it*. By no means do I intend to reintroduce a mind/body dichotomy within the philosophical analysis of computation systems. In order to avoid doing so, it is useful to use Whitehead's terminology, and to talk of physical and mental poles in order to refer to affective and logical capacities. However, the point remains: the incomputable is to be grasped through logic, not through affect.

This last assertion pushes Turing's logical breakthrough in a direction that Turing himself may not have endorsed. Just as I used Gödel earlier to go beyond Gödel, I am now attempting a similar manoeuvre in relation to Turing. For Turing, computing stops where incomputable quantities begin. Here, however, I am drawing on Turing's discovery of incomputability in order to argue for a different position: that while the incomputable is certainly that which cannot be successfully counted, it does not lie outside or beyond computation and should instead be seen as a defining, albeit indeterminate, element of its operation. Indeterminacy is, then, a fundamental component of computational processing. In this sense, incomputability expresses the indeterminacy of computation's formal and axiomatic logic, as it discloses the unknown dimension of computation's logico-quantitative character. Incomputability thus breaks with a Deleuzian ontology of the virtual (and also with related attempts, inspired by Deleuze's work, to virtualise digital computation), insofar as it confirms that the maximally indeterminate does not uniquely pertain to sensibility or to the thinking that emerges from the affective plane. Indeterminacy, to put this otherwise, is not uniquely tied to the virtual matter-flows of life, but also pertains to the rationalising functions of counting (i.e., to formalisation-as-discretisation).

Having advanced these contentions, it may now be useful to return to my proposed distinction between abstractness and abstraction. This is a distinction that, I claimed in chapter 2, was implicitly stated but centrally located in Deleuze's advocacy of aisthesis. For Deleuze, thought is immanent to sensation insofar as it is abstract or virtual thought. Abstractness is the status of those unmediated relations with the sensible dimension that thought entails when it does not represent anything. Abstraction, on the other hand, only represents. According to Deleuze, abstractive techniques hinder the dynamism of abstract thought via cognitive stratification and epistemic reduction. In contrast to this Deleuzian stance, I now wish to argue that the incomputable destabilises such an opposition between the abstract and the abstractive. Incomputability demonstrates that abstraction, in computation, is not a stopping point for computational systems' capacity to relate to indeterminacy. Abstraction in computation is, in fact, the manner in which an intelligible relation with indeterminacy—as opposed to a sensible relation—is established. Formalisation-as-discretisation is a fundamental functional feature of procedures of deductive abstraction. The formal discretisation of computation can be understood as the *abstractive structuring* specific to the computational method. However, while computation always constructs an abstractive matrix of discrete points, the incomputable reveals that these points are discrete and yet also infinite. Alan Turing's 1936 work founded the notion of computability upon a quantification of logico-mathematical infinity. Computer science (and Turing himself) might have pragmatically adopted a posture of seeming indifference towards this quantitative infinity. Nonetheless, my contention is that this quantitative infinity in computation should be understood as the motor of Turing's model for the mechanisation of deductive abstraction. Computation is an abstractive method that produces and manipulates quantifiable entities into a sequence of procedures. Although computation divides the infinity of counting into finite steps through formalisation, the possibility that these steps are infinite ingresses each and every computational process. The infinity of the incomputable is always present; it cannot be avoided.

The relevance of these points is that they help us to develop one of this book's central aims: that of establishing an aesthetics of computation according to which abstractive operations are not obstacles to the prospect that computation could be dynamic and complex vis-à-vis indeterminacy, but are in fact crucial to that possibility. On the one hand, it becomes clear, via Turing, that to construct a discrete, and yet infinite, abstractive matrix is something that a computational system must do in order to be functionally operative. On the other hand, it is possible to draw on Turing's work to argue that it is precisely because computation abstracts through discretisation that this formal indeterminacy ingresses into the actuality of computational processing. Abstraction in computation is therefore not an epistemic simplification that blocks infinity, but a means of constructing a logico-quantitative relation with infinity. The analysis of the ontological aspects of deductive abstraction and the argument against metacomputational perspectives that I have introduced in this second part of the book were both presented with a view towards developing that contention. Having engaged with incomputability, I can now ground this hypothesis, because I have demonstrated that computational abstraction affords access to indeterminacy. By reworking Turing's discovery of the incomputable as evidence of the indeterminate condition of computation, I want to propose that computation is defined by the indeterminacy that makes it *contingent*. An ontology of contingency is to be found at the formal level of computational systems. Contingency here is an ontological status that is not uniquely predicated upon the empirical. I mobilised Gödel's conception of incompleteness to argue for the extra-empirical character of formal axiomatic systems. With Turing's incomputability, I can now go further and fully divorce the contingent from the empirical. Computational systems might interact with the empirical world and open up to the environmental input that brings lived variability into the algorithmic procedure. Algorithms themselves might also be considered to be empirical by virtue of their very concrete and material applications, implementations, and performances. Nonetheless, my point is that one truly breaks with metacomputation only if it is demonstrated that computation is *already* contingent, at its formal level, because of the indeterminacy of axiomatics.

My discussion of contingency should not be understood as attributing a chaotic or irrational element to computing. Contingency in computation is not opposed to structure; on the contrary, it results from it. Contingency is the ontological status of algorithmic operations of ordering and systematising the real through logico-quantitative means. The latter are algorithmic operations that are preset, but which are always ultimately contingent because of their internal indeterminacy. This contingency means that formalisation-as-discretisation never exhausts indeterminacy. Computation is made of quantities, yet these are quantities that cannot be fully counted; an ever-increasing number of axioms can be added to the system, and an ever-increasing number of steps can be added to the calculation. This contingent status then undermines Universal Computation, insofar as it shows that to formalise is not merely to reduce or to compress. The infinity of counting is there to stay, and for this reason it is possible to say that, within the formal axiomatic systems of computing, there is not a reduction of complexity to simplicity, but complexity in its own right. This contingent situation does not, however, deny the functionality of this (always already complex) computational method. As I indicated earlier, the formal and axiomatic method of computing works. Historically, the legacy of Hilbert's metareasoning encountered its fair share of setbacks and bitter disappointments. Still, as the mathematician Gregory Chaitin remarks, 'while formal axiomatic systems are a failure, formalisms for computers are a brilliant success'.[26] In light of what has been discussed so far, it can be suggested that to welcome this success means conceding that computation's rationalising processes would not exist if it were not for the indeterminacy (and the consequent complexity) that always subtends them. Acknowledging the significant presence of indeterminacy within computation must thereby change the way in which one is to understand the preprogrammed character of computing. The presence of indeterminacy within computation, which is engendered by the ingression of infinity, demonstrates that computation's matrix of abstraction is not entirely given beforehand, and that it is in fact always an *event*: it is constructed *within the actuality* of computational processing. The contingency of formal axiomatic systems thus shows us that, although computation may well be preprogrammed, it can never be entirely predetermined.

A clarification is required here. The proposed conceptualisation of contingency in computation does not imply that the latter is equal to a game of chance in which one merely expects something to go wrong. Contingency in computation is not the abrupt upshot of an informational Russian roulette, with users gambling on an algorithmic procedure that either could or could not halt. Of course, incomputability involves the ambiguity of an input that might not return the promised output, and thus contingency might be seen as the possibility of a computational procedure being something other than that which it has been programmed to be, of not finding the intended result, or of not producing an outcome. Nonetheless, although the incomputable also involves the risk of unpredictability (and a consequent dose of risk taking is thus permanently embedded in computing practices), contingency in computation is more than this. The contingency of computational systems should not be understood in terms of a capacity for accident, wherein the terms of the algorithmic process can deviate from the preset rule. The preset rule does not in fact have to be other than itself in order to be contingent: it does not have to deviate from formal logic or axiomatic deduction in order to embrace indeterminacy, because it is contingent already, at its logical, formal, and axiomatic level, thanks to the infinity that is inscribed in its being preprogrammed.

Following on these points, what I argued to be the autonomy of formal axiomatic systems can now be cast as a *process of determination* that continually undergoes the ingression of indeterminacy. The key ontological manoeuvre here involves abandoning the metacomputational project that wanted to establish total determinism and considering instead the autonomy of formal axiomatic structures in terms of computational processing's internal striving for determination. This striving has not been compromised by incompleteness and incomputability. In fact, the opposite is the case: incompleteness and incomputability have strengthened it. The ontological operation that I am attempting thus follows from the consideration that although the incomputable dismantles the ontological and epistemological dream of a *mathesis universalis*, it does not undermine the functional self-sufficiency of computational systems. This self-sufficiency simply becomes something other than metacomputational necessity. To affirm the self-sufficiency of computation amounts to saying that computation, strictly speaking, needs nothing but itself in order to determine itself. This affirmation, however, does not exonerate computation from having to confront indeterminacy in each and every iterative process. In the self-sufficiency of computation's method of abstraction, one discovers that preprogrammed computational rules contain an inherent level of undecidability that remains unknown. This is an undecidability that cannot be systematised by discretising and counting, despite the fact that these actual procedures of systematisation are what engenders the very possibility of such undecidability. Some things will not be computed; the self-sufficiency of computation means that the formal process will discover anew, in the actuality of computational processing, what these things are. Consequently, to argue for the autonomy of the computational process is to claim that the maximally unknown, which the incomputable expresses, is the indeterminacy that defines computation's drive towards its own realisation. In other words, computational processing, as a self-sufficient process of determination, cannot be separated from the indeterminacy that it is always tending towards.

To argue that computation is to be understood not in terms of total determinism but in terms of a process of determination involves putting contingency at the heart of axiomatics. By doing so, I am avoiding the inscription of an idealist and transcendent sufficient reason into computing. However, since I am not only affirming indeterminacy, but also the self-sufficiency of computation, my position here is distinct from philosophies of absolute contingency, such as that of Quentin Meillassoux, who would claim that 'contingency *alone* is necessary'.[27] Meillassoux has been described as 'the thinker most responsible for initiating a renewed debate around the concept of contingency',[28] so it may prove useful to explain how and why my position differs from his. First of all, it should be noted that Meillassoux's work may seem similar to some of my claims, because it does not identify contingency with the merely accidental, and because it frees this concept from any subordination to probability. Crucially, Meillassoux also presents contingency as an event: as '*something that finally happens*'.[29] Beyond these similarities, however, Meillassoux's absolute contingency and my understanding of contingency in computation remain distinct. This can be illustrated by emphasising the way in which necessity and contingency are, in my view, to be articulated in computational systems. According to Meillassoux's cosmological perspective, there is no place for necessity: everything is contingent; only the contingent is therefore truly necessary. When looking at computational systems, however, I believe that it is not possible to get rid of necessity so drastically, due to their preprogrammed and axiomatic nature. Evidently, I cannot extend Meillassoux's absolute contingency to computational systems because of the self-sufficient character of axiomatics that I have stressed. Although my critique of metacomputation is intended to demonstrate that total determinism cannot be achieved, it also acknowledges that computational processes tend towards a necessary completion, and that they do so not despite indeterminacy, but by virtue of it. My proposal that we should understand computation in terms of processes of determination is, then, at odds with Meillassoux's '*principle of unreason*',[30] according to which everything might or might not be without a reason. Computation's processes of determination do have a reason to be what they are. However, instead of finding this reason outside of themselves, and thus falling into an infinite regress towards an ultimate necessary being, computation's processes of determination are *causa sui*.

The causality and finality of computation will be discussed at length in the third part of the book. Nonetheless, it can be stressed here that it is precisely the relation between necessity and contingency in computation that needs to be reassessed. We should not conceptually discard the self-sufficiency of computation, precisely because we are affirming the functional as well as the ontological autonomy of formal axiomatic systems. At the same time, however, this autonomy has been argued for by dismantling the meta-computational assumption of a closed circle of determinism. Considering computation as a process of determination (and not as a matrix of total determinism) points to an ontological struggle between determinacy and indeterminacy, according to which computational forms are not preformed and static but are instead always eventual, and in a process of becoming. It is to this struggle and to this becoming that we should now turn. In order to pursue this, however, we need to draw upon Whitehead's ontological schema.

ACTUAL EVENTS OF THOUGHT

How can this ontological manoeuvre from determinism to determination that I am proposing be viewed through the lenses of Whitehead's philosophy? We can begin to answer this question by returning to the Whiteheadian characterisation of actuality. Whitehead's philosophy is aimed at uncovering the true nature of the world. This world is always actual: in Whitehead's own words, 'apart from things that are actual, there is nothing—nothing either in fact or efficacy'.[31] Whitehead's actuality expresses itself as a multiplicity of concrete entities, all of which are different from each other. Whitehead's actuality could then be said to be the Cartesian *res vera*.[32] To put this otherwise, actuality is *reality*. This reality, however, is never just given. Reality is to be achieved. Although the actuality of occasions is fundamental, it is not simple, for it results from a complex procedure of realisation. According to Whitehead, the actual is also *process*. The processual nature of the real implies the internal development of the actual occasion and involves this occasion's change of status in relation to other actual occasions. Actuality can be seen, therefore, as a full-fledged act of becoming. This becoming, in turn, is a coming to be, or a coming into existence. Ultimately, for Whitehead, processes correspond to *self-actualisations*. On this view, existence does not transcend the process of realising actual occasions. Rather, process and existence are the same thing.

This condition seems strikingly true for computation too: the existence of computational processes corresponds to their coming into being. In chapter 3,

I proposed that we should consider computational processes in terms of Whiteheadian actual occasions. I can now add that *to be* a computational actual occasion is always *to become* such an occasion. In other words, to look at computation as a self-constitutive process of determination means to understand this process of determination in terms of its self-actualisation. This is a central contribution that Whitehead's philosophy offers to the onto-logical study of computation. Whitehead permits a refinement of my pro-posed understanding of computation's own processes of determination be-cause his actual occasions are themselves processes of determination. The parallel that can be established between the picture of computation that I am drawing and Whitehead's account of reality does, however, need to be devel-oped further.

Whitehead's philosophy of actuality offers a way of refining my under-standing of computation's non-representational relation with indeterminacy. It is possible to fully sustain a non-metacomputational approach to computa-tional systems only when another understanding of abstraction in computa-tion has been introduced. This is precisely what Whitehead permits us to do. Via Whitehead, it can be demonstrated that abstraction in computation is not a departure from the reality of the event of thought, but is rather constitutive of such eventuality. The most significant issue in Whitehead's characterisa-tion of actuality is that the actual occasion's process of determination, in order to achieve both its aim and its end point, requires the ingression of indeterminacy in its own constitution. Whitehead wrote clearly about this: the constitution of an actual entity is 'a process of transition from indetermi-nation towards terminal determination'.[33] To determine oneself, or to self-actualise, is to do so through and thanks to indeterminacy. In this sense, it is the actual that entails a functional relation with indeterminacy, not vice ver-sa. For Whitehead, to make a structure is the only way in which potentiality passes into actuality. Constructing a structure is also the only way in which indeterminacy becomes determinate. This construction is the very activity of actuality, as only actuality is active and generative. Whitehead's indetermi-nacy is thus addressed and resolved within actuality by actuality itself. It is my contention that this condition is true of computational systems too. Hav-ing engaged with incomputability and with the consequent contingent status of computation, I can now explain why.

I argued earlier that, while the points that compose computation's matrix of abstraction may well be discrete, they are, nonetheless, infinite, and if they are infinite, indeterminacy must be inherent within computational axiomat-ics. The maximally indeterminate thus forms a crucial part of computation's operations of formalisation-as-discretisation. In the context of the present discussion, I will now add that these operations of formalisation-as-discret-isation are not potential or ideal. They are actual. The observation that inde-terminacy underpins all computation thus allows us to contend that computation's matrix of abstraction is constructed within the actuality of computational processing. This actuality results from a discretisation of infinity that is characterised by a residue of infinity. Incomputability attests to the presence of this indeterminate residue. Nonetheless, it is the actuality of computation that maintains a relation with that residue, since it is the actuality of operations of formalisation-as-discretisation that opens up to it, and which is ingressed by it. In the light of these comments, I can now return to the metaphorical open-endedness of computational axiomatics that I advocated earlier in this chapter, and specify that this open-endedness should be understood as computation's aperture towards its own self-actualisation. Computation's actual operations of formalisation-as-discretisation are open not because they let things in, which would transform them into a transitory and fluid patchwork composition. The openness of the formal system that I am describing is thus not the openness that assemblage theories, among others, would promote. This is due to the fact that computational processes remain teleologically closed, as they are finite processes of determination that always tend towards producing themselves. Their axiomatic openness is thus not the openness of something without an end. Instead, it is the metaphysical open-endedness of a process that, in verging towards its end, is always ingressed by indeterminacy.

Understanding computation as a process of determination that is always ingressed by indeterminacy, as is the case with Whitehead's actuality, affords a means of articulating a central contention of this book: that the maximally unknown that the incomputable expresses points to a non-human capacity to render indeterminacy intelligible. Whitehead fully envisaged such a capacity. He called it 'conceptual prehension' and attributed it to all actuality. Conceptual prehensions are a seizing of ideality, or a mode of selecting it. This is the ideality possessed by what Whitehead called 'eternal objects': ideas that are infinite and disconnected from each other, and whose nature is maximally unknowable if taken in distinction from the actualities that seize hold of them. Eternal objects have the function of determining an actual occasion; they inform its coming into existence. However, because they cannot be known and hence cannot be represented, eternal objects are to be understood as the indeterminacy that determines the realisation of the actual occasion. For Whitehead, indeterminacy is, therefore, a fundamental ingredient of actuality's determination. Moreover, one can note that for Whitehead, and differently from Deleuze, the maximally indeterminate does not pertain only to sensibility, or to the thinking that arises from it. The analogy that can be drawn with my previous discussion of the incomputable is evident here: with Whitehead, it becomes possible to theorise computation's capacity to logically and formally address the unknown—a capacity that, however, does not aim to represent this unknown through preformed and universal functions of valid reasoning. Whitehead helps us to do so because he himself theorised such capacity in terms of actuality's activity of conceptually prehending the indeterminacy of eternal objects.

My proposal is now as follows. I intend to understand formalisation-as-discretisation in terms of Whiteheadian conceptual prehensions. This is the new role that I wish to assign to formal abstraction, against its metacomputational interpretation. To put this otherwise, incomputability demonstrates that computation is *not just* a physical manipulation of data, and that neither does it only involve the infinite continuous intensive transformation of these data through affects and intensities. Algorithms are procedures through which to logically think, and *not just* to affectively feel, the unknown. The incomputable also shows, however, that formal operations of abstraction, and the thinking of this unknown, are *not just* representations, insofar as they confront what cannot be represented without reducing or simplifying it, but by fully embracing its unpresentable complexity. By thinking abstraction in computation in terms of conceptual prehensions, I am thus departing from Deleuze's ontology of thought. Computation's conceptual activity cannot be the abstract thought that Deleuze advocated, for it does not correspond to a sensuous or affective processuality. Instead, it points to a logical and formal processuality. Retaining a Deleuzian terminology, the incomputable could be called an 'event of thought'. However, this event of thought does not stem from a clash with the being of the sensible (as would be the case in a Deleuzian ontology), but from computation's generating, in each process, its own logical limits. The incomputable, as an actual—and not virtual—event of thought, is hence conditioned by computation's logical and formal contingency (that is, by the inherent indeterminacy of computation itself). In this sense, it is exactly the occurrence of the incomputable that challenges the conception of computation as an all-encompassing representational 'image of thought' (to rephrase another of Deleuze's expressions). In the process of determining computation's actuality (i.e., in the computational processing itself), the abstractive method of computation has to think beyond what is already known (i.e., beyond what is preprogrammed). While Deleuze famously argued that axiomatics is a stopping point for thought, what has been discussed here can offer a way of arguing that axiomatics in computation might constitute another modality of thought altogether: one that is processual yet impersonal, non-existential and extra-empirical. Although this processual thought is preprogrammed, it cannot be considered to be totally preconstituted or preformed, precisely because it is processual.

For Whitehead, thinking is aesthetic because it is a mental activity that is nonetheless prehensive. Conceptual prehensions express a mental activity that is, in Whitehead's view, aesthetic insofar as it is a feeling of ideality. By understanding formalisation-as-discretisation in terms of conceptual prehensions, a different way of theorising an *aesthetics of the intelligible* can be proposed. The consideration of computational idealism that has been conducted in this second part of the book has provided a means of studying the role that logical formulation and deductive abstraction entertain in a mathematically focused understanding of computational aesthetics. The idealist aesthetics of a priori computational forms is grounded on a deductive 'preformulation' of intelligibility that computational axiomatics would seem to instantiate. Arguably, computational idealism is an aesthetics of the intelligible because it puts logic at the heart of aesthetics. However, if computational abstraction is to be understood in terms of conceptual prehensions (as I have claimed it should be), and if (as I have also claimed) axiomatics does not compress or simplify reality, but rather expands and complexifies it, then the opposite operation becomes conceivable, and another aesthetics of the intelligible appears to be possible. From the perspective of the open-ended axiomatics that I am advancing here, aesthetics is at the heart of logic, not vice versa. By virtue of its prehensive relation with infinity, logic steps out of its representational and reductionist role and opens to its own inexhaustibility. On this view, the fracture between aesthetics and logic in contemporary computational culture begins to heal. Or, at least, one can begin to envisage how it is to be repaired. This reconciliation avoids turning computation's logical matrix of discrete and infinite points into an aesthetic flux of affective continuity. The quantitative is not made qualitative. By understanding formalisation-as-discretisation in terms of conceptual prehensions, we find a way to address the construction of computation's matrix of abstraction as immanently constitutive of the actualisation of the computational process itself.

Having made that last contention, I can now return to a claim that I advanced earlier: the limits of computational axiomatics should not be understood as restrictions or constraints, or as an inadequacy of sorts. On the contrary, they should be understood as evidence of computation's potential. I have already indicated how Whitehead envisaged two types of potentiality: one that he called 'real' because it concerns some particular state of affairs of the actual world, and one that he referred to as 'pure' insofar as it pertains to the ideality of eternal objects. We should now focus on the latter. For Whitehead, the pure potential of eternal objects is a mode of indeterminacy that crucially contributes to the final determination of the actual occasion. Pure potentials become realised only in such a determination, as a result of their ingression into the actuality of the occasion. The speculative proposition that I suggest is now as follows: it is possible to understand the quantitative infinity that always ingresses computational procedures in the Whiteheadian terms of eternal objects' pure potentiality. This is because the infinite quantities of the incomputable have the same function as Whitehead's eternal objects. They are the *unknown condition* that is integral to the realisation of the actual occasion (or, in computation's case, of the algorithmic actual procedure). As eternal objects are pure potentialities from the standpoint of the actual occasion that selects them, so too are the infinite quantities of the incomputable from the standpoint of an actual procedure of calculation that always engenders them. There cannot be actual events without the ingression of pure potentiality, as Whitehead's actuality needs the ideality of the eternal objects. Similarly, there cannot be computational events without the indeterminacy of the incomputable that conditions the computational determination, insofar as the conclusion of a computational process has to be informed by the quantitative infinity that it is always tending towards. In every computation, there is an actualisation of this infinity.

Both the infinity of the eternal objects and the infinity of incomputable events do not transcend or regulate actuality; they are immanent to it. This immanence is of a particular kind. In the sections above, I discussed the disparity between the indeterminacy of Turing's incomputable and the indeterminacy of Deleuze's virtual. I can now add that the pure potentiality of Turing's incomputable (which is akin to that of Whiteheadian eternal objects) and the pure potentiality of Deleuze's virtuality are markedly different. In order to explain this point, one needs to consider that Deleuze and Whitehead advocated distinct types of pluralism, which presupposed different conceptions of part-whole relations and dissimilar ontological principles of connection between all things. For Deleuze, the virtual is a sort of metaphysical glue that holds everything together. There is no ontological singularity, but only univocity of the virtual, despite the multiplicity of its infinite faces. In Whitehead's philosophy, however, there is no such whole of virtual ideas: eternal objects are an infinite heterogeneity of disjointed idealities. These eternal objects are not connected among themselves. They do not communicate between each other prior to their ingression into actualities. So, while for Deleuze virtuality and actuality are to be engaged along a continuum, insofar as they are reciprocal ontological dimensions to be multiplied along a whole in becoming, for Whitehead there is no such whole of continual differentiation, but rather a stretching out or an extending over of separate ontological units of actuality that happen once and never again, and which select idealities that are themselves discrete yet infinite. This is a very striking difference. Because he envisaged the discreteness of actuality and the discrete potential thereof in this manner, Whitehead's model offers the concrete possibility of successfully addressing the infinite quantities of the incomputable in terms of the pure potential of counting. The passage from potential to actual is achieved not by plunging into the whole of virtuality's plane of immanence, but instead by doing what computation always does: constructing a complex schema of abstraction according to which certain quantities enter the actualisation and others do not. While the virtual is immanent to all actuality via sensation, the infinite quantities of the incomputable need a conceptual activity to ingress computation's actuality, just like eternal objects. In this sense, the legitimacy and irreversible specificity of the logico-quantitative character of computing is maintained: it is only thanks to this logico-quantitative character of computation that this pure potentiality ingresses the actuality of the computational procedure in the first place.

NOTES

1. See Alan M. Turing, 'On Computable Numbers, with an Application to the Entscheidungsproblem', *Proceedings of the London Mathematical Society* 42 (1936): 230–65, https://doi.org/10.1112/plms/s2-42.1.230.

2. *Completeness* meant that any true or false statement within an axiomatic system could be proved or disproved in formal terms; *consistency* indicated that within the same system no invalid statements could be derived from a correct proof process; *decidability* referred to the notion of an *effective method* within the system, by means of which a statement's truth or falsity could be established.

3. According to Hilbert's programme, formal axiomatic systems present accurate accounts of mathematical argumentations and are provided with the power to justify the epistemological questions of the discipline. At an appropriate level of generality, the power of the axiom is the power of *metamathematics*: a fully mechanical mathematics that studies the rules and strength of what mathematics itself can or cannot achieve, and which is characterised by the application of secure 'finitary' methods to prove the validity of the metatheory itself.

4. See Kurt Gödel, 'On Formally Undecidable Propositions of the Principia Mathematica and Related Systems I', in *The Undecidable: Basic Papers on Undecidable Propositions, Unsolvable Problems and Computable Functions*, ed. Martin Davis, trans. Elliott Mendelson (Mineola, NY: Dover, 2004), 4–38.

5. Constance Reid, *Hilbert* (New York: Springer, 1996), 198.

6. Ernest Nagel and James R. Newman, *Gödel's Proof* (London: Routledge, 2005), 3.

7. Hilbert first addressed the idea of a procedure for decidability during the 1900 Second International Congress of Mathematicians in Paris, where he announced a list of twenty-three open problems in mathematics that he believed the coming twentieth century would need to address and resolve. The *Entscheidungsproblem* was formulated in connection with the solvability of Diophantine equations. The heart of what goes under the name of 'Hilbert's tenth problem' concerns the possibility of 'devis[ing] a process according to which it can be determined by a finite number of operations whether the equation is solvable in rational integers'. David Hilbert, 'Mathematical Problems: Lecture Delivered before the International Congress of Mathematicians at Paris in 1900', *Bulletin of American Mathematical Society* 8, no. 10 (1902): 458. Thanks to the combined work of the mathematicians Emil Post, Martin Davis, Hilary Putnam, Julia Robinson, and Yuri Matiyasevich over the last thirty years, Hilbert's tenth problem has been proved to be unsolvable and, therefore, undecidable. See Martin Davis, 'Hilbert's Tenth Problem Is Unsolvable', *American Mathematical Monthly* 80, no. 3 (March 1973): 233–69, https://doi.org/10.2307/2318447.

8. There is a great affinity between Gödel's and Turing's respective proofs. The two men, however, never met. On the relation between Gödel and Turing as regards the notion of computability, and on the consequent issues involved, see Wilfried Sieg, 'Gödel on Computability', *Philosophia Mathematica* 14, no. 2 (June 2006): 189–207, https://doi.org/10.1093/philmat/nkj005.

9. Turing, 'On Computable Numbers', 249.

10. Jean-François Lyotard, *The Postmodern Condition: A Report on Knowledge*, trans. Geoff Bennington and Brian Massumi (Manchester: Manchester University Press, 1984), 43.

11. This misconception is discussed in David Wayne Thomas, 'Gödel's Theorem and Postmodern Theory', *Publications of the Modern Language Association* 110, no. 2 (March 1995): 248–61, https://doi.org/10.2307/462914. See also Torkel Franzén, *Gödel's Theorem: An Incomplete Guide to Its Use and Abuse* (Wellesley, MA: A K Peters, 2005); Rebecca Goldstein, *Incompleteness: The Proof and Paradox of Kurt Gödel* (New York: Norton, 2006).

12. In the philosophy of mathematics, *ontological realism* is the view maintaining that (at least some) mathematical entities exist objectively, and that our mathematical theories can describe such entities. This position is also known as *mathematical Platonism* because it entails that mathematical entities can be understood as sharing the proprieties of Platonic forms. Gödel's mathematical Platonism is discussed at length in Richard Tieszen, *After Gödel: Platonism and Rationalism in Mathematics and Logic* (Oxford: Oxford University Press, 2011). See also Charles Parsons, 'Platonism and Mathematical Intuition in Kurt Gödel's Thought', *Bulletin of Symbolic Logic* 1, no. 1 (March 1995): 44–74, https://doi.org/10.2307/420946; Hao Wang, *A Logical Journey: From Gödel to Philosophy* (Cambridge, MA: MIT Press, 1996), 209–46. For Gödel's conceptual realism, see Donald A. Martin, 'Gödel's Conceptual Realism', *Bulletin of Symbolic Logic* 11, no. 2 (June 2005): 207–24, https://doi.org/10.2178/bsl/1120231631.

13. Andrew Hodges, 'Alan Turing: A Short Biography', 1995, http://www.turing.org.uk/bio/part3.html.

14. Hilbert, 'Mathematical Problems', 445.

15. I am alluding to the cognitive scientist Douglas Hofstadter's self-referential structures, which he calls 'strange loops'. See *Gödel, Escher, Bach: An Eternal Golden Braid* (London: Penguin, 2000). However, while Hofstadter uses strange loops to explain—in explicit reference to Gödel's incompleteness—his vision of consciousness and first-person existence, I am using this analogy to emphasise how axiomatic systems do not come full circle.

16. Goldstein, *Incompleteness*, 50–51.

17. Kurt Gödel, 'On Undecidable Propositions of Formal Mathematical Systems', in *Collected Works*, vol. 1, *Publications 1929–1936*, ed. Solomon Feferman, John W. Dawson Jr., Stephen C. Kleene, Gregory H. Moore, Robert M. Solovay, and Jean van Heijenoort (Oxford: Oxford University Press, 1986), 370.

18. Kurt Gödel, 'What Is Cantor's Continuum Problem?', in *Philosophy of Mathematics: Selected Readings*, 2nd ed., ed. Paul Benacerraf and Hilary Putnam (Cambridge: Cambridge University Press, 1983), 484.

19. Kurt Gödel, 'The Modern Development of the Foundations of Mathematics in the Light of Philosophy', in *Collected Works*, vol. 3, *Unpublished Essays and Lectures*, ed. Solomon Feferman, John W. Dawson Jr., Warren Goldfarb, Charles Parsons, and Robert N. Solovay (Oxford: Oxford University Press, 1995), 383.

20. Gödel, quoted in Wang, *A Logical Journey*, 167. For an analysis of Gödel's later philosophical turn towards Husserl's phenomenology, see Dagfinn Føllesdal, 'Gödel and Husserl', in *From Dedekind to Gödel: Essays on the Development of the Foundations of Mathematics*, ed. Jaakko Hintikka (Dordrecht: Kluwer Academic, 1995), 427–46; Richard Tieszen, 'Gödel's Path from the Incompleteness Theorems (1931) to Phenomenology (1961)', *Bulletin of Symbolic Logic* 4, no. 2 (June 1998): 181–203.

21. Gödel, quoted in Tieszen, *After Gödel*, 5. Gödel's views on minds and machines are summarised and discussed in Wang, *A Logical Journey*, 183–208. In order to contextualise debates about the relation between incompleteness and computational theories of mind, it can be mentioned here that the physicist and philosopher Roger Penrose has famously made his case against computational models of the mind while basing his argument exactly upon Gödel's incompleteness theorems. Penrose contends that Gödel's incompleteness is an insuperable deadlock for artificial intelligence, and he uses that claim to prove that human mental activities are subject to physical laws that cannot possibly be accounted for mechanistically. See *The Emperor's New Mind: Concerning Computers, Minds, and the Laws of Physics* (Oxford: Oxford University Press, 1989). A similar (but not identical) claim to Penrose's was originally advanced in John R. Lucas, 'Minds, Machines and Gödel', *Philosophy* 36, no. 137 (April 1961): 112–27, https://doi.org/10.1017/S0031819100057983.

22. Goldstein, *Incompleteness*, 122.

23. Gödel, 'What Is Cantor's Continuum Problem?', 483–84.

24. Wang, *A Logical Journey*, 169.

25. Gödel, 'On Undecidable Propositions of Formal Mathematical Systems', 370.

26. Gregory Chaitin, *Meta Maths: The Quest for Omega* (London: Atlantic, 2005), 55.

27. Quentin Meillassoux, *After Finitude: An Essay on the Necessity of Contingency*, trans. Ray Brassier (London: Continuum, 2008), 80.

28. Robin Mackay, 'Editorial Introduction', *Collapse: Philosophical Research and Development* 8 (December 2014): 34.

29. Meillassoux, *After Finitude*, 108.

30. Meillassoux, *After Finitude*, 60.

31. Alfred North Whitehead, *Process and Reality: An Essay in Cosmology* (New York: Free Press, 1978), 40.

32. See René Descartes, *Meditations on First Philosophy, with Selections from the Objections and Replies*, ed. and trans. John Cottingham (Cambridge: Cambridge University Press, 1986).

33. Whitehead, *Process and Reality*, 45.

Part 3

Experience

Chapter Seven

Computational Empiricism

UNCONVENTIONAL, NATURAL, AND NON-CLASSICAL COMPUTING

In May 2011, the Canadian start-up company D-Wave Systems announced the sale of its then newest computational device: D-Wave One. Generally, in the fast-paced technological present, where the computer that you really need is the computer that appeared on the market the day after you bought your last one, a piece of news such as this would have gone relatively unnoticed. In the case of D-Wave One, however, the announcement was memorable, for the device was—according to its constructors—the first quantum computing system on the market. The price tag of D-Wave One was $10 million, and its buyer, the global defence and security corporation Lockheed Martin, stated that they would use it to attempt to overcome some of their firm's most daunting computational challenges.[1]

The idea of harnessing the laws of quantum mechanics into a computing machine was first advanced by various physicists in the early 1980s.[2] To date, however, quantum computing is still in its infancy. Quantum computing devices are extremely difficult to build; so difficult, in fact, that the use of these machines in an everyday context appears to be much more than a leap away. The academic world was thus sceptical towards D-Wave Systems' claim to have constructed a 'practical quantum computer', as Geordie Rose (the co-founder of D-Wave Systems) called his computing technology.[3] When D-Wave Systems first publicly demonstrated its early prototypes in 2007, it attracted criticism for not having provided the scientific community with enough evidence of the inner workings of its processors. A heated debate followed the 2011 release of D-Wave One. D-Wave Systems defended their results by publishing a paper in the journal *Nature*, which dem-

onstrated that the approach that the company pursues (called 'quantum annealing') is consistent with the expectations of quantum mechanics.[4] This
approach discards the paradigmatic quantum gate model (a quantum mechanical reversible version of the logic gates found in conventional computing
machines, which is the most established theoretical model in quantum computing but which also entails many unresolved practical difficulties) in favour of the quantum annealing of the adiabatic model.

Of course, my aim here is not to assess D-Wave Systems' claims. I am
referring to this piece of scientific news because it epitomises some of the
ways in which computation, in the twenty-first century, is interwoven with
various gradations of empirical commitments, constraints, and consequences.
I see these empirical entanglements to be predicated on the assumption that
the contingent is an ontological status that pertains uniquely to the plane of
sense-data reception. Against this view, I want to propose that contingency
pertains to formal systems too, due to the inherent logical indeterminacy of
their axiomatic structures. In order to fully divorce the contingent from the
empirical, it is thus necessary to engage theoretically with those computational models that conflate the two. The core set of arguments that I am
endeavouring to advance in this book renders such an engagement even more
necessary. This is because one of my central claims is that an aesthetics of
contingent computation can only be established when this divorce is fully
accomplished.

A declaration made by Rose can serve to exemplify the extent to which
computational models today are entangled with the empirical realm. Rose
asserted that D-Wave Systems' engineers use an 'empirical approach' when
designing the company's quantum processors.[5] This empirical attitude entails 'not just following the theory', as D-Wave Systems senior vice president
of processor development Jeremy Hilton explained,[6] but rather developing
quantum technology in response to particular computational problems and
situations, as opposed to doing so according to the general principles of
quantum theory. In regards to the proclaimed empirical methodology of D-
Wave Systems, and to how this methodology has attracted investors while
alienating academics, one could note that the alleged dispute between a theoretical versus practical quantum computing mirrors the genesis of computer
science itself, which is partly a mathematician's theoretical construction and
partly an engineer's practical architecture. As can be seen from the example
of D-Wave One, an empirical attitude to quantum computing means refusing
to fit with the prescriptions of theoretical physics when these directions do
not result in viable practical results. The adiabatic model of D-Wave One
challenges the dominant model of the 'quantum logic gate': while the gate
model lies at the basis of a multipurpose quantum computer (which, however, at the time of writing, has yet to be successfully built), the engineers at D-
Wave Systems prefer to design specialised computing machines in order to

tackle particular algorithmic tasks and problems. The empiricism of this design choice resides in its a posteriori attention to real-world optimisation and in its disregard of the general purposiveness of an a priori theoretical model. Equally, this explicitly hands-on approach echoes the empiricist epistemology of the natural sciences and of the scientific method: a general formal model follows direct observation of the workings of nature and experimentation with these specific natural conditions, not vice versa.

On a further level of analysis, it is also possible to remark that the empiricism of D-Wave One was engendered by the physical existence of the computing system. Definitely not your next mobile device, D-Wave One is a bulky computing machine, whose performance is strictly conditional upon its material circumstances. D-Wave One's processor inhabits a cryogenics system, hosted within a ten-square-metre room. Liquid helium circulates to keep the system at a temperature near to absolute zero, and the device has to be protected by a shield in order to avoid the interference of magnetic radiation. It can be argued, then, that D-Wave One intensifies the interdependency between the logical abstraction of a mechanical procedure and its physical realisation in actual machinery. Surely this interdependency between software and hardware is true for every computing device. However, this is even more the case for quantum computing, as D-Wave One's computational operations are only viable when paired with the happening of specific subatomic conditions. D-Wave One's condition of existence is hence empirical because it relies on physical reality: on its life support system of cooling gases and radiation shields, but also on the physical reality of quantum mechanics. Some systems, procedures, and instruments can be said to 'sense' these physical conditions of existence directly or indirectly. Clearly, this sense reception operates at a scale beyond the threshold of human perceptual awareness. Nonetheless, the attainment of descriptive and procedural knowledge about quantum computation is predicated upon the concrete possibility of the reception of these sense-data, as well as upon the possibility of their accurate objective representation (that is, upon those scientific measurements that can be carried out without probing the quantum state).

Having set out some of the important empirical aspects of this chapter's opening example, a consequent level of empiricism can now be identified within it. This level of empiricism has to do with the specific type of relation between abstraction and experience that is put forth by those *alternative* computing methodologies (of which quantum computing is but one example) that consider computation to be a fact of the empirical world. This specific type of relation, which I will characterise below as *associative* and as grounded upon the *externality* between thought and sense-data, underpins the approach to computation that is to be critically investigated in this third part of the book. I have named this approach *computational empiricism*. It is thus important to unfold the assertion slowly, through a series of sequential steps in the argument. Once again, the case of D-Wave Systems can provide a useful entry point to these issues. According to the company's old commercial slogan, D-Wave Systems' engineers 'have a problem with the impossible'. Arguably, this impossibility refers to the complications of constructing a quantum computer. The impossible, however, also brings to mind the *hard problems* of computer science, the solutions of which are deemed to be extremely difficult to calculate because they require algorithms capable of accounting for high computational complexity (i.e., for the elevated number of resources that an algorithm must employ in order to reach a solution). Although these tasks are logically viable, their intractability is related to the allocation and the management of computational means such as time or memory space.[7]

Among other possible examples, the case of the travelling salesman problem (or TSP, for short) is a good instance of the many concerns that computational complexity has to deal with. This intensively studied problem in combinatorial optimisation requires the identification of the shortest path for visiting all the cities among a set of given cities, with given distances between each pair of them. The task sounds relatively modest and simple, but it is not. The TSP could be solved by brute force, in the sense of a search that would check every round-trip route until the shortest one is found. Very large instances of this problem, however, are extraordinarily hard to solve via this method, for the total number of possible tours grows exponentially. As the TSP case thus shows, computationally complex problems involve a different type of difficulty to that posed by Turing's notion of incomputability. The incomputable defines the logical existence of well-defined tasks that cannot be resolved by a finite automated procedure. With computational complexity, however, what comes into question is not whether there is an algorithm that would be capable of providing us with a result, but whether this algorithm can give us a solution efficiently. Rather than 'effective calculability',[8] it is *efficient computation* that is pursued here, insofar as efficiency is 'captured by corresponding resource bounds'.[9] This assertion finds support in a seminal paper by the mathematician and theoretical computer scientist Alan Cobham, in which he describes the class of efficient computations known as the complexity class P (where 'P' stands for polynomial time). 'The problem', Cobham writes, 'is reminiscent of, and obviously closely related to, that of the formalization of the notion of effectiveness. But the emphasis is different in that the physical aspects of the computation process are here of predominant concern.'[10]

While there have been numerous attempts to resolve the intractability of hard computational problems with clever heuristics, these efforts have often produced only relative advances. In order to tackle these computationally complex tasks, novel understandings of what it means to compute have also been advanced. This is the historical and conceptual perspective from which one should read D-Wave Systems' commercial slogan. From this view, the D-Wave Systems case is a contemporary example that has to be inscribed into the larger technoscientific tendency to look for alternatives to 'classical computation'. The latter expression refers to Turing's 1936 formalisation of the notion of computability, as defined by the Turing machine: a finite calculation, determined by a well-defined sequence of deductively determined steps, from input to output. Against the seeming rigidity and artificiality of the Turing machine, non-classical computational approaches propose bottom-up methodologies that address physical reality in order to extrapolate the laws of computational abstraction.[11] Their goal is to uncover and promote novel principles, models, and methods of efficient information processing that are largely induced from the observation and simulation of physical, biological, and chemical systems, with a view towards developing non-standard computing architectures. The opposition between classical and non-classical models of computation could then be seen to be based on a perceived contrast between, on the one hand, a certain formal indifference on the part of traditional computational systems towards the real world and, on the other, the privilege given to factual existence by more unconventional paradigms, which are therefore said to be reality based. This divergence has often resulted in the (declared or tacit) intent to bring the unpredictable behaviour of observed empirical facts back into the computational model, and to thus move from the a priori prescriptions of immutable formulation to the a posteriori descriptions of emergent formations.

These alternative approaches to computation comprise (yet are not limited to) the following: quantum, molecular, neural, cellular, DNA, and membrane computing; collective intelligence; parallel computation; cellular automata; chaos, dynamical, evolutionary, and self-assembled systems; relativistic and collision-based computing; swarm intelligence; photonic logic; amorphous computing; physarum machines; and hypercomputers. The exotic names of these technologies might recall a sci-fi novel, but this is not fiction. *Unconventional, natural,* and *non-classical computing* are very active fields of technoscientific inquiry, which contribute to the development of experimental computing systems as well as to that of more ordinary consumer products. Although the adjectives 'unconventional', 'natural', and 'non-classical' are not synonymous, since their fields of enquiry, techniques, and aims often overlap, it is not rare to find them used interchangeably. 'Unconventional computing' is a broad umbrella expression that encompasses research into computational structures and methods other than the computer architecture of von Neumann and the Turing machine. 'Non-classical' computational systems are those that differ significantly from the classical concept of a computing machine (i.e., from the digital electronic computer). Among other factors, the universality and the sequential determinism of traditional digital electronic computers are challenged, and so too is the consequent traditional algorithmic and output-oriented understanding of what it means to compute. Finally, 'natural computing' is a more specific expression, which indicates the study and development of (1) human-designed methodologies that take inspiration from the natural world for information processing and problem solving, (2) computational techniques that employ natural elements or agents (such as DNA, photons, or neurons) to compute, and (3) computations that actually take place spontaneously in nature.

The relation between non-classical computation and computational complexity is far from being univocal and exclusive; one cannot make the claim that research in the former field originates uniquely in response to the difficulties of the latter field. Obviously, a multiplicity of factors has to be taken into account, such as, for instance, the innovations and advancements in biology and physics over the last decades. Nevertheless, the connection between computational complexity and alternative computational paradigms often seems undeniable and is predicated on the following question: could the contingency of empirical facts and situations be the inspiration for solving computational problems that are more dependent on concrete spatiotemporal resources and constraints than they are on logical determinations? Could or should, in this sense, computational complexity be modelled upon the complexity of those concrete, chaotic, adaptive, and non-linear systems that are observed empirically by the natural sciences?

From the perspective of a large part of the unconventional computing approaches mentioned above, the answer to both questions would be yes. In this respect, the predominant physical aspect of computation, which Cobham identified at the core of a definition of computational efficiency, is part of a broader investigation into the true character of the physical world—a true character which unconventional, natural, and non-classical computing understands as mutable yet inherently quantifiable, and which, as such, could be (at least in theory) incorporated into the formalisms of computing machines. Some of the evidence that these alternative approaches to computation could offer to support their proposition include DNA's encoding of genes, ants in a colony organising themselves among tasks to solve problems, and neurons transmitting information to other neurons. The fact that the process of protein folding, which is spontaneously carried out by biological molecules within milliseconds, takes dozens of years for a digital computer to simulate is one instance, among many others, that has made scientists wonder whether this efficiency can be mimicked by nature-inspired computational models and whether these would be able to exhibit a similar information-processing and problem-solving power. From this view, one can understand how the question of differentiating what might be said to compute from what does not has become a leading investigative point for unconventional computing practices. Largely favoured by the convergence of the natural, mathematical, and computational sciences into unified informational frameworks, non-classical models of computing confront this issue by widening contemporary understandings of what a computational system might be and might do.

ASSOCIATIONS

Computational empiricism understands experience as the reception of sense-data. The assignment of epistemological primacy to sense experience is a central empiricist thesis, and one that appears in philosophy textbooks to characterise empiricism at large. In the context of the theories and practices of alternative computing, this epistemological priority of sense experience is mirrored in the attention paid to physical reality by alternative computing, and this likeness suffices to justify why I am talking of empiricism in relation to computation. In computational empiricism, the sense-data of experience are assumed to be essential to the activity of science (computer science included). From this perspective, sense experience is considered to be the site of genuine and original epistemological evidence, and data collected from it are viewed as the benchmark for scientific validity. A closer look at this empiricist focus on sense-data would reveal that the reality of computational systems (natural and artificial) is a collection and organisation of associated *res*: namely, circumstances, conditions, or 'things' as they manifestly occur. According to computational empiricism, reality is a reception of qualitative and quantitative factual records to be measured, parameterised, and put into variables. An empirical epistemology of computational sciences aims to find better computational methods, descriptions, models, and simulations that accord with the organisation and systematisation of the facts of the sensible world, in the hope that the operation of empirical reality itself could be used to solve problems.

This flattening down of experience onto sense experience also characterises the particular school of empiricist philosophy that I am taking as a philosophical reference for my description of the empiricism of alternative computing. In what follows, I will compare unconventional, natural, and non-classical computing to the traditional empiricism of sensory experience, as this has been developed in the early modern philosophy of the seventeenth and eighteenth centuries by the British philosophers Francis Bacon, Thomas Hobbes, John Locke, George Berkeley, and David Hume. There are many differences in beliefs, themes, and scope between these writers. For this reason, the utility of grouping these names together under the conventional label of British empiricism might be doubted or even contested. Nonetheless, this standard classification is also justified: common traits between the exponents of the British school of empiricism can be recognised, the foremost of which is their understanding of experience as a reception of sense-data. Early modern British empiricism is a belief about the foundations of knowledge, but also about the content of human minds, which are both supposed to be attained and secured upon sense-based experience. British empiricism arose during a tumultuous time in intellectual history: that of the Scientific Revolution, the Reformation, and the Enlightenment. These are events that originated from, but also resulted in, changed worldviews. The mechanistic new science that surrounded Bacon, Hobbes, Locke, Berkeley, and Hume emphasised observational and experimental procedures and overruled the Scholasticism of the Middle Ages. Natural phenomena were thenceforth explained *scientifically*—that is to say, via a compilation of proprieties and features that could be expressed in quantitative terms, or, as Galileo phrased it, by reading that 'all-encompassing book that is constantly open before our eyes, that is the universe', which 'is written in mathematical language'. [12]

My aim here is to trace an intellectual trajectory within the ways in which what is given or received in experience has been conceived as a sense-datum: a sense-datum that has become extremely important for the alternative computational systems of the twenty-first century. Of course, to determine how sense-data could be incorporated into a general model of valid reasoning is a task that is central to computer science in general. My point, however, is that this sense-datum becomes even more crucial for the unconventional, natural, and non-classical methods of computing indicated above, due to their explicit involvement with the physical world. The parallel between the empiricism of the early modern period and contemporary stances in alternative computing should thus be emphasised. This is not only because the British empiricist school interprets experience as an enquiry into sense-data reception, but also because it understands these sense-data as *external* to the source of their reception and consequent elaboration. Arguably, an explicit attention to how the datum of experience (namely, an object) is presented to thought (or to the thought of a subject) is also proper to other philosophical frameworks. One of these other interpretative philosophical frameworks that comes to mind, for instance, is Husserl's eidetic phenomenology, with its reduction of the perceptual particulars of experience to their essences and its intentional binding between the world and consciousness. [13] It should thus be stressed that the cornerstone for composing the proposed parallel between British empiricism and contemporary unconventional, natural, and non-classical computing is precisely based on the characterisation of externality that early modern empiricism assigned to sensory access to reality. This feature, in my view, is tacitly assumed by non-classical computation too. The character of externality, however, does not denote merely external things per se, but instead indicates an exteriority of thought (and of the source of this thought) from sense-data.

While this exteriority is generally a common assumption among early modern empiricists, my primary point of reference is one of the most influential of these philosophers: David Hume. This focus is not arbitrary. Hume aimed at uncovering the requirements and limitations under which legitimate beliefs about experience are generated. The epistemology of British empiricism culminates in his work, but it does so in a manner that produces a destabilising assessment of the tradition from which it emerged. Developing, but also correcting, John Locke's terminology, Hume divided the contents of the human mind into *impressions* and *ideas*. Impressions are 'our more lively perceptions, when we hear, or see, or feel, or love, or hate, or desire, or will'.[14] They are 'all our sensations, passions and emotions, as they make their first appearance in the soul'. Ideas are defined as 'the faint images of these [impressions] in thinking and reasoning'.[15] Hume argued that 'all the materials of thinking are derived either from our outward or inward sentiment'.[16] The difference between ideas and impressions is in fact not of kind but of degree: while impressions are our most immediate and lively perceptions, ideas are said to be 'more feeble',[17] as they are less vivid copies of those impressions.

For Hume, there is no intrinsic and interior purpose or reason to things that accounts for the relation between ideas and impressions. Impressions are a collection of separate and distinct perceptions, and they have no necessary, essential, or objective connection between each other. In this respect, sense-data are external to the actions of the mind on these data. Such a view of perception characterises Hume's epistemology, and it informs his ontology too: for what Hume depicted is a world in which everything is external to everything else. The Humean framework of thought/sense-data externality is also clearly far removed from the Platonic endorsement of the a priori that I analysed in the second part of this book. In Hume, there are no necessary truths of reasoning. The relation between thought and data collected through a sensing capacity is, on the contrary, naturalised into an associative rapport, and this association constitutes the act of reasoning itself. Hume argued that 'there appear to be only three principles of connexion among ideas': 'namely, *Resemblance*, *Contiguity* in time or place, and *Cause* or *Effect*'.[18] These principles of connection are not theoretical or logical norms: they are psychological attitudes exposed to empirical discovery and assessment. Such an associative relation between thought and sense-data inevitably recalls the *associationism* of some psychological theories, according to which the mind is organised from simple thoughts to more complex ones, and mental content is arranged according to similarities between ideas. Hume's epistemology (and that of British empiricism in general) is indeed a fundamental reference for associationist theories of the mind.[19] However, moving now from a psychological terrain to the crux of my argument, it is important to stress that, from the perspective of this associative rapport, abstraction is not endowed with any autonomy or legitimacy. Abstraction is dependent upon the cognitive dispositions of human nature and not on any finalistic necessary connection.

As noted above, a conceptual terrain similar to the landscape of early modern empiricism can be found in unconventional, natural, and non-classical computing. This similarity is most evident in the way in which physical reality, in most alternative computational paradigms, is related to the formal rules of computation. Following the traditional empiricist precept, this physical reality is considered to be made up of records that are 'loose and separate'.[20] In unconventional, natural, and non-classical computing, computational rules are naturalised upon their association with data and behaviours extracted from the observation of the physical universe. Despite the fact that unconventional computing certainly promotes a study of concrete particularities, its focus is thus still on the production and validation of general formalisms, which are now, however, to be *induced* from the fabric of manifest reality. Inductive reasoning is central to the comprehension and command of this exterior reality. The qualities and quantities of this reality become the measurable data of natural and artificial computational systems alike. In this sense, the inductivism of unconventional, natural, and non-classical computing practices is not an antithesis to computational formalisation; on the contrary, it is best viewed as broadening it. However, there is no intrinsic causation or internal regulation between the reality of computational abstraction and the reality of their empirical referent; again, there is only association.

Famously, Hume himself expressed concerns about the extent to which we should trust the inductive process of abstracting generalisation from experiential instances, and about the extent to which we can consider these instances to be sufficiently reliable to employ them as grounds for making predictions and conducting actions. He concluded that there is no justification for supposing that what has happened in the past will happen again in the future.[21] In an alternative computing context, however, one can comment that the uniformity of nature, which Hume identified as the required assumption of inductive reasoning, is considered acceptable (and perhaps also vindicated) by virtue of the fact that the inferential jump from the observed to the unobserved is established on the describability and predictability of empirical instances through computational means. Different non-classical computational models select different empirical instances in the world, from which to extract their computational formalisations. For example: genetic algorithms simulate natural selection, and artificial neural networks simulate the firing of neurons in the organic brain. These computational models are, nonetheless, able to produce findings that correspond to a uniform and predictable nature, as they construct computational formalisms on the basis of the inductive inference that what they tend to replicate and simulate will happen again. In other words, on this view, the uniformity of nature with which Hume was concerned becomes that which can be established via the explanatory power of computation, and of the capacities for prediction and action that computation aims at.

THE CONTINGENCY OF THE SENSES

The treatment of unconventional, natural, and non-classical computing set out above affords a return to the key conceptual difference that I propose between the empirical and the contingent. In computational empiricism, there is no such distinction: the contingent is tied to the empiricism of the senses, inasmuch as it is a status that pertains uniquely to the objects of sense-data reception. Indeterminacy, in this respect, is an ontological status tangled with the universe of physical possibilities to be received, collected, and elaborated by the computational system.

This sense-empiricist understanding of contingency is best explained by drawing once again on a parallel with Hume. The aspect of his work that is most relevant here is his theory concerning the provisional and fortuitous character of the universal principles of association between ideas (contiguity, resemblance, and causation). These principles, Hume argued, are established empirical occurrences that cannot be demonstrated deductively and universally. On the contrary, they can only be observed as a 'custom or habit'.[22] No 'idea of necessary connexion'[23] among, for instance, a cause and its effect can be found in the external object without trespassing beyond the confines of sensory experience. I believe that, in a computing context, an equally empirical acceptation of contingency, which echoes Hume's, is noticeably typified in debates about the physical limits of computation. These debates sit at the core of computational complexity theory and also inform much of the experimentation in unconventional computing. In order to clarify this conceptual passage about empirical contingency, it is useful to consider quantum computation again, as this is a computing proposition that arises as a response to the physical limits of digital machines.

In 1965, Intel co-founder Gordon Moore anticipated that the number of transistors on an integrated circuit would double roughly every two years.[24] Moore's prediction of an exponential growth of computer power ended up holding true for the next five decades and acquired the status of an informal rule in Silicon Valley and elsewhere. Of course, while the number of components on a chip has doubled approximately every two years since 1965, the scale of a transistor has become markedly smaller. This constant miniaturisation of silicon electronics, however, also prompted the possibility of an unsettling consequence: what will happen when we approach the very limit of this scaling down (a limit at which it becomes impossible to go smaller), when transistors will be the size of atoms? Scale seems to put an upper boundary on the power of computation. Is there a point, not so far in the future, when computers will not be able to compute faster due to their physical limits? Quantum computing is an attempt to overcome these physical limits by trying to make computation work on an atomic scale. It dared to ask the question, why not use atoms themselves—these basic components of the physical universe—to compute? This hypothesis consequently raised another daring question about the possibility of devising a new kind of computer upon the principles of quantum mechanics. While traditional computing machines obey the principles of classical physics, quantum computers are subject to the laws of the physics of the subatomic world. Similarly, where traditional electronic digital computers work with bits (namely, basic units of information that can have the value of either one or zero), in quantum computing the fundamental measure of quantum information is the qubit (also known as the quantum bit), which can be one, zero, or any mixture state of both values. This spooky characteristic of superimposition, together with other equally unusual features, prompts the requirement that quantum computers should involve not only an entirely new type of design architecture, but also a totally new way of programming, based on the probabilistic scenarios of the quantum scale.

This description of quantum computation has, of course, been greatly simplified. Yet, even from this brief overview, one should be able to see why it effectively amounts to a modern holy grail for science and technology. If successful, it promises a new class of algorithms that could solve the hard problems of computing, performing calculations much faster than any existing or future traditional computing device. Rather than going through all the possible solutions sequentially, like a traditional computer does, a quantum algorithm would instead check all possible solutions of a set simultaneously. Multiple operations could then be performed at once. The physicist David Deutsch has described quantum computation as 'the first technology that allows useful tasks to be performed in collaboration between parallel universes'.[25] 'A quantum computer', Deutsch comments, 'would be capable of distributing components of a complex task among vast numbers of parallel universes, and then sharing the results.'[26] Drawing on Deutsch's consideration, I would argue that the dream of exploiting quantum physics' inherent exponentiality is the dream of exploiting the accidental nature of physical reality. In attempting to solve a problem, traditional computing systems would look for a logical shortcut. Quantum computing, however, embraces the full manifold of physical possibilities allowed by quantum mechanics. The power of quantum computing is that it combines the strength of a computational model with the wealth of possibilities of the physical universe (or, to be more specific, of the physical universe's energy states) by looking for what might happen, but which need not occur.

I can return now to the empirical understanding of the contingency of alternative computing, which is the contingency of the physical conditions of the world or, to use a famous image that recurs in many accounts of quantum theory, the contingency of the roll of the dice. This understanding of contingency should not be confused with the contingent encounter with the being of the sensible that Deleuze advocated. Similarly, it should not be taken as the clash with sensibility that engenders, from a Deleuzian perspective, a shock to thought. Instead, the contingent nature of the physical world denotes the mutability and unpredictability of particular sensible beings, which are brought to intelligible recognition via the reception of sense-data. At both a macro- and a micro-scale, this sense-empirical acceptation of contingency is considered to be the basic character of all physical events, and it is studied by the natural sciences that alternative computing explicitly addresses. From this perspective, in order to explain and replicate physical phenomena (such as, for instance, those described by quantum mechanics), computing has to juggle the many variables of real-world problems, bypassing straightforward distinctions between true and false, and must give its assent to solutions that are probabilistic. Efficient computation attempts to defeat its own physical limits by addressing the factual existence of these limitations. Any gain is achieved on the grounds that spatial and temporal resources can be amplified, stretched, and finally matched out by pairing up with the contingent character of the physical universe. Even from this perspective, however, for the sake of applicability, computational rules must exceed their observational basis and repeat, once again, the old cybernetic quest for prediction. Yet the very idea of computational projection has changed: it is not subsequent to a simple a priori logical necessity, but instead turns to the highly complex a posteriori in order to find its strength. In other words, it takes on the plethora of possible physical eventualities and, at best, it leaves us with the frequency of Humean habits and customs.

NOTES

1. See Michael Feldman, 'D-Wave Sells First Quantum Computer', *HPCwire*, 26 May 2011, https://www.hpcwire.com/2011/05/26/d-wave_sells_first_quantum_computer.

2. See Paul Benioff, 'The Computer as a Physical System: A Microscopic Quantum Mechanical Hamiltonian Model of Computers as Represented by Turing Machines', *Journal of Statistical Physics* 22, no. 5 (May 1980): 563–91, https://doi.org/10.1007/BF01011339; David Deutsch, 'Quantum Theory, the Church-Turing Principle and the Universal Quantum Computer', *Proceedings of the Royal Society of London A* 400, no. 1818 (8 July 1985): 97–117, https://doi.org/10.1098/rspa.1985.0070; Richard P. Feynman, 'Simulating Physics with Computers', *International Journal of Theoretical Physics* 21, nos. 6–7 (June 1982): 467–88, https://doi.org/10.1007/BF02650179.

3. Quoted in Jason Pontin, 'A Giant Leap Forward in Computing? Maybe Not', *New York Times*, 8 April 2007, http://www.nytimes.com/2007/04/08/business/yourmoney/08slip.html.

4. See Mark W. Johnson et al., 'Quantum Annealing with Manufactured Spins', *Nature* 473 (12 May 2011): 194–98, https://doi.org/10.1038/nature10012.

5. Quoted in Edwin Cartlidge, 'Quantum Computing: A Commercial Reality?', *Physics World*, 2 April 2007, https://physicsworld.com/a/quantum-computing-a-commercial-reality.

6. Quoted in Tom Simonite, 'The CIA and Jeff Bezos Bet on Quantum Computing', *MIT Technology Review*, 4 October 2012, https://www.technologyreview.com/s/429429/the-cia-and-jeff-bezos-bet-on-quantum-computing.

7. Computationally hard problems are technically classified as NP-hard (where 'NP' stands for 'non-deterministic polynomial time').

8. Alan M. Turing, 'On Computable Numbers, with an Application to the Entscheidungsproblem', *Proceedings of the London Mathematical Society* 42 (1936): 231, https://doi.org/10.1112/plms/s2-42.1.230.

9. Oded Goldreich, *Computational Complexity: A Conceptual Perspective* (Cambridge: Cambridge University Press, 2008), 7.

10. Alan Cobham, 'The Intrinsic Computational Difficulty of Functions', in *Logic, Methodology, and Philosophy of Science: Proceedings of the 1964 International Congress*, ed. Yehoshua Bar-Hillel (Amsterdam: North-Holland, 1965), 29.

11. The relation between traditional and alternative computing is usually formulated in terms of the broader opportunities for computational practices offered by the latter. This broadening of computational possibilities involves asking 'questions that the TM [Turing Machine] model is unsuited to answer'. Bruce J. MacLennan, 'Natural Computation and Non-Turing Models of Computation', *Theoretical Computer Science* 317, nos. 1–3 (June 2004): 116, https://doi.org/10.1016/j.tcs.2003.12.008.

12. Galileo Galilei, 'From *The Assayer* (1623)', in *The Essential Galileo*, ed. and trans. Maurice A. Finocchiaro (Indianapolis: Hackett, 2008), 183.

13. See Edmund Husserl, *Ideas: General Introduction to Pure Phenomenology*, trans. William Ralph Boyce Gibson (London: Allen and Unwin, 1967).

14. David Hume, *An Enquiry concerning Human Understanding* (Oxford: Oxford University Press, 2007), 13.

15. David Hume, *A Treatise of Human Nature* (Oxford: Clarendon Press, 1975), 1.

16. Hume, *An Enquiry concerning Human Understanding*, 13.

17. Hume, *An Enquiry concerning Human Understanding*, 13.

18. Hume, *An Enquiry concerning Human Understanding*, 16.

19. Robert M. Harnish notes that 'the *basic idea* behind associationism seems to be this: *items that "go together" in experience will subsequently "go together" in thought'*. *Minds, Brains, Computers: An Historical Introduction to the Foundations of Cognitive Science* (Oxford: Blackwell, 2002), 16. Contemporary connectionist models in cognitive science can also be seen as a development of classical associationism. Connectionism, which became a popular theory of the mind in the 1980s, stresses that causal links between neural nodes (links that can indeed be understood as associations) are the basis for mental processing.

20. Hume, *An Enquiry concerning Human Understanding*, 54.

21. Hume addressed what is known in the history of philosophy as the 'problem of induction' (an expression that, however, Hume never used) in Book I, Part III, Section VI of *A Treatise of Human Nature*, and also in Section IV, Part II of *An Enquiry concerning Human Understanding*.

22. Hume, *An Enquiry concerning Human Understanding*, 32.

23. Hume, *An Enquiry concerning Human Understanding*, 44.

24. See Gordon E. Moore, 'Cramming More Components onto Integrated Circuits', *Electronics* 38, no. 8 (19 April 1965): 114–17, https://doi.org/10.1109/N-SSC.2006.4785860.

25. David Deutsch, *The Fabric of Reality* (London: Allen Lane, 1997), 195.

26. Deutsch, *The Fabric of Reality*, 195.

Chapter Eight

Factuality

The empiricism of unconventional, natural, and non-classical computing is meant to account for a physical world marked by *change*. According to the sense-empiricist approach to computation described in chapter 7, change is an empirical accident that is to be measured and explained through variables, parameters, and functions. The sensible has to be suitably synthesised as data so that it can be fed into the computational rule. Yet, since the physical world is always in process, computational empiricism aims to endow formal axiomatic systems with a capacity for adaptation, mutation, and evolution. In unconventional, natural, and non-classical computing, one does not have to choose between a logico-mathematical description or a biophysical one. Instead, one has to look for the ways in which logico-mathematical entities and symbolic operations can lean towards the uncertainty of contemporary physics, adjust through biological metaphors, and yet still qualify as effective and efficient computation. Within this sense-empiricist framework, therefore, one has to look for the ways in which computational abstraction can encompass and replicate worldly actualities and the formal logic inherent to computation can thereby be made *morpho*-logical.

In computational empiricism, the notion of form does not designate the predetermined representation of an a priori realm of intelligibility. Rather, it is akin to an a posteriori act of form giving, or indeed to a *formation*. The latter term suits the point that I wish to make, for it denotes a visible shape as much as a tendency, and thus accounts for the sensory and dynamic nature of morphological constructions. In his pioneering nineteenth-century study of botanical morphology, Goethe distinguished between *Gestalt* (German for 'form') and *Bildung* (German for 'formation'). While *Bildung* denotes 'what has been brought forth' or 'what is in the process of being brought forth', *Gestalt* indicates that 'the element of mutability is left out of consideration', and a composite whole is thus considered to be 'fixed in its character'.[1] Despite its seemingly anachronistic nature, Goethe's classification is useful here because it can help us to describe the a posteriori mobility and plasticity of the inductive forms (which, following Goethe's sense of the term, should perhaps be called *inductive formations*) that unconventional, natural, and non-classical computing has to deal with. These forms/formations are not Platonic immutable essences; instead, they are variable configurations that exist in a context (whether that be the anatomical, the geophysical, the urban, or the living), that exhibit certain behaviours (rules arise from the unruly, via growth and mutation), and that generate other configurations themselves.

From this morphological perspective, 'to study form is to study change.'[2] Change, in turn, is in this context the most public and recognisable facet of that ordering principle that goes under the name of *emergence*. This is a notoriously slippery concept, as it is often used to describe phenomena, behaviours, and proprieties, and yet it remains ambiguously defined.[3] Commonly, emergence is summarised with the holistic motto 'the whole is more than the sum of its parts'. It can be broadly defined using the words of the mathematician and physicist James P. Crutchfield, who describes it as 'a process that leads to the appearance of structure not directly described by the defining constraints and instantaneous forces that control a system'.[4] The detractors of emergence lament the latter term's status as a buzzword. This status grew as a result of the concept of emergence's popularity, which has taken it, since the 1990s, beyond its original philosophical use, and which has given it a far more common currency. Its advocates, on the other hand, claim that emergence offers great potential as regards the need to understand natural phenomena scientifically, and hold that it might also be of great utility in attempts towards advancing a viable technological programme for the realisation of sophisticated artificial systems.

Emergence indeed provides an attractive justification of the ways in which human societies, for example, or water currents, clouds, brains, immune systems, migrating birds, hurricanes, financial markets, and coastlines, all transform themselves, together with their constitutive elements, into different wholes. In these *complex adaptive systems*, a macro-structure emerges from the local micro-behaviours of their components. Change is viewed as a non-linear vector of accumulation. Small differences magnify into much greater consequences, in a butterfly-effect chain reaction of divergences, convergences, and arising patterns. One of the key characteristics of emergence is the impossibility of determining, from the initial conditions of the system, what its final outcomes will be. The best way to describe this feature is to observe that emergent proprieties are reliant on some more fundamental and basic proprieties, yet also maintain a degree of independence from them.

Because of this inherent margin of changeability, the deductive method is not the best candidate to provide us with knowledge of emergent systems. With emergence, we can only hope for reasonably correct inductive predictions. In this sense, emergence is often welcomed as the rightful affirmation of *chance* over the predeterminations of deductive reasoning. Since it develops from the interactions of its components, the behaviour of an emergent system cannot be predicted deductively. Emergence is therefore applauded as an inductive explanatory framework, oriented towards the indeterminacy of empirical phenomena. Most interestingly, this emergent explanatory framework is considered to have enough power to account for how *empirical novelty* manifests itself, thus promising routes towards a level of variation that would be inaccessible to deductive axiomatics, insofar as the latter can only make explicit that which is implicit in its premises. From this perspective, the new is the unexpected, but also that which remains indeterminate because it is unpredictable. The descriptive powers of this sense of novelty are applied as an alternative to the reductionism that reigns in the life sciences as well as in culture, society, and economy. To put this otherwise, emergence is applied as an explanatory account that guarantees a significant revision of micro/macro dynamics, as well as an ontological reorientation of the particular/universal and order/disorder dichotomies. These reworkings are meant to explain human creativity and natural creation, and to account for the ways in which the universe and humankind can generate anything new at all.

It is here, in my opinion, that the debate about alternative computational formalisation stands today: it has turned to emergent proprieties and phenomena in order to test their versatility for moving beyond deduction, and it has thereby introduced chance and empirical novelty into the formal constraints of computation. Alternative computing's fascination with emergence has much to do with the special appeal of the behavioural unpredictability that emergence describes. This behavioural unpredictability rests upon a strange and unforeseen affiliation between dependency and autonomy. In order to be made computational, it requires formal structures that would be highly robust and fault tolerant (that is to say, structures that would not be plagued by the determinism of Turing's notion of computability), and which would be able to accommodate the variable interactions of emergent systems.[5] Emergentism (which is the belief in, or the theory of, emergence) pledges to have done with the reductionist dream of distilling reality into a set of a priori rules that would be generally applicable to being, thinking, and doing.[6] Significantly, emergentism suggests focusing instead on playing along with the simple local instructions and thereby seeing, a posteriori, how complex strategies of conduct might stream out of a situation where no appearance of organised behaviour was initially to be found. It is precisely in the context of the possibility of studying such variation that the computational appears to be the ideal habitat for form-finding experimentations, geared towards the artificial generation of emergent regulation. This compatibility is partly due to the ability of computational systems to run successful simulations. For the scientist, the computer is a pivotal ally in the study of emergent systems; through computational modelling, the rules of emergence can be imitated, understood, and replicated in manners that would be largely impossible otherwise.[7] Equally, those computational efforts that are largely based on the observation of empirical phenomena and which, despite being rich in computational content, have baffled programmers' hopes of ever being fully encompassed within the deductive constraints of Turing-computability, could finally find their formal and mechanical systematisation via the devising of alternative understandings of what it means to compute, which would exploit the proprieties and conducts of emergent regulations.

The generation of high-level sophistication by low-level rules, procedures, and processes is a functional principle of emergence. This functional principle, however, also plays a big part in the rationale of alternative explorations of computability. Such shared characteristic between emergence on the one hand, and unconventional, natural, and non-classical computing on the other, is one of the reasons why scientists, engineers, programmers, artists, and cultural theorists have been drawn to consider the possibility of a form of computational emergence that could close the gap between the deductions of logico-mathematical sciences and the inductions of the natural sciences. Because it is 'more protean in its manifestations', and 'more theoretically deconstructable', emergence is thought to be 'more likely to give rise to a basic theoretical model of wide application'.[8] It is also worth noting here that unconventional, natural, and non-classical computing approaches endorse the prospect of replicating emergent behaviour on the basis of a shared concern with the complexity of concrete chaotic, adaptive, and non-linear systems. In chapter 7, I considered how one of the most promising ways of resolving computational complexity is to attempt to model it on our scientific knowledge about the complexities of the natural world. I would now add that emergence is an explanatory framework that arises from the observation and simulation of those physical, biological, and chemical systems from which unconventional, natural, and non-classical computing extracts new methods of information processing. The implication for scientists and programmers is as follows: if emergence is a successful explanatory framework able to account for natural complexity (i.e., complexity about unpredictable behaviour in nature), then the generation of its features by algorithmic means can also be employed to solve computational complexity (i.e., complexity about computational resources, such as memory space and time). Of course, there are difficulties, mostly because computation involves finite procedures and reductions, while emergentism, by principle and necessity, entails a disregard for both. However, the potential reward would arguably afford compensation for such difficulties, as it could produce a computational system that returns more than what you put into it.

The formal study of emergence has already produced considerable insights. Among the most pressing tasks for computer science today, however, is that of developing a formal framework able not only to accommodate a generalisation of emergence's prescriptions, but also to give emergence in computation enough independence from deduction and simulation so as to be truly spontaneous. Undoubtedly, both tasks are not easy and invite many questions. What understandings of algorithmic rules and of computational procedures do we need in order to generate emergent regulation within a formal system? Can the notion of emergence help us to induce, rather than deduce, inferences, decisions, and instructions in computation? These questions are important, for they point towards the recognition of a certain level of autonomous agency of computation (a *design without a designer*, as it is often said). This desired autonomous agency of emergent behaviour in computation also translates into a further hypothesis: computational systems can deliver, in the guise of a simple rule or procedure that gradually builds up complexity, the self-organising character of emergent behaviour. There is, in emergence, a sense and use of the principle of simplicity that differs greatly from the notion of simplicity that I discussed in relation to computational idealism (see chapter 4). The simplicity of emergence is not the aristocratic minimalism of a terse, compressed, self-referential logical and mathematical formulation, but the rather more common straightforwardness of the building block. Perhaps it is a little plain and ordinary; yet, with admirable persistency, the simple makes up a whole from its parts. According to the emergentist framework, the path from simplicity to complexity encompasses empirical occurrences, regardless of size or kind. What characterises both the very small and the very big is that proximate, interactive processes among lower-level basic components breed higher and higher degrees of difficulty, density, and convolution. In emergent self-organisation, the movement is thus from determinacy to indeterminacy.

The prospect of a computational generation of emergence seems to contradict my earlier claim that emergence is an appealing explanation by virtue of its capacity to move outside the directions of deductive preprogramming and, therefore, outside the confines of algorithmic systems. This is, though, just an apparent conceptual discrepancy. The point that I wish to convey is this: emergence can be (and, in fact, is being) studied in info-theoretic terms; the central issue, however, is that there are also circumstances and situations in which emergence appears as distinctively computational. As highlighted by N. Katherine Hayles in her study of what she calls 'the Regime of Computation', the assumption is that computational systems not only simulate the behaviour of complex systems, but they can also truly generate it 'in everything from biological organisms to human social systems'.[9] My contention is that this native type of computational generation provides us with a specifically ontological approach to computation, which I call *computational emergence*. The latter expression is usually employed by computer scientists 'to mark some feature of a process which the software designer did not intentionally code into the algorithms which generate the process'.[10] However, I will adopt it hereafter to describe a proper ontology of computation (that is, an account of how the computational exists, or indeed a justification of computation's reality), according to which the latter is capable of self-organisation, and of doing so thanks to the employment of local, simple rules that encompass empirical facts, which themselves become variables of the much more global and complex phenomenal realm.

Emergence, to conclude, occurs in the physical world, and it can be simulated within a computational system through the creation of an adequate inductive formal model. Nonetheless, the key consideration to make in this regard is that emergence can also occur autonomously, in a purely computational manner. My argument, then, is that there is a particular type of emergence in computation, and that this type of emergence is specific to such a formal context. In order to understand how emergence can appear autonomously in computing systems, a reassessment of the very ontological categories of computation has to be in place. Let us now see how and why.

AN EMPIRICAL PHENOMENON AMONG EMPIRICAL PHENOMENA

By phrasing the deductive form/formula in the guise of an inductive formation, the ontology of computational emergence invests heavily in the idea of *construction*. In their edited collection on the use of computer modelling in developmental biology for the study of self-organisation, Sanjeev Kumar and Peter J. Bentley advance a claim that partially resonates with this assertion. 'The main goal of developmental and evolutionary biologists', they write, 'is to understand construction.' Computer science is 'equally obsessed with construction'. Whether this is 'the construction of life-like entities or complex designs or solutions', construction stands out as 'the unifying theme between the two subjects'.[11] I believe that one can take this consideration out of the context of computational development to extend it to the ontological debate about computation. Logico-mathematical reasoning aims to achieve a systematisation of procedures of thought. Computation attempts the same thing through its formal axiomatic structures. Computation's logic of construction can go too far; this much has been discussed in the second part of this book, where I examined how the computational rule is often assigned the metacomputational task of measuring and systematising the whole of reality itself (both culturally and technologically). Formal abstraction, in that metacomputational context, becomes the transcendent regulator of the empirical realm. In the context of the present discussion, however, it should be noted that the idea of construction in unconventional, natural, and non-classical computing practices reverses this order. On the one hand, when attempting to replicate emergence, unconventional computing takes empirical phenomena as its direct source for and of abstraction. The organisation of a computational structure is abstracted from the observation of an empirical one; computational construction happens at a sense-empirical level first, and on a logical one second. Formal abstraction is thus less regulative than imitative. On the other hand, however, in their capacity to produce emergence that is specific to the formal system, the computational structures of unconventional computing are themselves made empirical *res* of reality: things among other things. Computation therefore becomes *an empirical phenomenon among empirical phenomena*.

To the empiricist question 'What is given in experience?', computational emergence can be imagined to reply, 'All there is.' This answer is quite different to that which would be provided by Universal Computation. In chapter 4, I coined the expression 'Universal Computation' to denote the onto-epistemological principle that grounds the metacomputational organisation of reality. Computational forms, according to Universal Computation, are assigned an independent ontological reality: they stand as a metaphysical dimension that transcends and regulates the realm of empirical phenomena. In computational empiricism, however, a computational structure is less a form of intelligibility than a formation of sensibility. While Universal Computation thus implies a sort of two-tier metaphysics, with the intelligible as an ontological layer on top of the sensible, the ontologisation of computation through emergence needs nothing more than a one-level metaphysics. Interestingly, this is not a Deleuzian flat ontology, in which entities in different scales and levels of reflexivity and complexity are all accounted for in the same way.[12] On the contrary, this is a much less exciting metaphysical accreditation of only sense-empirical aggregations. The key idea is this: form is abstracted from the *factuality* of experience. This form ultimately conveys a self-organising formation. It expresses the tendency to produce structure—a structure that is inherent to the physical realm but that is also logically and chronologically dependent upon it. The ontology of computational emergence is therefore on one single level, because the abstract, as an ontological dimension, does not really exist. Only the factual exists.

There is not, at present, an explicit theoretical acknowledgement of this forms-from-facts ontological schema that I am foregrounding here. I must, therefore, be cautious when describing it, in order to avoid the risk of making my argument about computational emergence sound as if it is part of an accepted status quo. I am thus proposing the view that the computational empiricism of unconventional, natural, and non-classical computing is underpinned by an emergentist ontology. This is because, by addressing this ontology, I can expose the conceptual problems within such a sense-empiricist position. To this end, my claims about computational emergence should now be viewed in conjunction with my previous claims about computational empiricism. In computational empiricism, the components of the empirical realm from which the algorithmic formalisation is induced are the data (i.e., the givens) of reality. These are all external to each other. Relations between sensibility and intelligibility, and among sensibilities themselves, are the consequence of a subject's (whatever or whoever we take that subject to be) cognitive associations of these objects. A similar externality between thought and sense-data is also central to computational emergence: its ontological schema entails emergent discernible patterns (namely, a multifaceted uniformity that can be discerned or detected through empirical analysis and observation) that arise from the interaction among sensible facts. The latter remain, in Humean terms, *loose and separate*, with no internal connection. The facts of computational emergence are then computational empiricism's records of empirical factuality. They are atomic units of sensibility that would have no inherent connection among themselves—or with anything else—were it not for the capacity of an external source of sensory reception to collect and represent them as manifest empirical phenomena.

Admittedly, Hume is not the most obvious choice among possible modern philosophical reference points for the concept of emergence. Nevertheless, a certain degree of affinity between Humean empiricism and emergentism should be accepted, due to what I claim to be the *interactive externality* that both positions presuppose. Computational empiricism, qua an approach to computational formalisation that externally associates abstractive procedures to sense-empirical occurrences, is predicated upon an interactive atomic assortment of sense-data. Computational emergence, qua the ontology that subtends this approach, is equally externalist and interactive. Forms of intelligibility are the result of the interaction among external, unconnected facts of empirical factuality. Computation itself, according to this framework, is understood to be one of these unconnected empirical occurrences and assigned the quality of being a manifest, self-contained Humean matter of fact: a thing as it manifestly occurs, whose validity is not logical but rather assessed via sensory reception.[13] In this view, the actual becomes synonymous with the factual. The conceptual problems that I see with the computation-as-an-empirical-phenomenon approach can be summarised or epitomised by this equivalence.

The first problematic consequence that should be signalled here is that, if we accept that the actual existence of computation amounts only to its empirical factuality (i.e., to its being a thing of the empirical world that is to be received and elaborated), then we neglect the important conclusion advanced in the second part of this book—namely, that there is a degree of indeterminacy in computation that should not be relegated to an empirical dimension, but which is instead already to be found at the extra-empirical level of the formal axiomatic system. The forms-from-facts schema provides an ontological framework to justify, and also encourage, alternative computing's attempts to open up formal rules to the contingency of empirical data, thus moving from a determinist deductive paradigm to a more flexible inductive one. However, by considering this external indeterminacy and not its own, the inductive paradigm in computing flattens the contingent down to the level of the empirical once again, just as the deductive determinism of meta-computation does. Moreover, these alternative models, by implying that computation has to be made an empirical fact of the world in order to be endowed with the possibility of variation, also miss the capacity of computation to generate the new vis-à-vis the formal indeterminacy that computation's abstractive activity of discretisation encounters, via incomputability, in each and every actual process.

These reflections bring us then to a second problem with the forms-from-facts ontology of computational empiricism. Since it endows computation with functions and characters typical of the empirical dimension, the inductivism of alternative computing would seem to allow for the possibility of a computation that experiences. My claim, however, is that it does not. The experience to which it brings us close accounts only for sensory responsiveness, inasmuch as, in the reworking of formalism that unconventional, natural, and non-classical computing proposes, the abstractive capacity of the formal system is ontologically levelled out. In this respect, I would say that, just as it is misleading to flatten down contingency onto an empirical plane (because, by doing so, one overlooks the formal system's capacity to be exposed to its own indeterminacy), it is similarly deceptive to understand the experience of computation solely as the reception of sense-data. This is because such an understanding excludes from computation's conditions of experience the abstractive operations that are specific to the formal system.

I have already discussed how, for Deleuze, experience is not just empirical sense reception. It is useful here to discuss the Deleuzian perspective on this issue in greater detail, in order to clarify why it is problematic to understand experience solely in terms of sensory experience. Significantly, Deleuze's first book is on Hume.[14] However, as often happens with his work on fellow philosophers, Deleuze's reading goes far beyond Hume's original texts. Characteristically, Deleuze rephrased Hume's externalist epistemology as an ontological *externality of relations*. To claim, as Deleuze did, that 'relations are external to their terms' means to take a stand against ontologies of identity and the predetermined interiority of those philosophies grounded in representation.[15] Deleuze did exactly that, vis-à-vis Hume. The point that should be stressed, however, is that the external relations advocated by Deleuze do not imply an externality, of the associationist kind, between subject and object, or between thought and sense-data. Deleuze never supported associationism's primacy of a percipient subject over a perceived object. By distancing himself from an associationist epistemology, he brought Hume's empiricism, together with Kant's rationalist elaboration of it, to an idiosyncratic extreme. The experiential is not uniquely predicated upon empirical sense reception because, for Deleuze, it is not the mere senses but *transcendental sensibility* that grants us access to experience. On the one hand, therefore, Deleuze maintained Hume's empiricist principle that there is nothing outside experience; yet on the other, for Deleuze, this experience is a falling into the lived metaphysical reality of the 'being of the sensible' [16] and not an ordinary sense reception. Moreover, Deleuze also retained from Kant the view that the conditions of this metaphysical experience should be called 'transcendental' insofar as they are the ground of experiencing in the first place. Nonetheless, against Kant, Deleuze's transcendental operation takes place not within the mental faculties of a transcendental subject, but on the plane of immanence of thought and sensation: a plane that is metaphysical and not empirical, although still experienceable.

In contrast with early modern empiricism, a principle of internal and necessary connection thus remains in Deleuze. One can imagine Deleuze agreeing with Bergson, who argued that 'the capital error of associationism is that it substitutes for [the] continuity of becoming, which is the living reality, a discontinuous multiplicity of elements, inert and juxtaposed'. [17] In the Deleuzian 'transcendental' or 'superior' empiricism, [18] the continuity of becoming relies on (and is realised thanks to) a principle of internal connection. This principle is expressed by the plane of virtuality that cuts across all cognitive significations to unfold the actual in its potential for infinite difference. This is the internal connection of differential relations that coexist in experience, although they can be neither measured nor registered empirically. What Deleuze's transcendental empiricism described, therefore, is less an empty world of face-value empirical facts than the exact opposite: things are never as straightforward as they appear, for they are overflowing with a virtual potential to be different from what they are. In this respect, if Deleuze did not reduce experience to sense experience, then this is precisely because such a reduction would deny the possibility of an internal potential for generating ontological novelty. According to Deleuze, this ontological novelty does not derive from a priori laws or from the cognitive faculties of a percipient subject. On the contrary, in his view, the cause for novelty had to be understood as an internal principle of actualisation.

However, for Deleuze, such a principle is and remains on the virtual plane, and it is vis-à-vis this consideration that I can now explain how addressing the limits of sense-experience empiricism from a Deleuzian perspective ceases to be useful for my speculative purposes. With Deleuze I can show that the problem with computational empiricism is that its externalist interpretation does not allow for an internal principle of change, inherent to the conditions of real experience (of computation, as of anything else). I said that, for Deleuze, this principle is on the virtual plane, and these conditions are predicated upon affectivity and sensibility. I have, however, also stated that I am not pursuing a virtualisation of the discrete abstractive operations of computation, and that my argument is that the conditions for the real experience of computation entail both intelligible and sensible operations upon data. As I have mentioned already, the challenge is to think of them both not as equivalent but rather as consequent and also actual. Since this actuality is flattened out upon factuality, computational empiricism offers—differently from Deleuze—a way to address computation as actual (and this is why I had to discuss the sense-empiricist view and understand its underpinning emergentist ontology). However, I cannot pursue the sensationalist empiricist path either. What we are left with, then, is the task of rethinking the internal constitution of the actuality of computation so as to include an internal productive principle of dynamic eventuation.

PRESENTATIONAL IMMEDIACY AND THE BIFURCATION OF NATURE

Once again, the central operation that needs to be carried out involves advancing Gilles Deleuze's ontology via that of Alfred North Whitehead. To this end, I will now turn to Whitehead's theory of perception. Drawing on William James, Whitehead believed that any 'acquaintance with reality' is made of 'buds or drops of perception'.[19] Empiricism is thus correct: 'the ultimate test is always widespread, recurrent experience',[20] and 'all knowledge is grounded on perception'.[21] In this respect, Whitehead's theory of perception goes hand in hand with his philosophy of actuality. Ontologically as well as epistemologically speaking, actuality is the reality to be perceived. Yet, according to Whitehead, one needs to look at the internal constitution of such actuality. This is something that, in Whitehead's view, early modern empiricism failed to do, and so too did those stances in the history of philosophy that maintained that the immediate presentation of the world to our senses is the sole datum of perception.

I wish to argue here that the way in which computational empiricism and its emergentist ontological underpinning interpret and elaborate the actuality of computation (in other words, as factuality) is a direct consequence of the primacy that they both assign to *experience in the mode of presentational immediacy*. I take the latter expression directly from Whitehead, who used it to denote the familiar and proximate presentation of the external world around us 'by means of our projection of our immediate sensations'.[22] *Presentational immediacy* is a constitutive (although not basic nor foundational) form of 'direct recognition' that more sophisticated organisms enjoy;[23] it gives us 'a world decorated by sense-data dependent on the immediate states of relevant parts of our own bodies'.[24] It is what philosophy would describe as resulting from a sensationalist principle, and what helps to account, for instance, for how humans internalise their surroundings towards cognitive functioning. It is important to stress, however, that some 'limitations and extensions' entail that it would be misleading to posit a perfect overlap between presentational immediacy and sense awareness misleading.[25] In Whitehead's theory of perception, 'there are no bare sensations which are first experienced and then "projected" into our feet as their feelings'. 'The projection is an integral part of the situation, quite as original as the sense-data.'[26] Whitehead described presentational immediacy as 'introduc[ing] into human experience components which are again analysable into actual things of the actual world and into abstract attributes, qualities, and relations, which express how those other actual things contribute themselves as components to our individual experience'. 'These abstractions', for him, 'express how other actualities are component objects for us.' In other words, 'they "objectify" for us the actual things in our "environment"'.[27] According to Whitehead, in presentational immediacy, there is not just unmediated sensation or the consummation of it, but there is also the operation of a certain degree of cognitive scaffolding. Experience in the mode of presentational immediacy endows us with the ability to cognitively abstract and objectify. This element of perceptual objectification is key to understanding Whitehead's account of presentational immediacy; it is also what makes it very pertinent to computational empiricism. In presentational immediacy, one objectifies experience as the result of a direct perceptual representation. The very same type of *presentational objectification* that allows us to receive the world as composed of separate facts is also what occurs in unconventional, natural, and non-classical computing when this latter opens to the sensible datum: a datum that is received, but also determined, by an external point of reception. My contention is thus that the empirical reality that unconventional, natural, and non-classical computing inductively abstracts from, and to which it aims to belong, is not a neutral level of experience, but instead an ensemble of data that are already externally abstracted from the concreteness of what Whitehead would have called 'immediate' (and Deleuze, 'real') experience.

Insofar as it reifies what is already highly abstracted, alternative computing thus suffers from what Whitehead theorised as the *fallacy of misplaced concreteness*. This 'accidental error', to use Whitehead's words,[28] involves taking abstractions about actuality (e.g., the notion of time in physics) as true portrayals of these actualities in their concreteness (e.g., time as this is actually experienced). For Whitehead, the scientific method commits the fallacy of misplaced concreteness on a regular basis, divorcing entities from the web of internal relations that they entail with one another, and assigning them an isolated status of empty factuality. An example that Whitehead offered to illustrate this point is the positivist epistemologies of scientific materialism. Whitehead claimed that scientific materialism, with its focus on substances and accidents, does not look for reasons. On the contrary, it describes a world of matter that is 'senseless, valueless, purposeless'.[29] This matter is reduced to quantitative accounts of mechanically interacting and externally related elementary bits of reality, as if it was possible to simply locate these bits to specifiable points in space and time. Drawing from such a Whiteheadian claim, I would comment that the sense-data entering unconventional, natural, and non-classical computation are not actuality per se, but scientific material-ism's measurable factual records of this actuality. In this sense, the behaviour of the slime mould or of brain neurons (examples of facts that alternative computing takes as its immediate data) is, of course, part of actuality, yet it is also a high-grade abstraction that we make whenever we assume that this behaviour is an original part of the 'stuff' of the world. To accept (like unconventional, natural, and non-classical computation might do implicitly) that this is the real and immediate experience towards which one should orient the formal model means giving an abstraction an arbitrary status of concreteness. In Whitehead's terminology, it means to *misplace* the ab-stracted for the concrete.

At first glance, the problem with presentational immediacy is that the latter presumes that a representational picture of the real world can be ob-tained. Whitehead's criticism of presentational immediacy certainly address-es this point: presentational immediacy does provide us with a representation of the datum of experience, à la Locke or à la Descartes, and—in White-head's view—to take this representation for immediate experience is wrong. Nonetheless, I would suggest that this criticism cannot be limited to an attack on the representational character of traditional empiricist theories of sense-data reception. The core problem with the objectification of presentational immediacy is not its realism (that is, the assumption that the sensory experi-ence presents us with the real), but the fact that this realism is not realist enough. From a Whiteheadian perspective, the objectification of presenta-tional immediacy neglects the fact that actuality is always already too real to be separated out into what is purely physical and what is instead mind-dependent, or into an opposition between a perceived and a perceiver. To not be realist enough means to make a separation between an objective and a subjective reality. This is a separation that, from Whitehead's view, is non-sensical and just as absurd as a division between the primary and secondary qualities of the world (the former being independent from an observer, the latter being dependent). Such a misguided *bifurcation of nature*, as White-head would call it, is what makes presentational objectification possible in the first place: how to receive individual and separate data of experience if these data are not made part of an object that is already distinct from the source of this reception?

The separation between primary and secondary qualities is a traditional empiricist claim, but it is one that applies to computational empiricism too. In this respect, it is possible to say that both associationism and the externality between thought and sense experience that alternative computing encourages is a kind of collateral damage, caused by the division between primary and secondary qualities that a bifurcated nature entails. The separation of abstraction from experience is also a presupposition, as well as a by-product, of the very same bifurcation. As regards computational empiricism, the claim can be sustained by considering again the associationist principle between thought and sense-data that characterises this empiricism in the first place, and the way in which the latter reifies sensibility into a collection of factual records of empirical reality. To support the claim vis-à-vis computational emergence, on the other hand, one needs to take its ontological schema of forms-from-facts as the proof of the bifurcation. Were a structure of abstraction to result from the interaction among separate facts, this would be because these facts are *presentationally objectified*, in the sense that they are empty records of sense experience, to be received and synthesised as data by a source of reception that is, however, external to the data themselves. A sensory capacity and a conceptual one are bifurcated, therefore, in the reception of these data of experience. The abstracted structure of such data is also separated from the source of reception because it emerges as a consequence of the externalist interaction of these empirical elements.

This discussion of Whitehead's notion of presentational immediacy offers the opportunity to go into more depth as regards the problematic lack of an internal principle of connection in computational empiricism. Together with Deleuze, I argued that the lack of this internal principle amounts to a lack of an internal principle of change. Via Whitehead, I can now understand the absence of an internal dynamic principle as depending on the presentational manner in which the datum of experience is received and elaborated by and within actuality itself. It is worth considering Whitehead's attack on presentational immediacy's 'subjectivist bias' here.[30] Whitehead contended, in contrast to Hume, that what presentational immediacy takes to be the real world is not really immediate experience, but a perceptual given already abstracted (or objectified) by a preconstituted subjectivity. For Whitehead, the issue with presentational objectification is exactly this preconstituted subjectivity, external to its datum of perception. Such a subjective pole, bifurcated from its object, gives us an actuality that is fundamentally static, inasmuch as the datum of perception is externally received yet not internally elaborated. To sum up, presentational immediacy returns us to an actual/factual plane where there is only the illusion of change, and no real dynamism. Actuality, as an aggregate of objectified Humean loose and separate facts, is a collection of records devoid of any subjective interiority, and therefore incapable of initiating purposeful action. Whitehead could not agree with this depiction of actuality as passive factuality. For him, actuality is in act: both something that is happening, the constitution of which involves change, and something with a subjective pole that would perform, while also being the object of, this change.

In order to take these considerations further and develop them in the context of this book's onto-aesthetic investigation of computation's conditions of experience, the next chapter will look at how Whitehead's philosophy serves to conceptualise the problematic consequences, for computational aesthetics, of maintaining a sensationalist principle in computation, and affords a means of moving past them.

NOTES

1. Johann Wolfgang von Goethe, 'Formation and Transformation', in *Goethe's Botanical Writings*, trans. Bertha Mueller (Woodbridge, CT: Ox Bow Press, 1989), 23.

2. Michael Weinstock, *The Architecture of Emergence: The Evolution of Form in Nature and Civilization* (Chichester: Wiley, 2010), 9.

3. For a discussion of how, as yet, there is no comprehensive theory of emergence, see Mark A. Bedau and Paul Humphreys, 'Introduction', in *Emergence: Contemporary Readings in Philosophy and Science*, ed. Mark A. Bedau and Paul Humphreys (Cambridge, MA: MIT Press, 2008), 1–6; Jaegwon Kim, 'Emergence: Core Ideas and Issues', *Synthese* 151, no. 3 (August 2006): 547–59, https://doi.org/10.1007/s11229-006-9025-0.

4. James P. Crutchfield, 'The Calculi of Emergence: Computation, Dynamics and Induction', *Physica D: Nonlinear Phenomena* 75, no. 1–3 (August 1994): 12, https://doi.org/10.1016/0167-2789(94)90273-9.

5. It is important to note, however, that stressing an overly strict opposition between the logico-mathematical computing of Turing's model and a non-Turing biophysical computing could be misleading and also historically inaccurate. Turing never advocated a clear-cut distinction between the physical world on the one side and formal reasoning on the other. This has been discussed in Andrew Hodges's extensive reconstruction of Turing's life and legacy. See, for instance, 'Alan Turing, Logical and Physical', in *New Computational Paradigms: Changing Conceptions of What Is Computable*, ed. S. Barry Cooper, Benedikt Löwe, and Andrea Sorbi (New York: Springer, 2008), 3–15.

6. Emergentism most often denotes a position or movement in philosophy of mind that argues for the supervenience of mental proprieties over physical proprieties. See Jonardon Ganeri, 'Emergentisms, Ancient and Modern', *Mind* 120, no. 479 (July 2011): 671–703, https://doi.org/10.1093/mind/fzr038. I use the expression in a more general sense, so as to indicate the intellectual commitment to theories of emergence.

7. 'Models, especially computer-based models, provide accessible instances of emergence, greatly enhancing our chances of understanding the phenomenon. Moreover, the model can be started, stopped, examined, and restarted under new conditions, in ways impossible for most real dynamic systems (think of an ecosystem or an economy). We come full circle when we build computer-based models, providing the computer with a program that is fully capable of surprising its programmer.' John H. Holland, *Emergence: From Chaos to Order* (Oxford: Oxford University Press, 1998), 12.

8. S. Barry Cooper, 'Emergence as a Computability-Theoretic Phenomenon', *Applied Mathematics and Computation* 215, no. 4 (October 2009): 1352, https://doi.org/10.1016/j.amc.2009.04.050.

9. N. Katherine Hayles, *My Mother Was a Computer: Digital Subjects and Literary Texts* (Chicago: University of Chicago Press, 2005), 18–19.

10. John Symons, 'Computational Models of Emergent Proprieties', *Minds and Machines* 18, no. 4 (December 2008): 477, https://doi.org/10.1007/s11023-008-9120-8.

11. Sanjeev Kumar and Peter J. Bentley, 'An Introduction to Computational Development', in *On Growth, Form and Computers*, ed. Sanjeev Kumar and Peter J. Bentley (Amsterdam: Elsevier Academic, 2003), 9.

12. Because of his insistence on metaphysical wholes rather than on parts, as well as his antireductionist argument for the continuity of thought and life, Deleuze has often been read as a philosopher of emergence. See, for instance, John Protevi, 'Deleuze, Guattari and Emergence', *Paragraph: A Journal of Modern Critical Theory* 29, no. 2 (January 2008): 19–39, https://doi.org/10.3366/prg.2006.0018. To a greater or lesser extent, this reading involves stressing, on the one hand, the vitalist dimension of Deleuze's philosophy—his choosing *pneuma* (energy, spirit) above *logos* (representation, reason)—while, on the other, the vitalism that is inherent in certain theoretical approaches to emergence that focus on energetic matter in composition. In the chapter, however, I am not pursuing this affinity between Deleuze and philosophies of emergence. This is because I am not pursuing the vitalism of emergence either. My focus is not on the many cosmological or philosophical interpretations of emergence that have been given in literature, but rather on what happens when computational formalisms are endowed with some of the organisational properties that characterise emergent behaviour. In my proposed reading, alternative computing is understood as looking for an automated solution to a computational problem through the structural principles of emergent behaviour. This implies a level of mechanicism that makes a direct parallel with vitalism impossible.

13. See David Hume, *An Enquiry concerning Human Understanding* (Oxford: Oxford University Press, 2007), 18.

14. See Gilles Deleuze, *Empiricism and Subjectivity: An Essay on Hume's Theory of Human Nature*, trans. Constantin V. Boundas (New York: Columbia University Press, 1991).

15. Gilles Deleuze and Claire Parnet, *Dialogues II*, trans. Hugh Tomlinson, Barbara Habberjam, and Eliot Ross Albert (London: Continuum, 2006), 41.

16. Gilles Deleuze, *Difference and Repetition*, trans. Paul Patton (London: Continuum, 2004), 176.

17. Henri Bergson, *Matter and Memory*, trans. Nancy Margaret Paul and W. Scott Palmer (New York: Zone, 1991), 134.

18. Deleuze, *Difference and Repetition*, 68, 180.

19. William James, *Some Problems of Philosophy* (Cambridge, MA: Harvard University Press, 1979), 80. Also cited in Alfred North Whitehead, *Process and Reality: An Essay in Cosmology* (New York: Free Press, 1978), 68.

20. Whitehead, *Process and Reality*, 17.

21. Whitehead, *Process and Reality*, 158.

22. Alfred North Whitehead, *Symbolism: Its Meaning and Effect* (New York: Fordham University Press, 1985), 13.

23. Whitehead, *Symbolism*, 7.

24. Whitehead, *Symbolism*, 14.

25. Whitehead, *Symbolism*, 21.

26. Whitehead, *Symbolism*, 14.

27. Whitehead, *Symbolism*, 17.

28. Alfred North Whitehead, *Science and the Modern World* (New York: Free Press, 1967), 51.

29. Whitehead, *Science and the Modern World*, 17.

30. Whitehead, *Process and Reality*, 159. Whitehead credited Descartes for having made 'the greatest philosophical discovery since the age of Plato and Aristotle'. This discovery is the 'subjectivist bias' according to which 'subjects enjoying conscious experiences provide the fundamental data for philosophy'. Interestingly, Whitehead did not want to have done with the notion of subject per se. Instead, he wanted to reform it. 'Descartes' discovery on the side of subjectivism', Whitehead commented, 'requires balancing by an "objectivist" principle as to the datum for experience.' *Process and Reality*, 159–60.

Chapter Nine

Actuality

CAUSATION

Computational empiricism aims to introduce change and chance within computational formalisation. Yet, as we saw in chapter 8, the externality between subject and object that computational empiricism entails results in a dynamism that is devoid of an internal principle for the realisation of computation's actuality. The crux of the problem lies in computational empiricism's conflation of actuality with factuality. In what follows below, I will consider this problematic equivalence between actuality and factuality in order to overcome it. I will treat alternative computing's reduction of computational actualities to facts as a consequence of the kind of analysis of perception that is integral to its sense-empiricist approach. According to the 'sensationalist principle' of sense-data empiricism, and to appropriate Whitehead's theorisation of it, there is only 'the bare subjective entertainment of the datum', without 'any subjective form of reception'.[1] In Whitehead's view, such a 'doctrine of mere sensation' does not see that actuality is constituted by and via its inherent internal relations.[2] Whitehead attributed this mistake to British sense-data empiricism, and I will argue here that computational empiricism commits this very same error. Engaging with Whitehead's philosophy will allow us to correct this error and to address the physical reception of data in computation from a different perspective.

Whitehead's philosophy of actuality departs from the consideration of real and immediate experience. In this respect, Whitehead is undoubtedly an empiricist. The most significant dissimilarity between early modern British empiricism and Whitehead's empiricism, however, is that for the former all the *res verae* of reality are external to one another, while for the latter actuality is constituted by and via its internal relations. These internal relations are *causal* relations, which are always also *perceptual*. This is one of the most striking precepts of Whitehead's radical empiricism: although presentational immediacy is an important part of perceptual experience, it does not exhaust it. There is a more basic and primitive type of direct recognition, which Whitehead called *causal efficacy*. This is a ubiquitous modality of receptivity that is 'vague, haunting, unmanageable', yet all the same 'insistent'.[3] By Whitehead's own admission, this notion of causal efficacy contravenes 'the most cherished tradition of modern philosophy, shared alike by the school of empiricists which derives from Hume, and the school of transcendental idealists which derives from Kant'.[4] Hume wrestled with the notion of causality; his sharp analysis of induction led him to classify it as an association that the human mind constructs among conjoined events. In Hume, causation is secondary to the observation of a temporal succession: we perceive actual things (their qualities and substances), and then we construct causal relations. For Whitehead, by contrast, the causal relation is primary and dominant. We perceive causal relations and then we abstract away things, substances, and qualities. Whitehead also argued that Kant committed an analogous mistake to that of Hume when—despite wanting to correct the Humean conclusion that causality cannot be rationally justified—he ended up agreeing with Hume's belief that causal efficacy 'does not belong to the sheer data presupposed in perception'.[5] According to Kant, causation is part of the human cognitive systematisation of experience. Kantian causal relations are grounded in the cognitive faculties of the transcendental subject and are thus subsequent (as is also the case for Hume) to presentational immediacy. For Whitehead, instead, the type of experience proper to causal connection runs much deeper than Kant assumed, for causal efficacy is the condition—not the consequence—of presentational immediacy.

The importance that causal efficacy holds within Whitehead's philosophy is due not only to the central role that it plays in his theory of perception, but also to its significance within his ontology.[6] Causal efficacy is crucial to understand Whitehead's ontological argument about the internal relatedness of all things in experience. Experience in the mode of causal efficacy gives us a world 'where each event infects the ages to come, for good or for evil, with its own individuality'.[7] The past is always causally active as the *real potentiality* of the present. This point in Whitehead's ontology is undeniably complicated. An explanation can be attempted by stressing the relation of real potentiality to causality. Causal efficacy is a type of internal connection that occurs not because of the activity of the cause, but as a result of the activity of the effect. In other words, the core concern for Whitehead is not whether the past actively causes the present, but whether the present perceives its past as its own inevitable cause. For him, past data become active in the present because this present perceives those past data as causally significant for its own existence. The past is given *to* the present in experience (which means, the present receives the past), yet this past is also given as the real potential *for* the present to become its own future. In order to understand the depth of this proposition, which indicates the role of causal connection in the determination of actuality, it is useful to return to the Whiteheadian notion of actual occasion. First of all, it can be observed that actual occasions are not the simple building blocks of the emergentist paradigm; that is to say, they are not blocks that would accumulate in increasing levels of complication. Actual occasions are instead similar to Leibnizian monads of infinite complexity. Yet, whereas Leibniz's monads maintain their self-identity in the face of new acts and events, and would—with the provision of an underpinning cosmic harmony—coordinate themselves externally, Whitehead's actual occasions are always finite in space and time and 'interdependent'.[8] That is to say, actual occasions are constituted in virtue of their internal drive towards communication. Famously, a Leibnizian monad is isolated and windowless.[9] A Whiteheadian actual occasion, by contrast, has both windows and doors to facilitate the ingression of data that contribute to its determination. Actual occasions need other actual occasions, for they arise out of the data that they *inherit* from these other occasions. In this respect, 'causation is nothing else than one outcome of the principle that every actual entity has to house *its* actual world'.[10]

To fully appreciate how an actual occasion can causally house other actualities, let us consider again the 'underlying activity of prehension' that characterises the processuality of an actual occasion.[11] It is worth repeating here that, for Whitehead, a conceptual prehension is actuality's grasping or holding of ideality, and a physical prehension is instead actuality's grasping or holding of other actualities. Physical prehensions are strictly pertinent to the present discussion of causality, as for Whitehead they are in fact *causal feelings*. By virtue of a physical prehension, an actual occasion appropriates data from past actuality and reconstitutes these data in the present of its very own composition, eventually leaving them as the inheritance of future actualities. 'A simple physical feeling', in this sense, 'is an act of causation.'[12] Whitehead described the prehensive activity as having a 'complex constitution', which is 'analysable into five factors': (1) the *subject*, 'which feels'; (2) the *initial data*, 'which are to be felt'; (3) the *elimination* 'in virtue of the negative prehensions'; (4) the *objective datum*, which is what is felt; and (5) the *subjective form*—namely, '*how* that subject feels that datum'.[13] This description of the prehension's complex constitution reveals that a prehension is a mode of activity that exceeds the subject-object division. The actual occasion is neither the subject nor the object of its prehensions. For Whitehead, 'subject and object are relative terms': an occasion is 'a subject in respect to its special activity concerning an object; and anything is an object in respect to its provocation of some special activity within a subject'.[14]

Such a reworking of the subject-object relation is of primary importance to understand Whitehead's conception of actuality and should be emphasised vis-à-vis the distinction that Whitehead made between initial data and objective datum within prehensions. Every actual occasion prehensively inherits a multiplicity of initial data, constituting the givenness of experience. These initial data, however, are selected via eliminations and exclusions that take place by means of *negative prehensions*.[15] Lastly, an objective datum is obtained for each prehensive activity. This datum is entirely determined. In this prehensive process, the *subjective form* is the manner in which the subject feels its datum. The subjective form is thus produced in and by the integration of the manifold data into the atomic unity of the actual occasion. There is no subjective form that is equal or equivalent to another subjective form, since every prehension is different. Borrowing from the Latin *concrescere*, Whitehead used the term 'concrescence' to denote this process by which a multiplicity of discrete data grows together into a new concrete unity. The determination of an actual occasion (in other words, its self-actualisation) is marked by this concrescent activity of concretisation. More specifically, this growing together is the result of a causal process of objectification, which expresses 'the irreversible relationship of settled past to derivative present' that Whitehead saw as central to experience in the mode of causal efficacy.[16] This *causal objectification* effectively accounts for how actualities are 'original elements for a new creation'.[17] Causal efficacy is thus meant to explain how new actualities in the world come about. 'The functioning of one actual entity in the self-creation of another actual entity', Whitehead clarified, 'is the "objectification" of the former for the latter actual entity.'[18] Causal objectification, then, is an operation inherent to the becoming of new actual occasions, but also a crucial mode of their existence. In the prehensive activity a manifold is unified; this unity is the actual occasion. Upon its actualisation, an actuality is objectified for other actualities, and it enters the latter as the initial datum of their respective prehensions. The process of concrescence thus concludes with the new actual occasion having become the datum of future actualisations.

With causal efficiency, Whitehead managed to offer an alternative model to that of British empiricism. This alternative model explains the physical reception of data in experience by way of an internal causal connection among the *res* of reality. Whitehead's model of physical reception advances a reconceptualisation of the given of experience that also reshapes the relation between a subject and an object. The outcome of presentational immediacy is an empirical phenomenon because it has to be manifested to an already preconstituted subjectivity. A bare empirical fact always presupposes such a previously established subjectivity, and this bare factuality, therefore, maintains the subjectivist bias of the sensationalist doctrine of perception that Whitehead attacked. By contrast, the objective datum of the Whiteheadian prehensive process is the result of a process of internal objectification of actuality. This process from which objectivity develops is at the same time a process of subjectification, functional to the constitution of objective actuality itself. From the perspective of causal objectification, actuality is not just a bare fact, for it cannot be entrapped within the subject-object relationality that factuality presupposes. While in presentational objectifications (carried out via presentational immediacy) the subject must exist prior to the world, in causal objectifications (carried out via causal efficacy), neither subject nor object precedes the perceptive process. Instead, both are constituted within it. The objective datum is thus the result of the process of objectification of actuality itself. The subject of this objectification, however, is the very same actuality.

AN EMPTY DYNAMISM

The case of *evolutionary computation* offers an interesting opportunity to illustrate how Whitehead's presentational objectification and causal objectification can be said to operate within alternative computing methodologies. Evolutionary computation is about computational systems that can evolve over time. This is a biologically inspired range of theories and practices addressing computational systems that modify themselves over time by developing interactions, generations, iterations, and variations. Evolution, in the Darwinian sense of the term, is translated into computational procedures for sorting, searching, optimising, and problem solving. In order to achieve these evolutionary effects, many techniques are applied and perfected. Some of these techniques have been studied since the late 1950s and have been developed separately throughout the second half of the twentieth century. Most of these activities, however, were unified in the 1990s under the 'evolutionary computation' label. Today, they contribute to the shared efforts of a whole community of researchers in a steadily expanding field. Due to this multiple origin and multiple applications, evolutionary computation now encompasses a wide array of systems, processes, and procedures, such as evolutionary programming, genetic algorithms, evolutionary strategies, cultural algorithms, differential evolution, swarm intelligence, memetic algorithms, artificial immune systems, and DNA computing. This list could easily continue. Within this technological framework, evolution is a useful and powerful narrative to justify how empirical change and chance could be part of computation. For most computational systems, changing conditions would be lethal. However, this death sentence does not apply to those problems whose solutions are sought via evolutionary means. Accidental variation, on the contrary, increases the probabilities of success. In evolutionary computing, empirical change and chance infuse formal permanence via real values, thanks to the capacity of populations of individual algorithms to survive and reproduce. On the one hand, the measurable records of factuality (i.e., the data) that are fed to the systems change; on the other, however, the relation between the algorithmic instruction that manages these data and the data themselves also mutates. The system becomes adaptive and thereby continues to perform well under unforeseen conditions. In this way, evolutionary computation can solve problems that we do not fully understand. The basic idea is to generate a solution from the factual interaction of many computational parameters, as opposed to merely calculating this solution from a priori premises.

In what follows, I will argue that this evolutionary framework exemplifies my previous claims about the exteriority of subject and object in alternative computing, and also my contention that, in computational empiricism, the formalism of computation has not only been opened up to sense experience, but the abstractive operations of formalisation have also been ontologically neutralised to become part of such sense experience. Certainly, there are reasons to see evolutionary computing as simulative. Nonetheless, the importance of evolutionary computing for the present discussion does not stem exclusively from the striking similarities between the organic and the inorganic that evolutionary methodologies prompt. In my reading, these simulative features are left aside in order to stress the significant conceptual shift in how computation itself is conceived and spoken of: as an empirical phenomenon among empirical phenomena.

This point can be clarified by way of reference to one of the most widely used evolutionary techniques: *genetic algorithms*. The 'algorithmic' aspect of this technique has to be taken in the sense of Turing's 1936 formulation of an effective method of calculation for taking decisions. The specification 'genetic', however, also implies that these algorithms are endowed with a hereditary aspect that deviates from Turing's 1936 original a priori model of computation in order to encompass a posteriori elements of empirical change and chance. An algorithm that is genetic entails a generative imperative to produce new formations, along with a sense of temporal progression. This technique is robust, global, and easily implemented; for this reason, it is successfully applied to a variety of engineering sectors to solve practical difficulties. Beyond their engineering applications, however, genetic algorithms can also perform interesting forays into classification and prediction tasks, into scientific modelling, and into dynamic systems theory. Although there is no unanimous general description of the methodology of genetic algorithms, some fundamental traits can be identified as common to their use. In genetic algorithms, the programmer deliberately writes very simple instructions and lets complex behaviour emerge through an iterative selection process, which picks the best representations of solutions, rejects bad results, and produces new ones from those that survive the procedure. Natural selection and biological evolution are oversimplified into basic components, which reveal striking analogies between the biological and the computational. Within a computational system operating via genetic algorithms, one can count a *population* and witness *selection* according to *fitness* principles, while *crossover* and *random mutation* also promise variation among the offspring. With repeated iterations of the process, the population of genetic algorithms gets fitter and fitter, while the answers that they provide to a problem get better and better. A multiplicity of solutions can be generated and explored in this manner. The famous Darwinian survival of the fittest vouches for the quality of these solutions, as only the best algorithms can survive the genetic process. The evolution that this involves does not make predictions; instead, it works through probabilities by searching through them.

In this evolutionary spirit, genetic algorithms are operations on a population of possible solutions. Many computational problems require searching through a very large number of probable results. Unlike classical algorithmic optimisation models—which would determine, for every iteration, a single result, and which would then compose these results sequentially in order to reach an optimal point—genetic algorithms bring forth a population of results for each iterative generation, filling up the search space as much as possible. The margin of efficiency is thus both improved and enlarged. Chance, therefore, is particularly important for genetic algorithms, as they encode formal rules via the application of a bottom-up approach designed to encompass accidental variation over time. The biologically inspired proprieties of genetic algorithms are affected by choices in terms of population size or selection procedure, for instance. A few of these choices are stipulated a priori (for example, the programmer decides how to represent the information). Most of them, however, are impromptu agreements between circumstantial conditions and probabilities. These a posteriori choices are determined stochastically, which means that they are based on probability. The capacity of a genetic algorithm to adapt in time and through time is expressed, therefore, via instructions that are not deterministic but probabilistic.

It could be said that genetic algorithms summarise all that I have claimed so far about the inductive operations of alternative computing, about the empiricist character of these unconventional practices, and about the externality between thought and sense-data (or of subject and object) that characterises the ontology of emergence that underpins those practices. Genetic algorithms are a good example of factual interaction that builds up morphological change. Again, they are a good example of how programming wants to expose itself to empirical chance, and of how the scope of computation is being redefined so that it not only includes empirical phenomena into its formalisms, but also casts these formalisms as a fact of the world. In particular, it is interesting to address here how genetic algorithms are considered *dynamic processes* because they project a trajectory of development over time. A population of 'individuals' is evolved via the injection of useful variation and the introduction of guided random mutation that will protect the population against genetic stagnation. Elements of the current population are copied and mixed up into a younger generation, which gradually constitutes a whole new ensemble of individuals. This breeding is rapid and prolific; as a result, the composition of the genetic pool changes constantly. Mutation and crossover operate at a genotype level (that is, at the level of their genetic binary makeup). If the genotype (i.e., the binary script) changes, the phenotype (i.e., the correspondent solution) will change as well. The genotype could be interpreted as the *in-formation* that underpins and determines a certain phenotypical propriety. However, both the genotype and phenotype of an individual element of the population are facets of the same empirical plane that that element inhabits.

This aspect of genetic algorithms is curious. Genetic algorithms change, but they are praised for doing so because their formalism is turned on its head and treated as an empirical entity. This model thus implies the following inference: if genetic algorithms can change, then this is because they are bare facts of the world. It is hence possible to interpret genetic algorithms as adhering to the forms-from-facts ontological schema of computational emergence. The emergentist ontologisation of computation, I claimed earlier, underpins an empiricist approach to computation that is problematic insofar as (1) it reduces experience to sense experience; (2) accordingly, it interprets what is given in experience as a sense-datum; and (3) it then aims to encompass this sense-datum in the formalisms of computation via the association of intelligibility and sensibility, maintaining that the perceiver and the perceived are external to each other. Genetic algorithms reprise all of these problematic assumptions. Moreover, they also reinstate the equally problematic consequences of these assumptions: (1) that relations between sensibility and intelligibility are articulated as the percipient subject's objectifications of sense experience (presentational immediacy); (2) that the given of experience that computational empiricism inductively objectifies is not the concrete, but is always already abstracted (fallacy of misplaced concreteness); and (3) that reality is thus separated into primary and secondary qualities—that is, into fundamental, valueless constituents on the one hand, and mind-dependent additions on the other (bifurcation of nature).

My previous comments on the fallacy of misplaced concreteness in relation to alternative computing (see chapter 8) can now be developed further by adding that the factual interactions of genetic algorithms are themselves part of this fallacy. It is generally assumed that genetic algorithms replicate the behaviours of the physical world. Yet, following Whitehead, it could be remarked that these behaviours are not concrete bits of reality, but presentational objectifications that a percipient subject has extracted from reality. The computational structures of unconventional, natural, and non-classical computing do include empirical factuality successfully, although this empirical factuality is not, contrary to what computational empiricism would assume, the whole of experience. The key issue that needs to be underlined here is that the computational technique employed by genetic algorithms carries out presentational objectifications. The notion of computation itself (or, more precisely, that of genetic and evolutionary computation) is presentationally objectified whenever it is presented as an empirical phenomenon among empirical phenomena of the natural world, and as obeying the laws of genetics and evolution that are said to govern that natural world. The presentational world that genetic algorithms attempt to reproduce artificially is a world that has been emptied, in a similarly artificial fashion, of any interiority. In itself, it has no intelligibility, even though its future remains predictable (and therefore computable) because the totality of its behaviour is looked at from the point of view of an external percipient subject.

Change is thus taken to rely on behavioural uncertainty and is modelled upon the probabilities of the physical realm. From this perspective, change is the mutability that results from an aggregation of parts: simple building blocks combine to build up a whole of continuous variation. This is evolution as an aggregation of loose and separate bits of reality that are external to each other. Since everything is external to everything else, a computational procedure is the consequence of the interactive externality between elements in composition, the result of the addition of simple determinate units into a much more indefinite whole. In genetic programming, the optimisation of a solution follows an evolutionary and supposedly dynamic trajectory. The algorithmic processing of evolutionary computing is inserted into a wider interactive plane of parts that are in the process of constructing a whole of continuous change, moving from the local determination of a part (an input, for example) to the global indeterminacy of the whole (the output or final result, for instance, but also the overall trajectory of optimisation). The part itself, per se and in isolation from the whole, however, is not understood as being processual. Therefore, in the computational technique of genetic algorithms, there is no real elaboration of the datum of experience, nor of the algorithmic instruction that organises this datum. Elements are composed to create the continuity of variation that enables optimisation. It might help to think here of the animation of cartoons, or of the animation principles behind motion pictures. Single frames (or single records of factuality) are composed along the continuum of a temporal (yet not causal) narration. These frames are not related internally, but only externally. When the frames are played together, the illusion of a process or temporal movement of the single depictions is created. In each frame, however, there is no activity or process. This, figuratively speaking, is how change according to presentational immediacy works in evolutionary computing. Although there seems to be an animation, or indeed change, the datum is not elaborated internally. Instead, it is just fed to the algorithmic instruction, or the overall principle of organisation, as an already determinate entity that can increase the overall indeterminacy of the overall procedure and thus enlarge the pool of solutions for the final output. It is the role of the simple part to be determinate, and of the complex whole to be indeterminate.

THE INTERNAL ADVENTURE OF BECOMING

The empty dynamism that characterises computational empiricism contrasts starkly with the understanding of computation that I wish to propose. I too theorise computation as dynamic. Yet the dynamism that I aim to conceptualise is full of computation's potential to realise its own actuality. Let us return then to the characterisation of computation as a process of self-determination that I advanced in chapter 6, and let us do so in order to highlight a different, Whiteheadian theorisation of computational processing's hereditary and generative character.

According to Whitehead, actuality is complete and determinate, although this completion and this determination have to be accomplished. Any process of actualisation starts from multiple data to conclude with the unity of these data. This actual 'togetherness' itself becomes a datum that contributes to a new actualisation.[19] In Whitehead's actual occasions, change involves an internal momentum that has to be addressed *from within the part*, and not from the perspective of the overall external interaction of the many parts that create a final whole. Whitehead's philosophy, therefore, proposes a type of constructivism that is profoundly different from that which pervades emergentism, for Whitehead's construction is not a morphological self-organisation but an ontological self-realisation, expressing the 'creative activity belonging to the very essence of each occasion'.[20] 'The many become one, and are increased by one.'[21] This famous quotation from Whitehead emphasises how the part is not inferior to the final whole. The quotation can be read as a justification of the ontological legitimacy of discreteness. Moreover, it also shows that his philosophy of actuality can be employed to reverse the movement from determination to indeterminacy that characterises computational empiricism. In the emergentist ontology of computational empiricism, the part is determinate and the whole is indeterminate. By contrast, in Whitehead's ontological schema, the starting point for change is the indeterminacy of multiple parts in composition within actuality. Whitehead's reality passes from indeterminacy to determination; this determination then becomes a new indeterminacy for another process of determination. Equally, the trajectory of this composition is *from the complex to the complex*. Whitehead's emphasis on causal efficacy evidences that the objectification of the datum of experience does not depart from the simple record of factuality to result in a gradual complexification via accumulation. What is given in experience is rather already complex, because so too is its prehensive constitution.

The significance of stressing this directionality from indeterminacy to determination cannot be overstated. My aim in this book is to address the mode in which computation might be said to actualise itself. Via Deleuze and Whitehead, I understand this actualisation as a movement of determination from indeterminacy.[22] If I were to understand computational processing as moving in the opposite direction (from local determination to global indeterminacy), the possibility of attending to computation's self-actualisation would be precluded. Consequently, I cannot philosophically endorse those technical operations that attempt to enlarge computation's supposedly strict formalisms, and which thereby try to encompass the umpteenth variables of an apparently flexible empirical world. Nor, however, can I be theoretically content with those computing approaches that I discussed earlier, which intend to fabricate computational formalisms as simulative approximations of the chance probabilities of the physical world. Addressing computation's self-actualisation involves considering computation's very own indeterminacy, and thus its inherent contingent status. As long as indeterminacy in computation is modelled upon the unpredictability of empirical phenomena, one risks missing that computation's formal axiomatic systems are already ingressed by indeterminacy, at their formal level, and that this indeterminacy is not equivalent to the chance occurrences of factuality. This argument does not imply any dismissal of the technoscientific contribution of those theories and practices that have taken up the challenge of enlarging the threshold of contemporary computational resources. Still, what I am stressing is that, while taking up that challenge, some of these theories and practices have also developed a characterisation of computation that focuses misleadingly on empirical chance as the only principle of indeterminacy in computation.

A speculative experiment should then be proposed. Because genetic algorithms confirm computational empiricism's presentational immediacy, we should use them to prove the contrary: that there is another aspect of objectification in computation—one that is causal, not presentational. Thus, while earlier I analysed this evolutionary technique in order to demonstrate the fallacies of computational empiricism, I will now address it with a view towards surpassing these fallacies and towards redirecting the possibility of dynamism in computation. This is an important step towards demonstrating that *all* computational procedures can be understood as actual occasions that occur and determine themselves, not despite of, but because of their inherent indeterminacy. This step in the argument is also meant to show that, precisely because computational processes can be understood as actual occasions, an aesthetics at two levels can be proposed successfully. There is nothing intrinsically wrong in unconventional, natural, and non-classical computing theories and practices. What is perhaps mistaken, however, is the way in which they have been spoken of via the implicitly sense-empiricist assumptions that I have analysed so far.

In order to explain how genetic algorithms could be said to carry out causal objectifications, it is necessary to distinguish algorithms from data, and to understand the relation between the two in this instance of evolutionary computation. An 'algorithm' is a set of well-defined instructions for solving a problem in a finite number of steps. As regards 'data', the contextual ambiguity that surrounds that term partly serves my argument. According to the definition employed by computer science, data express information inputted into a computer: information that is to be managed, elaborated, and transformed in some way by the computer's program. In this sense, data are information that is received, processed, and outputted by the computer's algorithmic instructions. Yet, following the etymological roots of the term, one can also consider data as the *givens of experience*. The two designations are not incompatible, and they can be combined to describe data as those givens of experience that constitute the information that is to be processed by the algorithms.

In Whitehead's causal objectifications, a multiplicity of initial data is unified in the creation of a novel actual occasion. In my view, it is also the case that, in genetic algorithms, data ingress the constitution of a new algorithmic occasion. Data are a multiplicity of information that gets organised and ordered in the processuality of the genetic algorithm. The algorithmic occasion that these data enter is the very instruction that selects the data in the first place. To explain this otherwise, data enter and constitute those algorithms that in turn have selected them and operated upon them. What genetic algorithms treat as data (that is, their object) are thus those populations of solutions that also inform the rules of agency (in other words, the subjective principle) of the very same algorithms. Neither subject (algorithm) nor the object (the data) precedes the processuality of computation; both are constituted as such within it. The situation could be said to be contradictory, but it is only apparently so. The contradiction is resolved if this relation between algorithmic instructions and data is understood in the Whiteheadian terms of causal efficacy: not just a mere Humean temporal succession, but a relation that conveys the activity of incorporating the outputs of past algorithmic occasions as inputs for the present of a new algorithmic occasion. The present of the genetic algorithm thus participates in the algorithm's past. This past is present in the genetic algorithm as the data of previous generations that are inherited by the new generation, and which thus become causally significant for the present of this new generation, which draws from them in its becoming. On this view, data are not understood as mere probabilities, or solely in terms of measurable records of empirical factuality. Instead, data are objectified occasions of a settled past that become integrated and realised into the new algorithmic occasion. These objectifications 'constitute the efficient causes out of which *that* actual entity arises'.[23]

Certainly, causal efficacy conveys a sense of *inheritance*. However, the Whiteheadian understanding of hereditary relations is different from that which is often employed in Darwinian theories of biological evolution. Although Whitehead could be said to be 'post-evolutionary' (for he wrote after Darwin and accepted his theories), he believed that evolutionary models of change reiterate the problematic expectations of scientific materialism. According to the latter, change in nature depends upon the interaction of bits of material reality with other separated bits of material reality. Whitehead commented that evolution, from this materialist perspective, 'is reduced to the role of being another word for the description of the changes of the external relations between portions of matter'. 'There is nothing to evolve, because one set of external relations is as good as any other set of external relations.'[24] Against scientific materialism, Whitehead grounded inheritance in causal efficacy, and thus upon an internal relation that aims to explain how past actuality is present in future actualisations. By doing so, he offered not a theory of evolution of separate bits of matter, but a theory of the *act of becoming* of reality itself. According to this theory, every actuality (or every *res* of reality) is the product of the history in which it becomes. While every actuality holds a unique perspective on the history out of which it arises, that history is, however, also unique to the actuality that is generated from it. In Whitehead's theory of becoming, relations are not all as good as any other, and the principle of inheritance accounts not only for what is inherited, but also for the ways in which that which is inherited is transformed.

I now suggest to extend this Whiteheadian understanding of an act of becoming to genetic algorithms. As I have already indicated, I propose to address genetic algorithms in terms of actual occasions. By focusing on the causal efficacy of these algorithmic occasions, I am stressing the 'internal adventure of becoming' of their actual constitution.[25] Therefore, one of the most important conceptual consequences of my proposed differentiation between actuality and factuality is the possibility of reworking the category of change and reconsidering what the latter might mean for computational systems. If computational processes are to be conceived as actual algorithmic occasions, then change in computing should be considered as much more than an efficient and effective approximation of empirical variability. Change should instead be understood as equivalent to becoming, and this becoming should be understood as an ontological feature of computation's actuality. Change is thus something that is truly required by a computational procedure, inasmuch as the latter is a process that realises itself by virtue of its own activity of self-determination. As regards the specific example of genetic algorithms analysed here, this evolutionary technique is praised for being dynamic because it projects a trajectory of development over time via the introduction of random mutation modelled upon the unpredictability of empirical phenomena. From one generation to the next, what is accumulated is variation, which accounts for the improvement of a pool of results. This is not, however, just simulation: according to computational empiricism, computation itself is a legitimate empirical phenomenon among empirical phenomena.

Now my argument proceeds as follows. If computation is to be understood as actual rather than as factual, then what constitutes a *dynamic computation* differs drastically. In a Whiteheadian sense, a dynamic process is the activity of self-determination that takes place within an actual occasion, and which is initiated by causal objectifications. A computational procedure that is dynamic is thus not a computational procedure whose formalism bends underneath the weight of more and more variables approximating empirical variation. On the contrary, it is a computation that *becomes*. In other words, it is a computation whose activity consists in coming into existence. Of course, computational procedures can simulate nature, and we can stretch our conception of what computation is towards the empirical realm, so as to make the computational procedure a bare fact of the physical world. My point, however, is that if we are to consider computation's dynamic character as *truly computational*, then we need to include the possibility that this dynamism consists instead of a procedure of self-actualisation. Change is not something that computational processing might do if it is rendered less computational and more akin to an empirical phenomenon. According to the view that I am proposing here, change happens because computation does what it is preprogrammed to do: it actualises or determines itself via the objectification of data.

These claims are introduced via the example of evolutionary computation for a specific reason, additional to those already mentioned above. This computational technique, together with other unconventional, natural, and nonclassical methodologies, could be labelled with the qualification 'post-Turing' to indicate that the technology is not strictly concerned with the universalisation of a determinist method of calculation. Genetic algorithms aim to encompass the incidental complexity of factuality. Most interestingly, however, this technique still moves within the parameters of what is possible to do with computational formalisation. In this respect, the evolutionary optimisation of genetic algorithms attempts to make up for the most troublesome aspect of Turing's formalisation of computability. This is the fact that, in a Turing machine, an algorithmic procedure is a process in which everything is preprogrammed. Those alternative computational formalisations that want to exploit the power of evolutionary dynamics, combining the principles of natural evolution with those of genetics, must discard such a determinist scenario. Obviously, computing cannot operate exactly in the same way as natural and material systems do. Yet computing that is post-Turing must approximate facts as much as possible, so as to account for the information processing of empirical variability.

Having said that, however, in light of what has been discussed so far, the significance of any label that would signpost a conclusive break from Turing's model of computability appears to be limited. If computational processing is understood in terms of actual events of determination, then one does not need to move beyond the Turing machine via biological or physical metaphors, extensions, or simulations in order to find the inception of change in computation. By highlighting the conceptual shortcomings of those approaches that want to make computation a fact of the physical world, I can thereby advocate the view that computation is neither nature nor artifice. *Computation is computation*, and it should be addressed and assessed on the grounds that it is a process of self-actualisation. The determinism of computational axiomatics does not oppose dynamism in computation. Quite the opposite; it needs it. A central consequence of the emphasis that I am proposing we should place on Whitehead's causal efficacy can thus be brought here to the fore. For Whitehead, causal efficacy corresponds to a mode of perception. Causal relations are perceptual relations; they are Whitehead's physical prehensions. To engage in a physical prehension is to feel what there is, or what there has been, and to internalise this feeling into a unity that constitutes what there will be. Again, a Whiteheadian physical prehension is the way in which actuality relates to other instances of actuality. Past occasions are inherited and causally influence the constitution of the new occasion because they are physically prehended by it. Consequently, by speculating regarding the possibility of causal efficacy in computing, I am, in effect, endowing computation itself with such a physically prehensive activity.

Why is this important? Evidently, the Whiteheadian notion of physical prehension offers a means of understanding the transmission and influence of data beyond the associationism of sense-data empiricism, which considered any internal relation to be a subjectivist fiction. In the specific context of computational systems, affirming computation's physical prehensions also affords the possibility of opposing the cognitivism that saturates the field of computing. This is because the affirmation provides a way of saying that computation entails a physical operation upon data, and that it cannot, therefore, be reduced to the status of a merely mentalist affair. To put this otherwise, from the perspective of causal efficacy, it becomes possible to argue that in computation there is not just a cognitivist representation of preconstituted functions of intelligibility. Data are not just represented; there is always a physical grasping and ordering of data to be objectified and made constitutive of the actual computational process. Ultimately, to argue for causal efficacy in computation implies contending that the latter has prehensive powers of affecting and being affected. Algorithms too, in other words, entail a response to actuality that is predicated upon what could be called affective capacities: affective capacities that, in Deleuzian terms, would refer to a computational 'being of the sensible', and which—from a Whiteheadian perspective—allow computational actuality to enter directly into the constitution of other computational actuality.

Causal efficacy aims to explain 'the immanence of past occasions in the occasions which are future', or how 'the past has an objective existence in the present which lies in the future beyond itself'.[26] The difficulty arguably lies in explaining this immanence and this existence in terms of a subject-object relation. The notion of physical prehension attempts to address precisely this challenge. Brian Massumi correctly emphasises that 'the cognitivist paradigm equates the subject with the knower, and the object with the known',[27] and he also states that Whitehead's philosophy stands as an effective onto-epistemological move beyond the cognitivist paradigm because it successfully overcame this subject-object divide. In Whitehead's philosophy, objectivity is the '*activity* that has been left over in the world by previous events of change'. The subjective, in turn, 'is not something pre-existing to which an event occurs: it is the self-occurring form of the event'.[28] It is this non-opposition between perceiver and perceived, and between knower and known, that characterises physical prehensions, on the one hand, as truly innovative modes of relatedness of the actual and, on the other, as the foundation of the self-creating activity of actuality. By speculating about the existence of physical prehensions in computation, I am thus opening up the possibility that an algorithm is a procedure according to which computational actuality elaborates other computational actuality (i.e., what comes before and after it) as its object, and that, while doing so, it effectively constitutes itself as an active subject. To equate algorithms to actual occasions, then, also involves considering the *agency* of computation. This agency concerns the operations of determination of the algorithmic procedure itself.

We can develop these considerations by noting that one of the consequences of the claims made above is that the very sense of *generation* in computation can be reassessed. Computation might be said to be generative because it realises itself. In turn, the qualification 'genetic' might be used to denote the interconnection of these processes of actualisations, and not merely the informational simulation of biological genetics. In this respect, one of the most crucial speculative advantages that one gains from thinking of computation's internal adventure of becoming is the fact that it becomes possible to expose computation's *real potentiality*. Whitehead's ontological schema envisaged two types of potentiality: one that is 'pure' and that pertains to the ideality of eternal objects, and one that is 'real' and that pertains to the actuality of the process itself. Real potentiality is specific to actual events and their historical nature. It indicates how creativity is to be found only within actuality, for only the actual is in act, and therefore only it can create. In this sense, real potentiality suggests that 'the universe is . . . a creative advance into novelty'.[29] In the case of computation, if one understands the relation between the algorithm and the data as causal—as I have proposed one should do—it then becomes possible to see how the past of the algorithmic occasion is causally active in the present as the real potential of actuality to become something else. This potentiality is real because it conveys the propagative character of computational actuality itself: the capacity of a computational actual occasion to create new computational actual occasions from the 'components which are *given* for experience'.[30] Arguing for the real potentiality of computation, via causal efficacy, also offers further occasion for speculating on the ways in which indeterminacy in computing manifests itself. Causal objectification requires indeterminacy. This, however, is not the pure indeterminacy of ideality, but the real indeterminacy of a multiplicity of actual past occasions that might be inherited in the present, and which might be left over for future actualisation. Crucially, for Whitehead, 'objectification involves elimination'.[31] Something actualises itself because something else does not. The givenness of experience involves a *decision*, or a cutting off, of alternatives, according to which some data get selected and others do not. Upon the selection of its data, the actual occasion must become itself. Decision is not the arbitrary choice of a percipient subject, but the determination of an objective datum in the process of the subjectification of the actual occasion. There is no subjectivity prior to the decision; instead, the subject is constituted by virtue of the decision. The indeterminacy that this decisional capacity stands for is therefore inseparable from the actuality's self-determination: indeterminacy is the correlate of determination.

The emphasis that has been placed on computation's causal efficacy is particularly important in relation to my goal of offering an investigation of computational systems that could challenge the representational orientation that pervades the field of computing, while also advancing a viable theorisation of computation's potential to realise its own actuality. However, two problems should now be highlighted. These problems are encountered if both this challenge and this theorisation stop at the level of computation's causal efficacy (that is to say, at the level of its physical prehensions). First, throughout this book, I have often stressed that we should avoid discarding the logico-quantitative specificity of computational systems and that we should instead philosophically reconsider those formal operations that cannot be talked about solely in terms of affects. While I aim to subtract the method of abstraction that defines computation from the metacomputational project of symbolic reduction of reality, I also argue for the aesthetic legitimacy of this very same method. In this respect, it is crucial to emphasise that, if I were to remain focused on the affective aspect of computational reality that physical prehensions could explain, I would not be fulfilling this rationale. Rather, I would perhaps be participating in what I referred to, in the first part of this book, as an aisthesis of digital computation, according to which conceptual and physical operations are the same thing because thought and sensation are immanent to each other. I would thus neglect the logico-quantitative character of computational systems that I wish to bring to the foreground. I can avoid this potential neglect by following the contrasting Whiteheadian view that thought and sensation are not immanent to each other but consequent, and that conceptual and physical operations are related and yet distinct. Whitehead theorised conceptual prehensions as consequent to physical prehensions, yet also as essential to the realisation of actuality. It is precisely this aspect of his philosophy that makes it possible to argue that causal efficacy is not a sufficient explanation of how new actuality comes about. I must return here, therefore, to a point that was developed earlier: we need to build an aesthetic investigation of computation that would address the latter at two levels. To this end, Whitehead's ontological schema is doubly important and relevant. On the one hand, since it envisaged physical prehensions, this schema allows us to say that computation is not just an abstractive reduction via a priori representations. On the other hand, however, since this same ontology did not stop at the physical reception of actual data but envisaged conceptual operations upon ideal (or eternal, in Whitehead's terminology) data too, Whitehead's ontological schema also gives us a way to readdress the undeniable abstractive capacity of computation, beyond representation.

The second issue that should be brought to the fore follows from these considerations. Real potentiality is always potentiality 'relative to some actual entity'.[32] However, according to Whitehead's ontology, actuality is 'dipolar'.[33] This characteristic entails that, while real potentiality is relative to actuality, these actualities process data both physically and conceptually. Consequently, such a real potentiality expresses 'a twofold aspect of the creative urge. In one aspect there is the origination of simple causal feelings; and in the other aspect there is the origination of conceptual feelings.'[34] Along with the indeterminacy relative to a multiplicity of actual data that are to be physically prehended, actuality then also determines itself in relation to the indeterminacy of eternal data that are to be conceptually prehended. For Whitehead, the actual is never fully realised without the ingression of the latter. The important question to address is thus this: what is the role of the pure potentiality of ideality in relation to the real potential of actuality? The implications of this question concern the fact that the internal principle for computational actuality's realisation—which is at the basis of the computational dynamism that I wish to theorise by drawing on Whitehead's model of processual actuality—cannot be predicated uniquely upon causal relations, for conceptual prehensions are to be considered part of computational actuality's operativity as much as physical prehensions are. But how does the object of these conceptual prehensions (what I defined, in chapter 6, as the pure potential of the infinite quantities of the incomputable) relate to the real potential of computation to process data and thus actualise itself? The argument about the inadequacy of causal efficacy in explaining how new actuality comes about, and that concerning the integration of actual and eternal data in the expression of real potentiality, are closely related. Both translate into a call for investigating how, while being originated via physical operations, new actuality is never complete without a conceptual determination. If we are to fully understand computational processes in terms of Whitehead's actual occasions, these issues need to be addressed directly.

FORM OF PROCESS

The peculiar dynamism of the computational procedure characterises computation's condition of existence as truly processual, for it highlights how computational processing can be understood in terms of becoming. The internal adventure of this becoming offers a way to address computation as *an actual event among other actual events*. On this view, a computational process is something that happens. In a Whiteheadian sense, it is an actual event because it occurs, and because it begins and then finishes.

Whitehead's ontological schema thus helps us to refine the ontology of contingency that has been advanced in the second part of the book, where I proposed a novel philosophical interpretation of Gödel's and Turing's logical breakthroughs. In addition to being indeterminate, however, I can now describe computation as contingent because it is also *eventual*. Stressing this eventuality does not imply claiming that computation is an accident in the hands of chance. By contrast, and again following Whitehead, this eventual character shows that computation is a *processual occurrence*. Whitehead's ontological schema then provides us with an ontological framework through which to interpret indeterminacy and eventuality as crucial to the actualisation of the computational procedure. In order to arrive at this conclusion, it has been necessary to analyse those unconventional, natural, and non-classical computing attempts that aim to extend Turing's preprogrammed model towards empirical individuations. By criticising the insufficient attention that those attempts paid to the need for an internal principle of self-actualisation, I suggested another route towards the investigation of the ontological conditions of computational systems. Every stage in the argument was necessary if we are to finally consider how computing's preprogramming might be compatible with what Whitehead called 'the ultimate freedom of things'.[35]

For Whitehead, this ultimate freedom is the autonomy of the actual occasion that is in charge of determining itself. In the case of computational systems, this proposition can be appropriated to conceive the self-sufficiency of the computational procedure as grounded upon the internal contingency of the formal system. Throughout this book, I have argued that we should reconsider the relation between necessity and contingency in computation. I explained that the functional as well as the ontological autonomy of formal axiomatic systems should be affirmed and that this autonomy should be viewed as something other than the closed sufficient reason of metacomputation's total determinism. I can now develop these claims further and ask, what is the relation between the pure and real potentiality of computation? Why is causal efficacy not enough to account for the production of new computational actuality? In order to answer these questions, one needs to address how the physical and conceptual determinations of the computational actual occasion are consequent to each other. This means that we need to return to the findings presented in the second part of this book, where I argued that computation is a process of determination that is always 'ingressed' (to keep using Whitehead's term) by quantitative infinity, and that this quantitative infinity is an indeterminacy that should be grasped at a logical level, not an affective one. Looking at this issue again will allow us to rephrase the self-sufficiency of computation in relation to another issue that has to be considered: that of the *finality* of the computational procedure.

This argument can be introduced by emphasising first of all that, by considering computation as eventual, we are developing the speculative hypothesis of a *computation that experiences*. The inductivism of unconventional, natural, and non-classical computing is intended to bring forth the empirical dimension of computational procedures. However, since unconventional, natural, and non-classical computing conflates the contingent with the empirical and the actual with the factual, it is ultimately incapable of addressing computation's *own* experience ontologically. Implicitly following an early modern empiricist tradition, unconventional, natural, and non-classical computing considers experience in terms of sensory responsiveness. By contrast, the speculative manoeuvre that I believe should be carried out involves removing the investigation of experience from sense-data empiricism and understanding the meaning of experience as, I argue, Whitehead did: as self-actualisation. Theorising the eventuality of computation in connection to its becoming allows us to understand experience precisely in these terms, for a process can be conceptualised both in terms of what describes computation's experience and in terms of computation's self-actualisation. The Whiteheadian internal activity of becoming, therefore, presents the possibility of a computation that experiences insofar as this computation is a process of determination that will never be ontologically repeated in exactly the same way.

For Whitehead, actual occasions are 'drops of experience',[36] and an act of experience is an act of constructing reality. If experience is a process, and if that process is the actual event that objectifies the real and makes it transmissible, then experience corresponds to an ontological operation of synthesis of a given multiplicity into the actual occasion's *unity*. To experience is to self-constitute oneself as a new actuality in the world via the unification of many data from the standpoint of a subject that defines this unifying perspective. In this sense, 'apart from the experience of subjects there is nothing, nothing, nothing, bare nothingness'.[37] The subject, however, does not precede the unification of data: it also constitutes itself through it. Drawing on this Whiteheadian characterisation of experience, a computational process that experiences can be described as a computational process that is *concrete* and *concrescent*. This claim pertains to this book's central proposition that aesthetics constitutes a viable means of investigating computational systems. My contention is this: it is precisely because there is contingency (that is to say, indeterminacy and eventuality) within computation that one can think and speak of computation's experience. Moreover, since it is possible to conceptualise a computation that experiences, it is also possible to reconsider the significance of an aesthetic enquiry of computational systems.

In making these claims, I am continuing the ontological characterisation of aesthetics introduced by Deleuze, for whom aesthetics is an investigation into the conditions of real experience. From a Deleuzian perspective, this point is straightforward: experience is an unmediated immersion into the being of the sensible, and aesthetics is the science of sensation that addresses this immersion. Aesthetics, it follows, constitutes a privileged means of accessing experience and its ontological conditions. These are conditions that, for Deleuze, correspond to the virtual becoming of what is lived, and which are thus to be felt rather than cognised. This is worth repeating: according to this Deleuzian perspective, anything that separates us from affect and sensation (such as, for example, abstractive techniques like computing) not only stops experience but is also outside of what counts as experiencing altogether. Whitehead's proposition concerning this issue is quite different from that of Deleuze. For Whitehead, abstraction is not what blocks experience but what makes it possible. This reflection is of particular utility to my attempt to establish a novel aesthetics of the logical procedures of computation, because it offers a way to understand formal abstraction as central to the constitution of computation's own experience. In a Deleuzian spirit, this aesthetics would then look for computation's conditions of real experience. However, in contrast to that of Deleuze, this aesthetics would not limit these conditions to the transcendental infinite qualitative transformation of the real expressed through sensation, but would instead extend them so as to also encompass the logico-quantitative specificity of computation.

The positions that have been developed so far should allow us to offer responses to, and to perhaps fully overcome, two perspectives. The first one still concerns computational empiricism. The associationism that subtends the latter, I argued, understands computational procedures in terms of bare factuality and designates this bare factuality as the presentational objectifications of an external datum of perception. In the context of the present discussion, I would argue that computational empiricism is also problematic, for it characterises computation as a record of factuality with no conceptual capacity of its own: *a fact with no thought*. In the emergentist ontology of computational empiricism, there is no recognition of computation's conceptual activity qua its abstractive capacity, but only the dull repetition of what computing systems have sensed. Since it cannot think the relation between abstraction and experience beyond association, computational empiricism does not allow the speculative manoeuvre that I have proposed here: that of extending computation's conditions of experience (and therefore those of aesthetics) to include, in Whiteheadian terms, a physical and a mental pole, thereby allowing two levels of determination.

Deleuze could not agree with associationism due to its lack of an internal principle of connection. In this respect, it is possible to speculate that Deleuze would not have philosophically endorsed bare factuality either, inasmuch as he always defended the role that the abstract plays within experience. Because of his commitment to the lived metaphysical dynamics of the real, Deleuze would not have agreed with sense-empiricist depictions of reality as a collection of facts with no thought. These comments relate to my previous consideration of Deleuze's advocacy of the abstractness of thought, and to his attendant rejection of any representational image of such thought (see chapter 2). Arguably, this Deleuzian enthusiasm for abstract thought successfully disputes the early modern empiricist removal of a dimension of ideality from reality. Overall, this Deleuzian position thus offers a means to effectively conceive experience beyond a collection of Humean facts. Yet my point is that Deleuze's view is problematic too. In fact, it constitutes the second position that should be surpassed if one is to consider computation's logico-quantitative specificity as key to the constitution of computation's own experience.

First of all, for Deleuze, thought and sensation are immanent to each other. Such a Deleuzian position raises a difficulty in the context of the aesthetic investigation of computational systems, since if we retain this immanence, we risk flattening out the logico-quantitative specificity of computation onto an affective and continuous plane of virtual transformation. Ultimately, this flattening out results in the impossibility of establishing a successful relation between the aesthetic and the logical, and in the consequent impossibility of establishing a computational aesthetics that would fully engage with computation's formal and axiomatic character. Because of his commitment to the univocity of being, Deleuze did not ontologically differentiate thought from process. For Deleuze, thought is less an elaboration of process than an unmediated expression of what is felt in and through the becoming of the real. Thought is an expression of those unactualised virtual forces of becoming that spread themselves among all matter. On this view, thought is *flux*. Or, to say this in the terminology developed in this book, thought is abstract, yet not abstractive. I see this to be a problem because to attend to the logico-quantitative specificity of computation (and to consider this specificity as crucial to computation's self-actualisation) involves admitting that the dynamism of the computational procedure cannot correspond to the infinite field of continuous qualitative transformation of Deleuze's virtuality. Formal abstraction in computation is, above all, *structure*. It does not dislocate and deterritorialise. Rather, it orders and organises, and it does so through formalisation-as-discretisation.

Whitehead's reflections on what he called 'forms of process' must now be introduced. A *form of process* is 'the final mode of unity in virtue of which there exists stability of aim amid the multiple forms of potentiality, and in virtue of which there exists importance beyond the finite importance for the finite actuality'.[38] A form of process describes the organisation of data in the world. For Whitehead, in every actualisation—that is to say, in every process—a form is created. This form qua structure is not an a priori transcendent and regulative blueprint, nor is it an a posteriori accumulation of empirical individuations. This form or structure of actualisation is instead specific to the process itself, and an essential vehicle for past actuality and ideality alike to become constitutive of new actualities in the world. Because the Whiteheadian ontological schema that I am drawing from involves such a final mode of unity, the internal adventure of becoming of computational actual occasions cannot be equated to empirical individuations or transcendent representations. In addition, it is not comparable to Deleuze's understanding of becoming either. The dynamism that I am theorising is a process geared towards the realisation of a final state. This becoming does not exclude *permanence*, for it is the becoming of discrete occasions that, each conceived as a unity, are finite, fulfilled, and express a completed transformation. This becoming therefore ends with a moment of fixity. The form of the process is indeed such a moment, when the occasion's full potential for realisation has been depleted.

A direct reference to Whitehead might help again here. Whitehead believed that 'there is a becoming of continuity, but no continuity of becoming'.[39] While for Deleuze the conclusion of becoming is an illusion, and events remain in part unactualised (and by consequence, always fundamentally virtual), for Whitehead, a terminus is inevitable. Events are actual precisely because they do not endure indeterminately. Every actual occasion, conceived as a fundamental unit of reality, begins, actualises itself, and then perishes. Upon its actualisation, an actual occasion ends, and it is then objectified for future actual occasions as the datum of their respective prehensions. A concrescence is effectively concluded with the actual occasion becoming the datum for other actualisations. Upon perishing, the actual occasion develops into the data for future prehensions, future concrescences, and future actual occasions: a Whiteheadian process ends when it has unified, and thus concretised, multiplicity, when 'the universe of many things acquires an individual unity'.[40]

I want to argue that something similar to this 'perpetual perishing', as Whitehead called it,[41] is proper to computational processes too. By ordering data, computational actual occasions are leaning towards the unity of a resolution. This unity is the achievement of a final determination, the accomplishment of an internal dynamic. This is true of algorithmic procedures in general, but it is also very evident in this chapter's example of genetic algorithms, for the rationale of the genetic algorithmic procedure exhausts itself when an optimal result is reached. The processing of a genetic algorithm, like the process of other computational actual occasions, is a dynamism that tends towards an *end*—where end here denotes both a *completion* and an *aim*. Completion is precisely the aim of such a dynamism. In this sense, a computational process, like an actual occasion, 'never really is'.[42] It comes into being to perish, and hence to be replaced by new computational actualities. It is only with its birth, which always subsequently involves its death, that something new is possible: every computational self-actualisation is an addition of a new computational reality. Computational processing can be understood, therefore, in the Whiteheadian terms of the becoming of continuity, and thus differently from any Deleuzian continuity of becoming. Following Whitehead's characterisation of an actual occasion, computational self-actualisation is, in turn, to be understood as geared towards an attainment.

These comments are important speculative considerations as to how computation might be said to actualise itself. The suggested complementarity of the notions of completion and aim should now be addressed in connection to the statement that everything in computation's formal axiomatic systems is preprogrammed. Since an algorithmic procedure is, by definition, geared towards the fulfilment of a task, the approaching of an end is not opposed to its preprogramming but engendered by it. I do not understand this, however, to be a circumstance that limits computation's capacity for self-actualisation. Quite the opposite: precisely because of this somewhat teleological aspect of the computational function, the popular denunciation of the generative limits of this preprogramming becomes invalid, or it ceases to be relevant. Effectively, by understanding a computational procedure as an actual process of determination geared towards an end, I am assigning to it the responsibility of its own self-actualisation, and thus of its own generation. 'It is to be noted', Whitehead wrote, 'that every actual entity . . . is something individual for its own sake'.[43] Every actual occasion is self-creative: 'at once the product of the efficient past, and also, in Spinoza's phrase, *causa sui*'.[44] If computational processes are to be understood as actual occasions, as I claim them to be, then one should grant them not only causal efficacy, but also the same additional capacity for *self-causation*. Attending to this capacity for self-causation serves to foreground computation's self-sufficiency (i.e., the fact that computation needs nothing but itself in order to reach determination), and also to account for the central role that computation's inherent indeterminacy plays in such self-sufficiency. In other words, it affords a means to develop the proposed notion of contingent computation.

For Whitehead, every occasion is its own reason for being what it is, and this attests to the self-sufficiency of actuality in his ontological schema. Yet, despite its chronological primacy, causal efficacy is unable to fully account for the production of ontological novelty. Causal objectification is the affective basis from which experience (and, consequently, new actuality) arises. However, causal efficacy cannot bring processes of determination to conclusion. In order to achieve what Whitehead called *satisfaction*, an actual occasion needs to exhibit another type of causality: a *final cause*, expressed by a *subjective aim*, which directs the actual occasion's capacity for self-causation, and which is incorporated in every step of the occasion's determination. This subjective aim is the cause for the unity of the concrescence; it is also what guides the attainment of such a unity. It introduces 'a novelty of definiteness not to be found in the inherited data of [the concrescence's] primary phase', and thus accounts for what is 'inexplicable by any tradition of pure physical inheritance'.[45] The final cause is an appetite for completion that complements causal efficacy's chains of succession, so as to make the occasion a truly new actuality in the world, beyond its inherited elements. The final cause shows that, in order to fulfil its attainment, the actual occasion must not only select among the actual data inherited from past occasions, but also from the discrete multiplicity of eternal objects, which, as already explained, stand as the pure potentialities that inform the coming into existence of the actual occasion via the latter's conceptual prehensions. The finality of the occasion then indicates that genuine novelty arises only with the additional determination, further to sensibility, of conceptual functioning. Only with the ingression of the pure potentiality of eternal objects does the real potentiality of the actual occasion fully deplete itself. The objectification can then conclude in a 'final mode of unity'.[46] Here, then, is the second determination that we should be looking for: to every physical objectification there corresponds a conceptual eventuation of an ideal, thanks to which actuality truly becomes.

But what about computational actual occasions? Whitehead's argument for the purposive and creative character of reality affords a new consideration of the conditions under which ontological novelty might be produced in computation. I indicated earlier that the self-sufficiency of computation can be read in terms of computational systems' capacity for self-causation. Expanding on this claim, I now want to stress the role that finality might play in computation too. The computational actual occasion has a fundamental purpose, and this purpose corresponds to its self-realisation. In Whitehead's philosophy, final causality explains how an actual occasion could be a novel-

ty beyond its inherited elements, showing that 'even the physical world cannot be properly understood without reference to its other side, which is the
complex of mental operations'.[47] Insofar as finality is what directs the concrescent process, this finality also shows how a 'mental pole' that would
grasp such an ideal is fundamental for actuality's capacity for innovation,
and thus for what Whitehead called the 'ultimate freedom of things'.[48] That
is to say, 'the definition of each *res vera* as *causa sui*'.[49] Following on from
this point, it can be commented that, in order to argue for the purposive
character of computation, one has to make the case for the relevance of
computation's conceptual functioning, or, to put this otherwise, for the
weight that conceptual prehensions would have in computation's own realisation. What should be established, then, is whether computation's internal
adventure of becoming accounts not only for the indeterminacy of actual
data, but also for an indeterminacy that corresponds to the evaluation of a
pure possibility, or of what, in a Whiteheadian sense, could be called 'eternal
data'.

I have, however, already proved this. The fact that computation is not just
a physical manipulation of data is demonstrated by the presence, in every
algorithmic procedure, of the incomputable. The notion of incomputability
should be brought to the fore again here in order to consider that, just as
actual occasions conceptually prehend the ideality of eternal objects, so too
do computational actual occasions logically address the ideality of quantitative infinity. This quantitative infinity stands as the indeterminacy that is
inherent to computational logos, and it thus requires a logical (and not affective) mode of relation. Not a physical prehension then, but a conceptual one.
It is only because computation is an abstractive structure, or indeed because
it constructs a matrix of discrete yet infinite points, that it comes to address
logically—in fact, in Whiteheadian terms, to prehend conceptually—the unknown in each and every process. Just as actual occasions must conceptually
confront the unknown, or the pure possibility, of eternal objects, so too must
computational procedures logically confront the unknown, or the pure possibility, of incomputable quantities.

This contention brings us back to a claim that I have already advanced in
chapter 6: the condition of existence of computational procedures cannot be
detached from their inherent internal indeterminacy. However, we can now
add to that earlier claim by noting that a computational process is something
that happens, and truly becomes, only because of its inherent indeterminacy.
In other words, in order to be actual, computation must be contingent. To put
this in Whiteheadian terms once more, the real potentiality of computation
must always consider the pure potentiality that the incomputable stands for.
The propagative and generative character of the computational method is
expressed in the self-actualisation of computational actual occasions. This
self-actualisation unifies components that are inherited from other computa-

tional actual occasions. However, the self-actualisation is never concluded without the ingression of the pure indeterminacy of incomputable quantities. Again, to use Whitehead's terms: computation's conceptual prehensions of these incomputable quantities (or of these eternal data) should be considered as a constitutive part of the realisation of the computational procedure, just as its physical prehensions are.

Admittedly, these speculative propositions may seem to contradict Turing's characterisation of incomputability. It could be said that Turing understood incomputability as an inconvenience: as something that prevents us from clearly assessing which inputs will lead to an output, and which will not. In this sense, the incomputable makes it impossible to determine a priori if a computation will conclude. Turing's own theorisation of incomputability might thus be said to contradict my argument that it is precisely in virtue of the incomputable that a computational process reaches its 'final mode of unity'.[50] In this respect, I would acknowledge here that, certainly, my claims push incomputability in directions that differ from those implied by Turing's original conceptualisation of this notion. I believe, however, that this speculative operation is legitimate, because what I argue to be completion in computation does not correspond to the outputting of a calculatory solution (that is, to what Turing was looking for), but rather to the ontological production of a new computational actuality. While for Turing the finitude of the computational procedure (that is, the fact that it has inherent limits) means that this procedure only repeats what it has already been preprogrammed to do, from my perspective the same finitude opens up the procedure to the pure potentiality of infinite incomputable quantities. The distinctive logical relation (that is, conceptual prehension) that the procedure establishes with these infinite incomputable quantities endows the computational actual occasion with its uniqueness and purpose.

The incomputable is thus a crucial requirement for the computational process to be a form of process, and for this computational process to express logically (or, in Whiteheadian terms, *conceptually*) a form for realisation. In this sense, we could imagine each computational actual occasion to take a determinate stance in front of its internal indeterminacy. The finality of this computational actual occasion is carried out by a formal relation with an original ideal of completion, an ideal that is specific and unique to that particular computational actual occasion. The computational procedure, as a form of process, is a mode of unity of data and prehensions. Its structure of actualisation is not given a priori, yet it is not recounted a posteriori either. Rather, this form of actualisation is inherent to the actual event of the computational occasion. The logico-quantitative character of computational systems brings about a further level of determination of the computational procedure, and this further level of determination shows how computational occasions are realised both on a sensible and an intelligible plane. Along with affective capacities, this logico-quantitative character is thus key to computation's self-actualisation, and thereby to computation's own experience. Because of its centrality to computation's own experience, it becomes an unavoidable object of study for computational aesthetics, which, this book has argued, is an investigation into the ontological conditions of computation itself.

NOTES

1. Alfred North Whitehead, *Process and Reality: An Essay in Cosmology* (New York: Free Press, 1978), 157.
2. Whitehead, *Process and Reality*, 157.
3. Alfred North Whitehead, *Symbolism: Its Meaning and Effect* (New York: Fordham University Press, 1985), 43.
4. Whitehead, *Symbolism*, 31.
5. Whitehead, *Symbolism*, 37.
6. For Whitehead, human cognitive faculties integrate causal efficacy and presentational immediacy in what he called *symbolic reference*. Failing to acknowledge this would have weakened the account of Whitehead's theory of perception presented in the chapter. However, as the notion of symbolic reference does not add any essential element to the point that I want to make, I will not treat it further.
7. Whitehead, *Symbolism*, 47.
8. Whitehead, *Process and Reality*, 18.
9. 'The Monads have no windows, through which anything could come in or go out.' Gottfried Wilhelm Leibniz, *The Monadology, and Other Philosophical Writings*, trans. Robert Latta (Oxford: Oxford University Press, 1925), 219.
10. Whitehead, *Process and Reality*, 80.
11. Alfred North Whitehead, *Science and the Modern World* (New York: Free Press, 1967), 70.
12. Whitehead, *Process and Reality*, 236.
13. Whitehead, *Process and Reality*, 221.
14. Alfred North Whitehead, *Adventures of Ideas* (New York: Free Press, 1967), 176.
15. An actual occasion prehends much more than it feels. To account for this surplus, Whitehead distinguished between *positive prehensions* (occurring when data ingress and partake of the constitution of the actual occasion) and *negative prehensions* (which instead regard incompatible data, prehended by the actual occasion but then excluded from the latter's internal constitution).
16. Whitehead, *Symbolism*, 35.
17. Whitehead, *Process and Reality*, 210.
18. Whitehead, *Process and Reality*, 25.
19. Whitehead, *Process and Reality*, 21.
20. Alfred North Whitehead, *Modes of Thought* (New York: Free Press, 1968), 151.
21. Whitehead, *Process and Reality*, 21.
22. Whitehead wrote that 'indetermination, rendered determinate in the real concrescence, is the meaning of "potentiality"'. *Process and Reality*, 23. In his philosophy, Deleuze addressed the movement from indeterminacy to determination in terms of *individuation*, and according to the processes of *differentiation* and *differenciation*. See *Difference and Repetition*, trans. Paul Patton (London: Continuum, 2004).
23. Whitehead, *Process and Reality*, 87.
24. Whitehead, *Science and the Modern World*, 107.
25. Whitehead, *Process and Reality*, 80.
26. Whitehead, *Adventures of Ideas*, 191.
27. Brian Massumi, *Semblance and Event: Activist Philosophy and the Occurent Arts* (Cambridge, MA: MIT Press, 2011), 6.

28. Massumi, *Semblance and Event*, 8.
29. Whitehead, *Process and Reality*, 222.
30. Whitehead, *Symbolism*, 36.
31. Whitehead, *Process and Reality*, 340.
32. Whitehead, *Process and Reality*, 65.
33. Whitehead, *Process and Reality*, 45.
34. Whitehead, *Process and Reality*, 239.
35. Whitehead, *Process and Reality*, 47.
36. Whitehead, *Process and Reality*, 18.
37. Whitehead, *Process and Reality*, 167.
38. Whitehead, *Modes of Thought*, 86.
39. Whitehead, *Process and Reality*, 35.
40. Whitehead, *Process and Reality*, 211.
41. Whitehead, *Process and Reality*, 29.
42. Whitehead, *Process and Reality*, 85.
43. Whitehead, *Process and Reality*, 88.
44. Whitehead, *Process and Reality*, 150.
45. Whitehead, *Process and Reality*, 104.
46. Whitehead, *Modes of Thought*, 86.
47. Whitehead, *Process and Reality*, 239.
48. Whitehead, *Process and Reality*, 47.
49. Isabelle Stengers, 'Speculative Philosophy and the Art of Dramatization', in *The Allure of Things: Process and Object in Contemporary Philosophy*, ed. Roland Faber and Andrew Goffey (London: Bloomsbury Academic, 2014), 209.
50. Whitehead, *Modes of Thought*, 86.

Conclusion

Computational Actual Occasions

This book has engaged with, and has endeavoured to answer, the following question: is aesthetics a viable mode of investigating contemporary computational systems? I hope that I have succeeded in replying in the affirmative and that I have proved that computation can indeed be addressed in aesthetic terms. The computational aesthetics that I have advanced may, however, appear to be a rather unusual aesthetic proposition. It does not concern art made by or with computers, or artistic categories in general, but rather pertains to the modes of being and becoming of computational processes. The computational aesthetics that I have proposed is, in essence, a philosophical study of what computation is and does.

In developing this study, I have drawn on Gilles Deleuze's call for an aesthetic ontology (or an ontological aesthetics) that would be concerned with the production of the real. I argued, however, that Deleuze excluded abstractive techniques such as computation from this ontological production and restricted all generative potential to what he called 'the being of the sensible'. Since it is a science of sensation—and of the thought that is immanent to it—aesthetics is, for Deleuze, the privileged entry point to the metaphysical dynamic that this being of the sensible expresses. In discussing this, I showed that such a Deleuzian perspective renders it difficult to consider computation aesthetically. This book has responded to that difficulty and has offered a theoretical view that is intended to resolve it. I have thus claimed that, while addressing computation in aesthetics terms involves agreeing with Deleuze's reworking of the scope of aesthetic investigations, it also involves departing from Deleuze's argument for the ontological superiority of sensation.

The following contention has been central to this work: in order to successfully establish an aesthetics of computation, we should extend the field
of aesthetic enquiry from the sensible to the intelligible. That is, aesthetics
should be extended from the plane of sensuous reception and qualitative
transformation to that of the logico-quantitative operations of computation. I
do not deny that the sensible is important. When it comes to considering what
computation is and does, however, I believe that sensibility is not enough.
Computation is a method of systematising reality through logico-quantitative
means. An aesthetics of computational systems should account for this specificity. I have hence proposed that addressing computation in onto-aesthetic
terms involves considering whether the logico-quantitative character of computation could also engender ontological production. If this book's aesthetic
ontology (or ontological aesthetics) of computation is perhaps unusual—
even when compared to other aesthetic ontologies of computational systems
that are possible, but which would be more invested in materialism than my
own—then its unusual nature is due to that proposition.

Throughout this study, I have searched for an aesthetics of the computational process: not an aesthetics of the uses or the outcomes of computation,
but an aesthetics of the formal axiomatic system, of the logical function, of
the algorithmic procedure. I have engaged, therefore, with the creative potential that belongs to computational procedures, prior to any coupling of computation with a biological substratum, a human referent, a body, or indeed
with society and culture at large. Such couplings would qualitatively translate the abstractions and discretisations of computation, thereby missing or
sidestepping its logico-quantitative specificity. My aim was instead to offer a
theoretical view that would afford a move beyond the supposed incompatibility of logic and aesthetics as two opposing ways of relating to and structuring
the world. From a Deleuzian perspective, the logico-quantitative character of
computation is excluded from aesthetics because its discrete and discretising
nature blocks the metaphysical dynamic of the real. Against this view, I have
demonstrated that computation is in a condition of becoming, but that this
becoming does not correspond to a virtual plane of continuous differentiation. Rather, it corresponds to discrete processes of determination, and it is
engendered by the quantitative (and not qualitative) infinity that ingresses
each and every one of these processes. Crucially, I claimed that there can be
ontological production in computation, not despite computation's actual operations of abstractive discretisation, but rather because of them. This ontological production corresponds to computation's self-actualisation.

In order to propose an aesthetics of the computational procedure, I had to
take computational systems for what they are: formal axiomatic systems. I
engaged, then, with the logico-mathematical inception of the theory of computability that phrased the computational method in these formal and axiomatic terms. In doing so, I uncovered something unexpected: indeterminacy

dwells at the logical heart of computation. This book has recounted my effort to theorise this indeterminacy vis-à-vis what I have argued to be the self-sufficiency of computational axiomatics. I showed that this indeterminacy is not modelled upon empirical individualities and that it does not correspond to the virtual intensities of that which is lived. Instead, this indeterminacy is specific to the formal axiomatic procedures of computation and to the functional and ontological autonomy of the latter. The book's novel reading of the onto-aesthetic significance of Gödel's incompleteness theorems and of Turing's notion of incomputability has been key to this theorisation, and it is central to my contention that indeterminacy indicates computation's potential for self-actualisation. Because I have theorised how indeterminacy dwells at the heart of computational logic, and because I have introduced the concept of contingent computation, it has been possible for me to propose an aesthetic ontology of computational procedures in their logico-quantitative specificity. The kind of aesthetic account of computation that I have advanced follows from my central contention that computation is inherently and intrinsically indeterminate. My theorisation of computation as contingent thereby afforded the primary speculative thesis of this study, which concerns the possibility of addressing computational procedures in the Whiteheadian terms of actual occasions.

Whitehead's actual occasions are processes of self-determination that are always ingressed by indeterminacy. This self-determination corresponds to the occasion's self-actualisation, which is carried out both at the level of the sensible and at the level of the intelligible. For Whitehead, actual occasions involve both physical and conceptual operations, which convey distinct yet related ontological determinations. Most significantly, these operations are aesthetic, because they are not representational mediations or cognitivist reductions, but prehensions. They are actuality's grasping, seizing, or holding of other actualities (in physical prehensions), as well as of idealities (in conceptual prehensions). By considering computational procedures in terms of actual occasions, I assigned to them this same self-actualising capacity and prehensive disposition. I proposed that computational actual occasions determine themselves via the physical manipulation of data (that is, physically prehending other computational actualities), but also because they address logically—and not affectively—their own indeterminacy (which means they conceptually prehend the logical indeterminacy that Turing's incomputable stands for). By drawing on Whitehead's ontological schema, I developed a theoretical framework that has allowed me to extend the aesthetic investigation of computation from the sensible to the intelligible, and to understand these two dimensions as related and consequent, yet not immanent to each other. I thereby argued for a computational aesthetics at two levels, which corresponds to the way in which the self-determination of computational actuality also operates at two levels.

The issues addressed in this book cannot be contained within either the Deleuzian or the Whiteheadian philosophical projects. With this study, I intended to offer an original response to some of the theoretical challenges that contemporary debates about computational aesthetics are confronted with. While Deleuze has set the ground for some of the ways in which I responded to these challenges, Whitehead has allowed me to develop my propositions in directions that Deleuze could not provide. The questions that I have engaged with, however, cannot be considered to be concluded by simply choosing one proposition over another. That is why, in order to conceptualise the computational actual occasion, I had to enter the disciplinary domains of many diverse branches of knowledge and consider a variety of positions that do not ostensibly fit together. Likewise, I did not focus on a particular field in which the computational method is applied; rather, I took computation itself as this book's own field of investigation. I have thus studied what I considered to be the key to an exploration of the proposed notion of contingent computation, and to the subsequent development and deepening of the means of theorising it vis-à-vis the establishment of a computational aesthetics. In doing so, I have been unconcerned with restrictions as to where one discipline ends and another begins, and I have followed my hypotheses wherever they would lead me. In this sense, while I hope that this book will serve as a contribution to cultural and media theory, it remains primarily philosophical in both scope and intention. It has proposed that we should approach computation as a method of abstraction: a method that is inscribed in the history of thought, and which stands as a fundamental problem relating to questions about reality and knowledge. The enquiry into what computation is and does has been inserted into debates pertaining to explicitly philosophical issues, such as, for instance, those concerning the relation between being and thought, finitude and infinity, the rational and the empirical, and the ideal and the material. In accordance with what can be discussed as the true rationale of philosophical work, these problems have been not so much resolved as elaborated.[1] The system that I proposed might be seen to reflect this ambition of producing new philosophical knowledge, and so too does the fact that this study, in order to generate such knowledge, had to be an exercise in speculation. Phrasing this speculation as an aesthetic enquiry has allowed me to develop what I hope has served as a consistent and engaging framework upon which one can address issues that pertain to aesthetics, but which are not limited to it.

Some of the most prominent issues that one could thus address are questions concerning the onto-aesthetic significance of abstraction and experience, which came to the fore during the course of this study. I argued that in order to be able to advance an aesthetics of contingent computation, we must reconsider what abstraction and experience are in and for computation. On this point, the disparity between Deleuze and Whitehead—and why I had to use the latter as a means of advancing beyond the former—is most evident. For Deleuze, abstraction is an epistemic enframing that hinders and burdens experience, while for Whitehead, by contrast, abstraction is a method of construction that makes past actuality and ideality alike constitutive elements of experience. This is because what accounts for real and unmediated experience is also different for the two philosophers: for Deleuze, it is a movement away from determination; for Whitehead, it is a movement towards it. Therefore, in this respect too, Whitehead offered a view that would suit this book's rationale, and which afforded one of its key intentions: that of considering formal abstraction as central to computation's own ontological production. My aim to establish a computational aesthetics that would not reduce the logico-quantitative character of computation to an affective plane has to be read in conjunction with its attendant goal of offering an account of computational formalism beyond the representational role that has traditionally been assigned to it. It is useful here to point out, once again, that a Deleuze-inspired aesthetic response to the representational character that is embedded within computing would be resolved by prioritising what cannot be represented—namely, the intensive force of sensation, and those affective capacities that bring computational systems as close as possible to fluid states of matter and life. This book, however, has tried to turn the onto-aesthetic response to what I described as the crisis of formalism towards a different direction: a direction concerning the possibility of challenging computational formalism without disposing of the abstractions and discretisations that are specific to it. To this end, I assigned a pivotal ontological role in the production of new computational actuality to computation's formal capacity to abstract and discretise. I did so by advancing the notion of contingent computation and by thus placing in centre stage the unknown that is beyond representation, but which is still within computational logos.

For this reason, I had to confront the same logico-mathematical tradition from which a contemporary version of metacomputation (i.e., the belief that rational calculation can a priori represent, and thus explain, every element of reality) emerged. I have, however, drawn very different conclusions from that tradition. Against the metacomputational view, I have shown that computation's abstractive discretisations are not reductions of sensibility's complexities to the simplicity of preformed representations of intelligibility. These abstractive discretisations are, on the contrary, means of expanding and complexifying computation's actuality, and of opening up the computational procedure towards its own concrete inexhaustibility. By virtue of the open-ended character of axiomatics theorised in this book, computation's abstractive discretisations can be seen as crucial to the self-actualisation of the computational procedure. It is only because quantitative infinity ingresses the computational process by means of formal abstraction that computation realises its own self-determination. Or, in other words, the indeterminacy of computation makes its determination possible. In this sense, computation's abstractive discretisations are constitutive of computation's own experience—provided, drawing on Whitehead, that we understand 'to experience' as 'to actualise oneself'.

I followed Deleuze in considering aesthetics to be an investigation into the conditions of real experience. However, I also departed from Deleuze, in order to argue that these conditions are not predicated uniquely on sensibility. Equally, the meaning that I assigned to experience, through drawing on Whitehead, differs from that of Deleuze. This is because I did not assign any existential connotation to it that would implicitly make us favour a metaphysical dimension of the lived. My hypothesis of a computation that experiences has been theorised by drawing on the Whiteheadian characterisation of experiencing as self-actualisation. A computational procedure that experiences is thus a procedure that is concrete but also concrescent. That means it is a spatiotemporal process that begins and then perishes, and which results from the eventuation of an actual structure and an actual unification of multiplicity. Rather than a Deleuzian subtraction from determination, computation's own experience corresponds instead to the objectification of both actual data and idealities, and thereby to the self-determination of an atomic yet processual entity such as the computational actual occasion.

These speculative propositions have prompted what I hope might stand as a significant reconsideration of the preprogrammed character of computation. I have tried to build this reconsideration gradually, through this book's engagement with the approaches to computation that I named 'computational idealism' and 'computational empiricism'. I have also argued that it is possible to find, within the preprogrammed operations of computational processing, a peculiar dynamism. This dynamism is internal to the deductive constraints of the computational formal axiomatic system, and it indicates the generative potential of such a system. It is not a virtual movement, but the most fundamental character of the actuality of computation. Similarly, since this dynamism pertains to discrete processes, it is not akin to a continuous flow of differential transformation either. This dynamism, however, is neither based on a priori representations, nor is it modelled a posteriori upon empirical variation. My critical discussion of both idealist and empiricist approaches to computation has addressed these issues. On the one hand, the critique of computational idealism has targeted an idealist aesthetics, oriented towards Platonism, and it has exposed the problems implicit in considering computational structures as immutable, regulative, transcendent deductive forms with no process. On the other hand, by highlighting the shortcomings of what I described as computational empiricism, I showed what happens, at a conceptual level, when the processuality of computation is taken to simulate empirical individualities, or when it is considered solely in terms of its bare factuality. I have suggested that, because of its implied Humean externality between thought and sense-data, a sense-empiricist position misses the 'internal adventure of becoming', to use Whitehead's expression, of computation, and thus cannot provide us with the kind of ontological aesthetics of computation that this book has sought. By contrast, the dynamism that I have theorised is characterised by the computational process fulfilling its own finality: that of being a procedure of determination, possessed of an internal adventure of becoming that consists in coming into existence. In this sense, computational actual occasions are finite processes of actualisation that always tend towards producing themselves. This self-production is their end, where 'end' stands as both their aim and their completion. In my view, instead of discarding preprogramming as a constraint on computing, the onto-aesthetic investigation of computation should be concerned with conceptualising how the computational process has an internal potential for self-actualisation precisely by virtue of the fact that it does what it is supposed to do.

My point is thus that the contingency of computation does not contradict the functionality of computation. Quite the opposite: it is this contingency that makes computation work, albeit in a manner that might not always fit with the instrumental purposes and the metacomputational agenda that we have assigned to computing. It is important to stress here, once again, that the preprogrammed processes of computation do not have to deviate from formal logic in order to be contingent. They are already indeterminate simply by virtue of their own logico-quantitative character. This is because the formal axiomatic method upon which this character is predicated is similarly indeterminate. The strength of computation's dynamism is thus encapsulated in my proposed engagement with that unique relation between contingency and self-sufficiency in computation. What I have depicted is possibly a cold world, in which there are no people and no intermediary states of enaction to reconcile an informational and quantitative dimension with the energetic and the qualitative. This depiction was deliberate and, in fact, necessary. Addressing this cold world of computational logic was an indispensable operation in order to detach the aesthetic investigation of computation from ontologies of lived experience, which would prioritise the continuity of affect and sensation over formal and formalised determinations. However, I have by no means intended to deny that there are both uses and users of the computational. Certainly, computational processes are part of the fabric of contemporary society, economy, and culture. My point is that we can more effectively understand computation's role in constructing this fabric if we allow for the study of computation's very own and very specific contingent ontology. It will be necessary, in future work, to develop the theorisation of computation's contingent ontology in relation to the investigation of social, cultural, and economic relations that act upon—or are acted upon by—computation's indeterminacy and eventuality. That is to say, it will be necessary to open up the following question: how do we live with contingent computation? As is perhaps now apparent, such an enquiry can only be conducted on the basis of a foundational ontological work such as that advanced within this book.

The claims that have been presented throughout the preceding chapters are not intended to offer an apology for computational regimes of instrumental rationality. On the contrary, they have sought to advance a radical reworking of the manner in which it is possible to understand the involvement of contemporary automated systems of calculation with the intelligible. What is at stake here, therefore, is the possibility of addressing the 'conceptual capacity' of computational systems, a possibility to consider that capacity beyond the critique of the instrumental, and also beyond the attendant reduction of computation's logico-quantitative specificity to a cognitivist mirroring exercise or (to use a final Deleuzian phrase) an 'image of thought'. This intellectual task requires a study of discrete yet dynamic forms of automated thought and experience, coupled to the development of a theory that would directly consider the ontological conditions and epistemological implications of such modes of thought and experience. The notion of contingent computation is then ultimately broader than the onto-aesthetic framework within which this book has developed it. Deleuze has opened up the prospect of resolving the question of what thought is through aesthetics. By drawing on Whitehead's ontological schema, it became possible to radicalise Deleuze's aestheticisation of thought and to thus theorise computation's own conceptual prehensions. Aesthetics has been the speculative means through which I proved that computational abstraction could be addressed beyond the old yet still powerful cognitivism that permeates the field of computing. However, the theorisation of computation's conceptual capacity to prehensively relate with the unknown will have to be developed further. The speculative possibility of discussing a *computational thought* that is contingent, and yet does not break away from structure, will need to engage with the analytic character of computational modes of prediction, evaluation, and decision, and with the ways in which these modes rely on internal and external indeterminacy.

In conclusion, the world of contingent computation might be cold, yet it is also a world that is capable of surprising us. What surprises us is the peculiarity of computational actual occasions. This peculiarity is epitomised by the fact that these processes do not contravene or circumvent preprogramming, but rather actualise themselves through doing exactly what they are supposed to. It is because of this self-determination, however, that computational actual occasions find the freedom to be what they are. The wonder, then, is all ours: it derives from realising that the conditions for novelty in computation are to be found in the actuality of the computational process itself.

NOTE

1. 'In fact, a philosophical theory is an elaborately developed question, and nothing else; by itself and in itself, it is not a resolution to a problem, but the elaboration, *to the very end*, of the necessary implications of a formulated question.' Gilles Deleuze, *Empiricism and Subjectivity: An Essay on Hume's Theory of Human Nature*, trans. Constantin V. Boundas (New York: Columbia University Press, 1991), 106.

Bibliography

Adams, Douglas. *The Hitchhiker's Guide to the Galaxy*. London: Pan, 1979.

Agre, Philip E. *Computation and Human Experience*. Cambridge: Cambridge University Press, 1997.

Alliez, Éric. *The Signature of the World: What Is Deleuze and Guattari's Philosophy?* Translated by Eliot Ross Albert and Alberto Toscano. London: Continuum, 2004.

Badiou, Alain. *Being and Event*. Translated by Oliver Feltham. London: Continuum, 2006.

———. *Deleuze: The Clamor of Being*. Translated by Louise Burchill. Minneapolis: University of Minnesota Press, 2000.

Barker, Timothy Scott. *Time and the Digital: Connecting Technology, Aesthetics, and a Process Philosophy of Time*. Hanover, NH: Dartmouth College Press, 2012.

Baumgarten, Alexander Gottlieb. *Aesthetica*. Hildesheim: G. Olms, 1961.

Bazzichelli, Tatiana. *Networking: The Net as Artwork*. Translated by Maria Anna Calamia and Helen Pringle. Aarhus: Digital Aesthetics Research Centre, Aarhus University, 2009.

Bedau, Mark A., and Paul Humphreys. 'Introduction'. In *Emergence: Contemporary Readings in Philosophy and Science*, edited by Mark A. Bedau and Paul Humphreys, 1–6. Cambridge, MA: MIT Press, 2008.

Benioff, Paul. 'The Computer as a Physical System: A Microscopic Quantum Mechanical Hamiltonian Model of Computers as Represented by Turing Machines'. *Journal of Statistical Physics* 22, no. 5 (May 1980): 563–91. https://doi.org/10.1007/BF01011339.

Bergson, Henri. *The Creative Mind: An Introduction to Metaphysics*. Translated by Mabelle L. Andison. New York: Citadel, 1997.

———. *Matter and Memory*. Translated by Nancy Margaret Paul and W. Scott Palmer. New York: Zone, 1991.

Blanché, Robert. *Axiomatics*. Translated by G. B. Kleene. London: Routledge and Kegan Paul, 1966.

Brooks, Rodney A. 'Intelligence without Representation'. *Artificial Intelligence* 47, nos. 1–3 (January 1991): 139–59. https://doi.org/10.1016/0004-3702(91)90053-M.

Brookshear, J. Glenn. *Computer Science: An Overview*. 7th ed. Boston: Addison-Wesley, 2003.

Cartlidge, Edwin. 'Quantum Computing: A Commercial Reality?' *Physics World*, 2 April 2007. https://physicsworld.com/a/quantum-computing-a-commercial-reality.

Chaitin, Gregory. *Meta Maths: The Quest for Omega*. London: Atlantic, 2005.

Church, Alonzo. 'An Unsolvable Problem of Elementary Number Theory'. *American Journal of Mathematics* 58, no. 2 (April 1936): 345–63. https://doi.org/10.2307/2371045.

Clark, Andy. *Being There: Putting Brain, Body, and World Together Again*. Cambridge, MA: MIT Press, 1997.

Clark, Andy, and David J. Chalmers. 'The Extended Mind'. *Analysis* 58, no. 1 (January 1998): 7–19. https://doi.org/10.1093/analys/58.1.7.

Clark, Tim. 'A Whiteheadian Chaosmos? Process Philosophy from a Deleuzian Perspective'. In *Process and Difference: Between Cosmological and Poststructuralist Postmodernisms*, edited by Catherine Keller and Anne Daniell, 191–207. Albany: State University of New York Press, 2002.

Cloots, André. 'Whitehead and Deleuze: Thinking the Event'. In *Deleuze, Whitehead, Bergson: Rhizomatic Connections*, edited by Keith Robinson, 61–76. Basingstoke: Palgrave Macmillan, 2009.

Clough, Patricia T. 'The Affective Turn: Political Economy, Biomedia, and Bodies'. In *The Affect Theory Reader*, edited by Melissa Gregg and Gregory J. Seigworth. Durham, NC: Duke University Press, 2010.

Clough, Patricia Ticineto, and Jeane Halle, eds. *The Affective Turn: Theorizing the Social*. Durham, NC: Duke University Press, 2007.

Cobham, Alan. 'The Intrinsic Computational Difficulty of Functions'. In *Logic, Methodology, and Philosophy of Science: Proceedings of the 1964 International Congress*, edited by Yehoshua Bar-Hillel, 24–30. Amsterdam: North-Holland, 1965.

Colburn, Timothy. 'Methodology of Computer Science'. In *The Blackwell Guide to the Philosophy of Computing and Information*, edited by Luciano Floridi, 318–26. Oxford: Blackwell, 2004.

Colebrook, Claire. *Blake, Deleuzian Aesthetics, and the Digital*. London: Continuum, 2012.

Cooper, S. Barry. 'Emergence as a Computability-Theoretic Phenomenon'. *Applied Mathematics and Computation* 215, no. 4 (October 2009): 1351–60. https://doi.org/10.1016/j.amc.2009.04.050.

Cramer, Florian. 'Entering the Machine and Leaving It Again: Poetics of Software in Contemporary Art'. 2006. http://www.gwei.org/pages/press/press/Florian_Cramer/fullversion.html.

———. *Words Made Flesh: Code, Culture, Imagination*. Rotterdam: Media Design Research, Piet Zwart Institute, 2005. https://www.netzliteratur.net/cramer/wordsmadefleshpdf.pdf.

Crutchfield, James P. 'The Calculi of Emergence: Computation, Dynamics and Induction'. *Physica D: Nonlinear Phenomena* 75, no. 1–3 (August 1994): 11–54. https://doi.org/10.1016/0167-2789(94)90273-9.

Damasio, Antonio R. *The Feeling of What Happens: Body and Emotion in the Making of Consciousness*. London: W. Heinemann, 2000.

Dantzig, George B. 'Programming in a Linear Structure'. In *The Basic George B. Dantzig*, edited by Richard W. Cottle, 23. Stanford, CA: Stanford University Press, 2003.

Davis, Martin. *Engines of Logic: Mathematicians and the Origin of the Computer*. New York: Norton, 2000.

———. 'Hilbert's Tenth Problem Is Unsolvable'. *American Mathematical Monthly* 80, no. 3 (March 1973): 233–69. https://doi.org/10.2307/2318447.

DeLanda, Manuel. *Philosophy and Simulation: The Emergence of Synthetic Reason*. London: Continuum, 2011.

Deleuze, Gilles. *Bergsonism*. Translated by Hugh Tomlinson and Barbara Habberjam. New York: Zone, 1991.

———. *Cinema I: The Movement-Image*. Translated by Hugh Tomlinson and Barbara Habberjam. London: Continuum, 2005.

———. *Cinema II: The Time-Image*. Translated by Hugh Tomlinson and Robert Galeta. London: Bloomsbury Academic, 2013.

———. 'Control and Becoming'. In *Negotiations, 1972–1990*, translated by Martin Joughin, 169–76. New York: Columbia University Press, 1995.

———. 'Cours Vincennes: Spinoza; 24/01/1978'. Lecture given at the University of Paris 8, Vincennes, France, 24 January 1978. Translated by Timothy S. Murphy. http://www.webdeleuze.com/php/texte.php?cle=14&groupe=Spinoza&langue=2.

———. *Difference and Repetition*. Translated by Paul Patton. London: Continuum, 2004.

———. *Empiricism and Subjectivity: An Essay on Hume's Theory of Human Nature*. Translated by Constantin V. Boundas. New York: Columbia University Press, 1991.

———. *The Fold: Leibniz and the Baroque*. Translated by Tom Conley. London: Continuum, 2006.

———. *Foucault*. Translated by Seán Hand. London: Bloomsbury, 2013.

———. *Francis Bacon: The Logic of Sensation*. Translated by Daniel W. Smith. London: Continuum, 2005.

———. 'Immanence: A Life'. In *Pure Immanence: Essays on a Life*. Translated by Anne Boyman, 25–33. New York: Zone, 2001.

———. *The Logic of Sense*. Edited by Constantin V. Boundas. Translated by Mark Lester with Charles Stivale. London: Continuum, 2004.

———. 'The Method of Dramatization'. In *Desert Islands and Other Texts, 1953–1974*, edited by David Lapoujade, translated by Michael Taormina, 94–116. Los Angeles: Semiotexte, 2004.

———. *Nietzsche and Philosophy*. Translated by Hugh Tomlinson. London: Continuum, 2006.

———. 'On Nietzsche and the Image of Thought'. In *Desert Islands and Other Texts, 1953–1974*, edited by David Lapoujade, translated by Michael Taormina, 135–45. Los Angeles: Semiotexte, 2004.

———. 'On the Time-Image'. In *Negotiations, 1972–1990*. Translated by Martin Joughin, 57–61. New York: Columbia University Press, 1995.

———. 'Postscript on the Societies of Control'. *October* 59 (Winter 1992): 3–7.

———. *Proust and Signs*. Translated by Richard Howard. London: Allen Lane, 1973.

———. *Spinoza: Practical Philosophy*. Translated by Robert Hurley. San Francisco: City Lights, 1988.

Deleuze, Gilles, and Félix Guattari. *A Thousand Plateaus: Capitalism and Schizophrenia*. Translated by Brian Massumi. London: Continuum, 2004.

———. *What Is Philosophy?* Translated by Graham Burchell and Hugh Tomlinson. London: Verso, 1994.

Deleuze, Gilles, and Claire Parnet. *Dialogues II*. Translated by Hugh Tomlinson, Barbara Habberjam, and Eliot Ross Albert. London: Continuum, 2006.

Derrida, Jacques. 'A Certain Impossible Possibility of Saying the Event'. In *The Late Derrida*, edited by W. J. T. Mitchell and Arnold I. Davidson, translated by Gila Walker, 223–43. Chicago: University of Chicago Press, 2007.

Descartes, René. *Meditations on First Philosophy, with Selections from the Objections and Replies*. Edited and translated by John Cottingham. Cambridge: Cambridge University Press, 1986.

Deutsch, David. *The Fabric of Reality*. London: Allen Lane, 1997.

———. 'Quantum Theory, the Church-Turing Principle and the Universal Quantum Computer'. *Proceedings of the Royal Society of London A* 400, no. 1818 (8 July 1985): 97–117. https://doi.org/10.1098/rspa.1985.0070.

Dreyfus, Hubert L. *What Computers Can't Do: The Limits of Artificial Intelligence*. New York: Harper and Row, 1972.

Eco, Umberto. *On Beauty: A History of a Western Idea*. Translated by Alastair McEwen. London: MacLehose, 2010.

Elwes, Richard. 'The Algorithm that Runs the World'. *New Scientist*, 11 August 2012, 32–33.

Emmer, Michele. 'Art and Mathematics: The Platonic Solids'. In *The Visual Mind: Art and Mathematics*, edited by Michele Emmer, 215–20. Cambridge, MA: MIT Press, 1993.

Fazi, M. Beatrice, and Matthew Fuller. 'Computational Aesthetics'. In *A Companion to Digital Art*, edited by Christiane Paul, 281–96. Chichester: Wiley-Blackwell, 2016.

Feldman, Michael. 'D-Wave Sells First Quantum Computer'. *HPCwire*, 26 May 2011. http://www.hpcwire.com/hpcwire/2011-05-26/d-wave_sells_first_quantum_computer.html.

Feynman, Richard P. 'Simulating Physics with Computers'. *International Journal of Theoretical Physics* 21, nos. 6–7 (June 1982): 467–88. https://doi.org/10.1007/BF02650179.

Fishwick, Paul A. 'An Introduction to Aesthetic Computing'. In *Aesthetic Computing*, edited by Paul A. Fishwick, 3–27. Cambridge, MA: MIT Press, 2006.

Fodor, Jerry A. *The Mind Doesn't Work That Way: The Scope and Limits of Computational Psychology*. Cambridge, MA: MIT Press, 2000.

Føllesdal, Dagfinn. 'Gödel and Husserl'. In *From Dedekind to Gödel: Essays on the Development of the Foundations of Mathematics*, edited by Jaakko Hintikka, 427–46. Dordrecht: Kluwer Academic, 1995.

Franzén, Torkel. *Gödel's Theorem: An Incomplete Guide to Its Use and Abuse*. Wellesley, MA: A K Peters, 2005.

Fuller, Matthew. 'Elegance'. In *Software Studies: A Lexicon*, edited by Matthew Fuller, 87–92. Cambridge, MA: MIT Press, 2008.

———. 'Introduction: The Stuff of Software'. In *Software Studies: A Lexicon*, edited by Matthew Fuller, 1–13. Cambridge, MA: MIT Press, 2008.

Galilei, Galileo. 'From *The Assayer* (1623)'. In *The Essential Galileo*, edited and translated by Maurice A. Finocchiaro, 179–89. Indianapolis: Hackett, 2008.

Galloway, Alexander R., and Eugene Thacker. *The Exploit: A Theory of Networks*. Minneapolis: University of Minnesota Press, 2007.

Ganeri, Jonardon. 'Emergentisms, Ancient and Modern'. *Mind* 120, no. 479 (July 2011): 671–703. https://doi.org/10.1093/mind/fzr038.

Gere, Charlie. *Community without Community in Digital Culture*. Basingstoke: Palgrave Macmillan, 2012.

Gibson, William. *Mona Lisa Overdrive*. London: HarperCollins, 1994.

Gödel, Kurt. 'The Modern Development of the Foundations of Mathematics in the Light of Philosophy'. In *Collected Works*, vol. 3, *Unpublished Essays and Lectures*, edited by Solomon Feferman, John W. Dawson Jr., Warren Goldfarb, Charles Parsons, and Robert N. Solovay, 374–87. Oxford: Oxford University Press, 1995.

———. 'On Formally Undecidable Propositions of the Principia Mathematica and Related Systems I'. Translated by Elliott Mendelson. In *The Undecidable: Basic Papers on Undecidable Propositions, Unsolvable Problems and Computable Functions*, edited by Martin Davis, 4–38. Mineola, NY: Dover, 2004.

———. 'On Undecidable Propositions of Formal Mathematical Systems'. In *Collected Works*, vol. 1, *Publications 1929–1936*, edited by Solomon Feferman, John W. Dawson Jr., Stephen C. Kleene, Gregory H. Moore, Robert M. Solovay, and Jean van Heijenoort, 346–72. Oxford: Oxford University Press, 1986.

———. 'What Is Cantor's Continuum Problem?' In *Philosophy of Mathematics: Selected Readings*, 2nd ed., edited by Paul Benacerraf and Hilary Putnam, 470–85. Cambridge: Cambridge University Press, 1983.

Goethe, Johann Wolfgang von. 'Formation and Transformation'. In *Goethe's Botanical Writings*, translated by Bertha Mueller, 21–29. Woodbridge, CT: Ox Bow Press, 1989.

Goffey, Andrew. 'Algorithm'. In *Software Studies: A Lexicon*, edited by Matthew Fuller, 15–20. Cambridge, MA: MIT Press, 2008.

Goldin, Dina, Scott A. Smolka, and Peter Wegner, eds. *Interactive Computation: The New Paradigm*. Berlin: Springer, 2006.

Goldreich, Oded. *Computational Complexity: A Conceptual Perspective*. Cambridge: Cambridge University Press, 2008.

Goldstein, Rebecca. *Incompleteness: The Proof and Paradox of Kurt Gödel*. New York: Norton, 2006.

Golumbia, David. *The Cultural Logic of Computation*. Cambridge, MA: Harvard University Press, 2009.

Goodman, Steve. *Sonic Warfare: Sound, Affect, and the Ecology of Fear*. Cambridge, MA: MIT Press, 2010.

Grosz, Elizabeth. *Architecture from the Outside: Essays on Virtual and Real Space*. Cambridge, MA: MIT Press, 2001.

Halewood, Michael. 'On Whitehead and Deleuze: The Process of Materiality'. *Configurations* 13, no. 1 (Winter 2005): 57–67. https://doi.org/10.1353/con.2007.0009.

Hallward, Peter. *Out of This World: Deleuze and the Philosophy of Creation*. London: Verso, 2006.

Hansen, Mark B. N. 'Affect as Medium, or the "Digital-Facial-Image"'. *Journal of Visual Culture* 2, no. 2 (August 2003): 205–28. https://doi.org/10.1177/14704129030022004.

———. *Bodies in Code: Interfaces with Digital Media*. New York: Routledge, 2006.

————. *Feed-Forward: On the Future of Twenty-First-Century Media*. Chicago: University of Chicago Press, 2015.

Hardt, Michael, and Antonio Negri. *Empire*. Cambridge, MA: Harvard University Press, 2000.

Hardy, G. H. *A Mathematician's Apology*. Cambridge: Cambridge University Press, 2009.

Harnish, Robert M. *Minds, Brains, Computers: An Historical Introduction to the Foundations of Cognitive Science*. Oxford: Blackwell, 2002.

Harrah, David. 'The Influence of Logic and Mathematics on Whitehead'. *Journal of the History of Ideas* 20, no. 3 (June–September 1959): 420–30. https://doi.org/10.2307/2708119.

Hayles, N. Katherine. *My Mother Was a Computer: Digital Subjects and Literary Texts*. Chicago: University of Chicago Press, 2005.

Hegel, Georg Wilhelm Friedrich. *Aesthetics: Lectures on Fine Art*. 2 vols. Translated by T. M. Knox. Oxford: Clarendon, 1975.

Heidegger, Martin. *Being and Time*. Translated by John Macquarrie and Edward Robinson. London: SCM, 1962.

————. *Contributions to Philosophy (Of the Event)*. Translated by Richard Rojcewicz and Daniela Vallega-Neu. Bloomington: Indiana University Press, 2012.

————. 'The Question Concerning Technology'. In *The Question Concerning Technology, and Other Essays*, translated by William Lovitt, 3–35. New York: Harper and Row, 1977.

Henry, Granville C. *Forms of Concrescence: Alfred North Whitehead's Philosophy and Computer Programming Structures*. London: Associated University Presses, 1993.

Hilbert, David. 'Mathematical Problems: Lecture Delivered before the International Congress of Mathematicians at Paris in 1900'. *Bulletin of American Mathematical Society* 8, no. 10 (1902): 437–79.

Hodges, Andrew. 'Alan Turing: A Short Biography'. 1995. http://www.turing.org.uk/bio/part3.html.

————. *Alan Turing: The Enigma*. London: Vintage, 1992.

————. 'Alan Turing and the Turing Machine'. In *The Universal Turing Machine: A Half-Century Survey*, edited by Rolf Herken, 3–15. Oxford: Oxford University Press, 1988.

————. 'Alan Turing, Logical and Physical'. In *New Computational Paradigms: Changing Conceptions of What Is Computable*, edited by S. Barry Cooper, Benedikt Löwe, and Andrea Sorbi, 3–15, New York: Springer, 2008.

Hofstadter, Douglas. *Gödel, Escher, Bach: An Eternal Golden Braid*. London: Penguin, 2000.

Holland, John H. *Emergence: From Chaos to Order*. Oxford: Oxford University Press, 1998.

Horkheimer, Max, and Theodor W. Adorno. *Dialectic of Enlightenment*. Translated by John Cumming. New York: Herder and Herder, 1972.

Horst, Steven W. *Symbols, Computation, and Intentionality: A Critique of the Computational Theory of Mind*. Berkeley: University of California Press, 1996.

Hume, David. *An Enquiry concerning Human Understanding*. Oxford: Oxford University Press, 2007.

————. *A Treatise of Human Nature*. Oxford: Clarendon, 1975.

Husserl, Edmund. *The Crisis of European Sciences and Transcendental Phenomenology: An Introduction to Phenomenological Philosophy*. Translated by David Carr. Evanston, IL: Northwestern University Press, 1970.

————. *Ideas: General Introduction to Pure Phenomenology*. Translated by William Ralph Boyce Gibson. London: Allen and Unwin, 1967.

Hyland, Drew A. *Plato and the Question of Beauty*. Bloomington: Indiana University Press, 2008.

James, William. *Essays in Radical Empiricism*. Cambridge, MA: Harvard University Press, 1976.

————. *Some Problems of Philosophy*. Cambridge, MA: Harvard University Press, 1979.

Jaromil. *'ASCII Shell Forkbomb'*. *Jaromil's Musings* (blog). 2002. https://jaromil.dyne.org/journal/forkbomb_art.html.

————. ':(){:|:&};: - Ou de la Bohème Digitale'. *Jaromil's Musings* (blog). 2002. https://jaromil.dyne.org/journal/forkbomb.html.

Johnson, Mark W., Mohammad H. S. Amin, Suzanne Gildert, Trevor Lanting, Firas Hamze, Neil Dickson, R. Harris, et al. 'Quantum Annealing with Manufactured Spins'. *Nature* 473 (12 May 2011): 194–98. https://doi.org/10.1038/nature10012.

Jones, Judith A. *Intensity: An Essay in Whiteheadian Ontology*. Nashville, TN: Vanderbilt University Press, 1998.

Kant, Immanuel. *Critique of Judgement*. Translated by James Creed Meredith. Oxford: Clarendon, 1978.

——. *Critique of Pure Reason*. Translated by John Miller Dow Meiklejohn. Mineola, NY: Dover, 2003.

Kay, Alan, and Adele Goldberg. 'Personal Dynamic Media'. In *The New Media Reader*, edited by Noah Wardrip-Fruin and Nick Montfort, 393–404. Cambridge, MA: MIT Press, 2003.

Keats, John. 'Ode on a Grecian Urn'. In *Complete Poems*, 282–83. Cambridge, MA: Belknap, 1982.

Kim, Jaegwon. 'Emergence: Core Ideas and Issues'. *Synthese* 151, no. 3 (August 2006): 547–59. https://doi.org/10.1007/s11229-006-9025-0.

Kitchin, Rob, and Martin Dodge. *Code/Space: Software and Everyday Life*. Cambridge, MA: MIT Press, 2011.

Kittler, Friedrich A. 'There Is No Software'. In *Literature, Media, Information Systems: Essays*, edited by John Johnston, 147–55. Amsterdam: Gordon and Breach, 1997.

Kiverstein, Julian, and Mark Wheeler. *Heidegger and Cognitive Science*. Basingstoke: Palgrave Macmillan, 2012.

Knuth, Donald E. *The Art of Computer Programming*. Vol. 1, *Fundamental Algorithms*. Upper Saddle River: Addison-Wesley, 1997.

——. *Literate Programming*. Stanford, CA: Center for the Study of Language and Information, 1992.

Kumar, Sanjeev, and Peter J. Bentley. 'An Introduction to Computational Development'. In *On Growth, Form and Computers*, edited by Sanjeev Kumar and Peter J. Bentley, 1–43. Amsterdam: Elsevier Academic, 2003.

Latour, Bruno. 'What Is Given in Experience?' *Boundary 2* 32, no. 1 (Spring 2005): 222–37. https://doi.org/10.1215/01903659-32-1-223.

Lazzarato, Maurizio. 'Immaterial Labour'. In *Radical Thought in Italy: A Potential Politics*, edited by Paolo Virno and Michael Hardt, translated by Paul Colilli and Ed Emery, 133–46. Minneapolis: University of Minnesota Press, 1996.

Leavitt, David. *The Man Who Knew Too Much: Alan Turing and the Invention of the Computer*. London: Phoenix, 2006.

Leibniz, Gottfried Wilhelm. 'Mathesis Universalis. Praefatio'. In *Mathematische Schriften*, vol. 7, *Die Mathematischen Abhandlungen*, 49–52. Hildesheim: G. Olms, 1971.

——. *The Monadology, and Other Philosophical Writings*. Translated by Robert Latta. Oxford: Oxford University Press, 1925.

——. *Theodicy*. Edited by Austin Farrer. Translated by E. M. Huggard. London: Routledge and Kegan Paul, 1952.

Lucas, John R. 'Minds, Machines and Gödel'. *Philosophy* 36, no. 137 (April 1961): 112–27. https://doi.org/10.1017/S0031819100057983.

Lyotard, Jean-François. *The Differend: Phrases in Dispute*. Translated by Georges Van Den Abbeele. Minneapolis: University of Minnesota Press, 1988.

——. *The Postmodern Condition: A Report on Knowledge*. Translated by Geoff Bennington and Brian Massumi. Manchester: Manchester University Press, 1984.

Mackay, Robin. 'Editorial Introduction'. *Collapse: Philosophical Research and Development* 8 (December 2014): 3–45.

Mackenzie, Adrian. *Cutting Code: Software and Sociality*. New York: Peter Lang, 2006.

MacLennan, Bruce J. 'Natural Computation and Non-Turing Models of Computation'. *Theoretical Computer Science* 317, nos. 1–3 (June 2004): 115–45. https://doi.org/10.1016/j.tcs.2003.12.008.

Maeda, John. *Creative Code: Aesthetics + Computation*. London: Thames and Hudson, 2004.

——. *Design by Numbers*. Cambridge, MA: MIT Press, 1999.

————. *The Laws of Simplicity: Design, Technology, Business, Life.* Cambridge, MA: MIT Press, 2006.

————. *Maeda@Media.* London: Thames and Hudson, 2000.

Manning, Erin. *Relationscapes: Movement, Art, Philosophy.* Cambridge, MA: MIT Press, 2009.

Manovich, Lev. *Software Takes Command.* New York: Bloomsbury Academic, 2013.

Marenko, Betti. 'Digital Materiality, Morphogenesis and the Intelligence of the Technodigital Object'. In *Deleuze and Design,* edited by Betti Marenko and Jamie Brassett, 107–38. Edinburgh: Edinburgh University Press, 2015.

Martin, Donald A. 'Gödel's Conceptual Realism'. *Bulletin of Symbolic Logic* 11, no. 2 (June 2005): 207–24. https://doi.org/10.2178/bsl/1120231631.

Martin, Robert C. *Clean Code: A Handbook of Agile Software Craftsmanship.* Indianapolis: Prentice Hall, 2009.

Massumi, Brian. *Parables for the Virtual: Movement, Affect, Sensation.* Durham, NC: Duke University Press, 2002.

————. *Semblance and Event: Activist Philosophy and the Occurent Arts.* Cambridge, MA: MIT Press, 2011.

————. 'Sensing the Virtual, Building the Insensible'. In 'Hypersurface Architecture', edited by Stephen Perrella, special issue, *Architectural Design* 68, nos. 5–6 (May–June 1998): 16–24.

————, ed. *A Shock to Thought: Expression after Deleuze and Guattari.* London: Routledge, 2002.

Meillassoux, Quentin. *After Finitude: An Essay on the Necessity of Contingency.* Translated by Ray Brassier. London: Continuum, 2008.

————. 'Potentiality and Virtuality'. *Collapse: Philosophical Research and Development* 2 (March 2007): 55–81.

Merleau-Ponty, Maurice. *Phenomenology of Perception.* Translated by Colin Smith. London: Routledge and Kegan Paul, 1962.

Moore, Cristopher, and Stephan Mertens. *The Nature of Computation.* Oxford: Oxford University Press, 2011.

Moore, Gordon E. 'Cramming More Components onto Integrated Circuits'. *Electronics* 38, no. 8 (19 April 1965): 114–17. https://doi.org/10.1109/N-SSC.2006.4785860.

Munster, Anna. *An Aesthesia of Networks: Conjunctive Experience in Art and Technology.* Cambridge, MA: MIT Press, 2013.

————. 'Digitality: Approximate Aesthetics'. In *Life in the Wires: The CTheory Reader,* edited by Arthur Kroker and Marilouise Kroker, 415–29. Victoria, Canada: NWP/CTheory, 2004.

————. *Materializing New Media: Embodiment in Information Aesthetics.* Hanover, NH: Dartmouth College Press, 2006.

Murray, Timothy. *Digital Baroque: New Media Art and Cinematic Folds.* Minneapolis: University of Minnesota Press, 2008.

————. 'Like a Prosthesis: Critical Performance à Digital Deleuze'. In *Deleuze and Performance,* edited by Laura Cull, 203–20. Edinburgh: Edinburgh University Press, 2009.

Nagel, Ernest, and James R. Newman. *Gödel's Proof.* London: Routledge, 2005.

Noë, Alva. *Action in Perception.* Cambridge, MA: Harvard University Press, 2004.

Olkowski, Dorothea. 'Deleuze's Aesthetics of Sensation'. In *The Cambridge Companion to Deleuze,* edited by Daniel W. Smith and Henry Somers-Hall, 265–85. Cambridge: Cambridge University Press, 2012.

Oram, Andy, and Greg Wilson, eds. *Beautiful Code: Leading Programmers Explain How They Think.* Sebastopol, CA: O'Reilly, 2007.

O'Sullivan, Simon, and Stephen Zepke. 'Introduction: The Production of the New'. In *Deleuze, Guattari, and the Production of the New,* edited by Simon O'Sullivan and Stephen Zepke, 1–10. London: Continuum, 2008.

Palter, Robert. 'The Place of Mathematics in Whitehead's Philosophy'. *Journal of Philosophy* 58, no. 19 (September 1961): 565–76. https://doi.org/10.2307/2023192.

Parikka, Jussi. *Digital Contagions: A Media Archaeology of Computer Viruses.* New York: Peter Lang, 2007.

Parisi, Luciana. *Abstract Sex: Philosophy, Bio-Technology and the Mutations of Desire*. London: Continuum, 2004.
———. *Contagious Architecture: Computation, Aesthetics, and Space*. Cambridge, MA: MIT Press, 2013.
Parsons, Charles. 'Platonism and Mathematical Intuition in Kurt Gödel's Thought'. *Bulletin of Symbolic Logic* 1, no. 1 (March 1995): 44–74. https://doi.org/10.2307/420946.
Penrose, Roger. *The Emperor's New Mind: Concerning Computers, Minds, and the Laws of Physics*. Oxford: Oxford University Press, 1989.
Piccinini, Gualtiero. 'Functionalism, Computationalism, and Mental States'. *Studies in History and Philosophy of Science Part A* 35, no. 4 (December 2004): 811–33. https://doi.org/10.1016/j.shpsa.2004.02.003.
Pisters, Patricia. *The Neuro-Image: A Deleuzian Film-Philosophy of Digital Screen Culture*. Stanford, CA: Stanford University Press, 2012.
Plato. *Phaedo*. Translated by David Gallop. Oxford: Oxford University Press, 2009.
———. *The Republic*. Translated by R. E. Allen. New Haven, CT: Yale University Press, 2006.
Pontin, Jason. 'A Giant Leap Forward in Computing? Maybe Not'. *New York Times*, 8 April 2007. http://www.nytimes.com/2007/04/08/business/yourmoney/08slip.html.
Portanova, Stamatia. *Moving without a Body: Digital Philosophy and Choreographic Thoughts*. Cambridge, MA: MIT Press, 2013.
Post, Emil L. 'Finite Combinatory Processes—Formulation 1'. *Journal of Symbolic Logic* 1, no. 3 (September 1936): 103–5. https://doi.org/10.2307/2269031.
Protevi, John. 'Deleuze, Guattari, and Emergence'. *Paragraph: A Journal of Modern Critical Theory* 29, no. 2 (January 2008): 19–39. https://doi.org/10.3366/prg.2006.0018.
Putnam, Hilary. 'Philosophy and Our Mental Life'. In *Philosophical Papers*, vol. 2, *Mind, Language and Reality*, 291–303. Cambridge: Cambridge University Press, 1975.
———. *Representation and Reality*. Cambridge, MA: MIT Press, 1988.
Reale, Giovanni. *Per una nuova interpretazione di Platone*. 21st ed. Milan: Vita e Pensiero, 2003.
Reid, Constance. *Hilbert*. New York: Springer, 1996.
Robinson, Keith. 'The "New Whitehead": An Ontology of the "Virtual" in Whitehead's Metaphysics'. In *Gilles Deleuze: The Intensive Reduction*, edited by Constantin V. Boundas, 45–81. London: Continuum, 2009.
Russell, Bertrand. *Autobiography*. London: Allen and Unwin, 1978.
Sayre, Kenneth M. 'Intentionality and Information Processing: An Alternative Model for Cognitive Science'. *Behavioral and Brain Sciences* 9, no. 1 (March 1986): 121–38. https://doi.org/10.1017/S0140525X00021750.
Schattschneider, Doris. 'Beauty and Truth in Mathematics'. In *Mathematics and the Aesthetic: New Approaches to an Ancient Affinity*, edited by Nathalie Sinclair, David Pimm, and William Higginson, 41–57, New York: Springer, 2006.
Searle, John R. 'Minds, Brains, and Programs'. *Behavioral and Brain Sciences* 3, no. 3 (September 1980): 417–57. https://doi.org/10.1017/S0140525X00005756.
Seibel, Peter. *Coders at Work: Reflections on the Craft of Programming*. New York: Apress, 2009.
Shagrir, Oron. 'The Rise and Fall of Computational Functionalism'. In *Hilary Putnam*, edited by Yemima Ben-Menahem, 220–50. Cambridge: Cambridge University Press, 2005.
Shaviro, Steven. *Without Criteria: Kant, Whitehead, Deleuze, and Aesthetics*. Cambridge, MA: MIT Press, 2009.
———. 'The "Wrenching Duality" of Aesthetics: Kant, Deleuze, and the "Theory of the Sensible"'. 2007. http://www.shaviro.com/Othertexts/SPEP.pdf.
Sieg, Wilfried. 'Gödel on Computability'. *Philosophia Mathematica* 14, no. 2 (June 2006): 189–207. https://doi.org/10.1093/philmat/nkj005.
Simondon, Gilbert. *Du Mode d'existence des objets techniques*. Paris: Aubier, 1958.
Simonite, Tom. 'The CIA and Jeff Bezos Bet on Quantum Computing'. *MIT Technology Review*, 4 October 2012. https://www.technologyreview.com/s/429429/the-cia-and-jeff-bezos-bet-on-quantum-computing.

Sinclair, Nathalie, David Pimm, and William Higginson, eds. *Mathematics and the Aesthetic: New Approaches to an Ancient Affinity.* New York: Springer, 2006.

Smith, Brian Cantwell. 'The Foundations of Computing'. In *Computationalism: New Directions,* edited by Matthias Scheutz, 23–58. Cambridge, MA: MIT Press, 2002.

Smith, Daniel W. 'Deleuze's Theory of Sensation: Overcoming the Kantian Duality'. In *Deleuze: A Critical Reader,* edited by Paul Patton, 29–56. Oxford: Blackwell, 1996.

Spinoza, Benedict de. *Ethics.* Translated by James Gutmann. New York: Hafner, 1949.

Stengers, Isabelle. 'Speculative Philosophy and the Art of Dramatization'. In *The Allure of Things: Process and Object in Contemporary Philosophy,* edited by Roland Faber and Andrew Goffey, 188–217. London: Bloomsbury Academic, 2014.

———. 'Thinking with Deleuze and Whitehead: A Double Test'. In *Deleuze, Whitehead, Bergson: Rhizomatic Connections,* edited by Keith Robinson, 28–44. Basingstoke: Palgrave Macmillan, 2009.

———. *Thinking with Whitehead: A Free and Wild Creation of Concepts.* Cambridge, MA: Harvard University Press, 2011.

Suchman, Lucy A. *Plans and Situated Actions: The Problem of Human-Machine Communication.* Cambridge: Cambridge University Press, 1987.

Symons, John. 'Computational Models of Emergent Proprieties'. *Minds and Machines* 18, no. 4 (December 2008): 475–91. https://doi.org/10.1007/s11023-008-9120-8.

Terzidis, Kostas. *Expressive Form: A Conceptual Approach to Computational Design.* London: Spon, 2003.

Thomas, David Wayne. 'Gödel's Theorem and Postmodern Theory'. *Publications of the Modern Language Association* 110, no. 2 (March 1995): 248–61. https://doi.org/10.2307/462914.

Thompson, Evan. *Mind in Life: Biology, Phenomenology, and the Science of Mind.* Cambridge, MA: Belknap Press of Harvard University Press, 2007.

Thrift, Nigel. 'Movement-Space: The Changing Domain of Thinking Resulting from the Development of New Kinds of Spatial Awareness'. *Economy and Society* 33, no. 4 (2004): 582–604. https://doi.org/10.1080/0308514042000285305.

———. *Non-Representational Theory: Space, Politics, Affect.* London: Routledge, 2008.

Thurtle, Phillip, and Robert Mitchell. 'Data Made Flesh: The Material Poiesis of Informatics'. In *Data Made Flesh: Embodying Information,* edited by Robert Mitchell and Phillip Thurtle, 1–23. New York: Routledge, 2004.

Tieszen, Richard. *After Gödel: Platonism and Rationalism in Mathematics and Logic.* Oxford: Oxford University Press, 2011.

———. 'Gödel's Path from the Incompleteness Theorems (1931) to Phenomenology (1961)'. *Bulletin of Symbolic Logic* 4, no. 2 (June 1998): 181–203. https://doi.org/10.2307/421022.

Toscano, Alberto. 'The Culture of Abstraction'. *Theory, Culture & Society* 25, no. 4 (July 2008): 57–75. https://doi.org/10.1177/0263276408091983.

Turing, Alan M. 'On Computable Numbers, with an Application to the Entscheidungsproblem'. *Proceedings of the London Mathematical Society* 42 (1936): 230–65. https://doi.org/10.1112/plms/s2-42.1.230.

Varela, Francisco J. 'The Re-Enchantment of the Concrete: Some Biological Ingredients for a Nouvelle Cognitive Science'. In *The Artificial Life Route to Artificial Intelligence: Building Embodied, Situated Agents,* edited by Luc Steels and Rodney Brooks, 11–22. Hillsdale, NJ: Lawrence Erlbaum, 1995.

Varela, Francisco J., Evan Thompson, and Eleanor Rosch. *The Embodied Mind: Cognitive Science and Human Experience.* Cambridge, MA: MIT Press, 1991.

Verostko, Roman. 'Algorithmic Fine Art: Composing a Visual Arts Score'. *Explorations in Art and Technology: Intersection and Correspondence,* edited by Linda Candy and Ernest Edmonds, 131–36. London: Springer, 2002.

———. 'Epigenetic Art Revisited: Software as Genotype'. In *Code: The Language of Our Time; Ars Electronica 2003,* edited by Gerfried Stocker and Christine Schöpf, 156–61. Ostfildern-Ruit: Hatje Cantz, 2003.

———. 'Imaging the Unseen: A Statement on My Pursuit as an Artist'. 2004. http://www.verostko.com/archive/statements/statement04.html.

Villani, Arnaud. 'Deleuze et Whitehead'. *Revue de métaphysique et de morale* 101, no. 2 (April–June 1996): 245–65.

Viterbi, Andrew. 'Error Bounds for Convolutional Codes and an Asymptotically Optimum Decoding Algorithm'. *IEEE Transactions on Information Theory* 13, no. 2 (April 1967): 260–69. https://doi.org/10.1109/TIT.1967.1054010.

Wang, Hao. *A Logical Journey: From Gödel to Philosophy*. Cambridge, MA: MIT Press, 1996.

Wegner, Peter. 'Why Interaction Is More Powerful than Algorithms'. *Communications of the ACM* 40, no. 5 (May 1997): 80–91. https://doi.org/10.1145/253769.253801.

Weinstock, Michael. *The Architecture of Emergence: The Evolution of Form in Nature and Civilization*. Chichester: Wiley, 2010.

Weiser, Mark, and John Seely Brown. 'The Coming Age of Calm Technology'. In *Beyond Calculation: The Next Fifty Years of Computing*, edited by Peter J. Denning and Robert M. Metacalfe, 75–85. New York: Copernicus, 1997.

Whitehead, Alfred North. *Adventures of Ideas*. New York: Free Press, 1967.

———. *Modes of Thought*. New York: Free Press, 1968.

———. *Process and Reality: An Essay in Cosmology*. New York: Free Press, 1978.

———. *Religion in the Making*. Cambridge: Cambridge University Press, 2011.

———. *Science and the Modern World*. New York: Free Press, 1967.

———. *Symbolism: Its Meaning and Effect*. New York: Fordham University Press, 1985.

Whitehead, Alfred North, and Bertrand Russell. *Principia Mathematica*. 2nd ed. 3 vols. Cambridge: Cambridge University Press, 1925.

Williams, James. 'A. N. Whitehead'. In *Deleuze's Philosophical Lineage*, edited by Graham Jones and Jon Roffe, 282–99. Edinburgh: Edinburgh University Press, 2009.

———. *Encounters and Influences: The Transversal Thought of Gilles Deleuze*. Manchester: Clinamen, 2005.

———. 'If Not Here, Then Where? On the Location and Individuation of Events in Badiou and Deleuze'. *Deleuze Studies* 3, no.1 (June 2009): 97–123. https://doi.org/10.3366/E1750224109000506.

Wilson, Stephen. *Information Arts: Intersections of Art, Science, and Technology*. Cambridge, MA: MIT Press, 2003.

Winograd, Terry, and Fernando Flores, *Understanding Computers and Cognition: A New Foundation for Design*. Norwood, NJ: Ablex, 1986.

Zagala, Stephen. 'Aesthetics: A Place I've Never Seen'. In *A Shock to Thought: Expression after Deleuze and Guattari*, edited by Brian Massumi, 20–43. London: Routledge, 2002.

Index

abstraction, 11, 28, 29, 32, 34, 41n1, 42n7, 47–51, 55, 61, 70, 73–75, 86, 87, 89, 92, 100, 102, 104, 106, 108, 127–128, 129, 133–137, 151, 167, 169, 193, 204, 207; computational, 55, 92, 136, 147, 157, 210; deductive, 40, 89, 90, 100, 101, 108, 117, 118, 125, 126, 128; and experience, 18, 86–87, 90, 111, 120, 145, 170, 194, 206; formal, 2, 6–7, 9, 12, 15, 16, 17, 54, 57–58, 65, 72, 73, 135, 136, 162–163, 194, 206; logico-mathematical, 92, 145; method of, 16, 55, 73, 101, 115, 130, 189, 193, 206; quantitative, 15, 31

abstractness, 11, 12, 47–51, 55, 67, 127, 194

actual entity, 69–70, 79n54, 133, 175–176, 185, 196. *See also* actual occasion

actual occasion, 15, 17, 65, 68–71, 72, 75–76, 78n17, 132–133, 134, 136–137, 175–176, 182, 183, 184, 185, 186, 188, 189, 191, 192, 195–196, 197, 198, 199, 200n15. *See also* actual entity; computational actual occasion

actuality, 12, 13–14, 18, 56, 57, 59n9, 64, 65, 67–72, 69, 75, 77, 79n54, 101, 109, 128, 129, 131, 132, 133–138, 168, 173–200, 205, 206, 208, 210; and factuality, 7, 167, 169–171, 173, 177; philosophy of, 7, 15, 62–63, 133, 167, 173, 182; production of, 4, 10, 66, 75,

192; and virtuality, 39, 59n9, 65, 69, 70–71

actuation, 92, 118

Adams, Douglas, 87, 98

Aesthetics + Computation Group (ACG), 91. *See also* Maeda, John

aesthetic ontology, 15, 61, 65, 203–204, 205. *See also* ontological aesthetics

aesthetics, 8–14, 24–25, 26, 32, 41, 58, 65, 72, 73, 84, 97; affective, 38–39; computational, 8, 9, 12, 14, 16, 18, 19, 49, 51, 57, 63, 75, 76, 84, 88, 90, 116, 118, 128, 171, 194, 200, 203–207; of computational idealism, 86, 97, 108, 110, 111, 117; of contingent computation, 8, 10, 12, 144; of continuity, 15, 30; Deleuzian, 9–10, 11, 12, 13, 27, 33–36, 43n39, 57, 62–63, 67, 193, 208, 209–210; digital, 23, 26, 28, 30–31, 40, 49; of digitality, 16, 30; of discreteness, 16, 26, 32; of the intelligible, 135–136; and logic, 11, 49, 73, 136, 204; of necessity, 17, 101, 103, 108; of thought, 10, 12, 27, 62, 210; at two levels, 12, 19, 61–65, 72, 183, 205; Whiteheadian, 12, 58, 62–64, 73, 76–77, 210. *See also* aesthetics-as-aisthesis; aisthesis; ontological aesthetics

aesthetics-as-aisthesis, 24–28. *See also* aesthetics; aisthesis aesthetic computing. *See* Fishwick, Paul

affect, 6, 9–10, 14, 15, 26, 35–41, 62–65, 67, 68, 72, 75, 127, 135–136, 187–188, 189, 191, 194, 200, 205, 207, 209; and intuition, 27; and sensation, 13, 23, 167, 193; Spinoza's definition of, 43n38. *See also* affective turn

affective turn, 36–41, 44n40. *See also* affect

agency, 98, 107–108, 161, 184, 188

Agre, Philip, 53

AI Infinity, 91–92, 95n27. *See also* Maeda, John

aisthesis, 8, 31–32, 64, 127; of the digital, 9–10, 31–32, 38, 56, 189; and logos, 73. *See also* aesthetics; aesthetics-as-aisthesis; fracture between aisthesis and logos

algorithm, 2, 5, 6, 17, 19, 54, 56, 92, 95n21, 102–105, 105–107, 109, 114, 115, 129, 135, 146, 154, 162, 184, 187–188, 189. *See also* genetic algorithm; necessity: algorithmic; Viterbi algorithm

alternative computing, 18, 145, 147, 149, 150, 152, 154, 155, 156n11, 159, 165, 169–170, 172n12, 173, 177, 178, 179, 180. *See also* natural computing; non-classical computing; unconventional computing

analogue, 24, 120; experience, 29; superiority of, 33–34, 37–38, 40

application, 6, 17, 105–106, 108–110, 177, 178, 179

architecture, 18, 36–37, 64, 77n4, 144, 147, 154

Aristotle, 65, 172n30

art, 9, 24, 26, 29, 30, 41n2, 57, 62, 83, 85, 90, 92, 102, 104, 160, 203; algorist, 103; computational, 91, 203; of computer programming, 85; and Deleuze, 27, 34, 51; and Heidegger, 42n7; media, 83, 108; new media, 29; philosophy of, 41n2; software, 37; theory of, 8, 24, 41n2, 43n39

artificial intelligence, 3, 29, 52–54, 139n21

ASCII Shell Fork Bomb, 83–87. *See also* Jaromil

assemblage, 25, 109, 134

associationism, 151, 156n19, 165–166, 170, 187, 193–194

automation, 2, 5, 26, 33, 53, 90, 98, 102, 103, 108, 121, 123, 124, 146, 172n12; of thought, 88, 210

autonomy, 40, 93n3, 151, 159, 161–162; of actual occasions, 191–192; of computation, 10, 17, 205; of formal axiomatic systems, 115–121, 130–132

axiom, 4, 98, 99, 111n1, 114, 118, 119–120, 124, 129, 138n3. *See also* axiomatic method; axiomatics; axiomatisation

axiomatic method, 4, 98, 99, 111n1, 114, 115, 118, 121, 123, 124, 129, 209. *See also* axiom; axiomatics; axiomatisation

axiomatics, 5, 97–111, 116, 117–119, 121, 124, 125, 129, 131, 135, 159, 207; computational, 4, 98, 101, 103, 105, 110, 119, 125, 134, 136, 187, 205; open-ended, 119–121. *See also* axiom; axiomatic method; axiomatisation

axiomatisation, 99. *See also* axiom; axiomatic method; axiomatics

Badiou, Alain, 26, 42n9, 66–67

Barker, Timothy Scott, 77n4

Baumgarten, Alexander Gottlieb, 41n2

beauty, 8, 16, 84, 85, 87, 92, 93n4, 93n5, 93n8, 97, 101, 102, 103, 109; and truth, 16, 83–87, 88, 90, 101, 103, 108, 109, 116, 118

becoming, 7, 10, 11, 18–19, 33–34, 36, 38, 50, 55–56, 58, 65, 69, 76, 77, 132, 137, 166, 185, 191, 192, 193, 194–196, 204; and being, 2, 4, 13, 14, 65, 75; of computation, 2, 14; internal adventure of, 182–191, 198, 209

Begriffsschrift. *See* Frege, Gottlob

behaviour, 31, 54, 103, 106, 152, 158, 159, 169, 180–181; automated, 53; complex, 178; emergent, 160–161, 172n12; social, 53; table of, 114–115, 122; unpredictable, 147, 159–160, 181

being, 10–11, 33, 34, 35, 36, 50, 67, 69–70, 84, 89, 99, 100, 108, 109, 132, 158, 159, 196; and becoming, 2, 4, 13, 14, 65, 75; modes of, 24, 58n5, 203. *See also* being-in-the-world; being of the

sensible; univocity: of being
being-in-the-world, 30
being of the sensible, 6, 11, 35, 40, 50, 56,
    72, 126, 127, 135, 155, 166, 188, 193,
    203
Bergson, Henri, 27, 62, 75, 166
bifurcation of nature, 167–171, 180
Bildung. See Goethe, Johann Wolfgang
    von
biology, 148, 162
biotechnology, 36–37
Blanché, Robert, 99
body, 3, 5, 23, 27, 28, 29, 31, 36, 37, 38,
    42n18, 64, 67, 204; and mind, 28, 72,
    76, 95n23, 126–127
body-area networking, 37
Boole, George, 98
brain, 52–53, 64, 95n23, 152, 158, 169. *See
    also* neuron
Brookshear, J. Glenn, 50, 107

calculability, 102, 125; effective, 89, 146
calculus: differential, 27, 42n10;
    infinitesimal, 76; propositional, 98;
    ratiocinator, 98
Cantor, Georg, 42n9, 120, 123
capitalism, 2–3, 33, 62, 99
Cartesianism, 53. *See also* Descartes, René
causa sui, 132, 196, 198. *See also* self-
    causation
causal efficacy, 174, 176, 177, 182,
    184–185, 187, 188, 189–191, 192,
    196–197, 200n6. *See also* causality;
    cause
causality, 132, 174–175, 197. *See also*
    causal efficacy; causation; cause
causation, 152, 153, 173–177, 196. *See
    also* self-causation
cause, 93n3, 101, 166, 174; and effect, 151,
    153; final, 19, 197. *See also* causal
    efficacy; causality
Chaitin, Gregory, 129
chance, 130, 157–162, 173, 191;
    distinction with contingency, 79n26;
    empirical, 177, 178–179; and
    Meillassoux, 79n26; of the physical
    world, 18, 183
change, 13, 18, 32, 35, 39, 64, 65, 67, 84,
    100, 107, 132, 157–162, 167, 170–171,

173, 177–178, 179–180, 181–182, 185,
    186, 187, 188
chaos, 84, 147
Church, Alonzo, 47–48, 94n20
Clark, Andy, 53
classification (computing), 178
closure, 92, 97, 104
Cobham, Alan, 146, 148
code, 38, 41n1, 83, 85, 86, 93n9, 108, 122,
    123, 162. *See also* script
codetermination, 40, 72
codification, 26, 32, 34. *See also* coding;
    encoding
coding, 38, 85. *See also* codification;
    encoding
cognition, 41n2, 52, 53, 64
cognitive science, 3, 29, 42n15
cognitivism, 2, 5, 12, 52, 54, 57, 58, 72,
    187–188, 205, 210
Cohen, Harold, 103. *See also* Algorists;
    art: algorist
communication, 40, 54, 97, 106, 107, 175;
    Deleuzian critique of, 9, 20n11, 51, 53
completeness, 69, 70, 113–114, 118,
    138n2, 182, 191
completion, 19, 68, 131, 182, 196–197,
    199. *See also* conclusion; end; perishing
complex adaptive system, 158
complexity, 1, 3, 29, 84, 129, 135, 148,
    160–161, 163, 175, 186; computational,
    146, 148, 153, 160; reduction of, 54,
    129
computability, 16, 17, 47, 48, 52, 89,
    94n20, 110, 114, 122, 124, 125, 128,
    138n8, 146, 159, 160, 186, 187; theory,
    4, 57, 123; Turing-computability, 160
computational actual occasion, 7, 72, 133,
    188–189, 192, 195, 196, 197–199,
    203–210. *See also* actual occasion
computational processing, 1, 5, 7, 10, 56,
    116, 124, 127, 129, 130–131, 135, 182,
    183, 186, 196
computational theory of mind, 15, 52, 58,
    59n17, 120. *See also* computationalism
computationalism, 52–53, 57–58, 59n17.
    See also computational theory of mind;
    post-computationalism
computer science, 3, 5, 50, 55, 56, 84–85,
    91, 95n21, 98, 99, 102, 110, 123, 144,

146, 149, 150, 161, 162, 184
conceptual capacity, 2, 11, 64, 210. *See also* prehension: conceptual
conclusion, 92, 93n7, 97–98, 100, 117–118, 122, 137, 195. *See also* completion; end
concrescence, 176, 193, 195, 197, 200n22, 208
connectionism, 53, 156n19. *See also* neural network
consciousness, 13, 29–30, 33, 69, 120, 139n15, 150, 172n30
consistency, plane of, 66
constraint, 57, 83, 117, 123, 136, 144, 148, 158, 159–160, 209
constructivism, 182
contiguity, 151, 153
contingency, 2, 4, 6, 8, 15, 17, 18, 68, 78n25, 84, 105–111, 116, 128–132, 144, 148, 165, 191–193, 209; ontology of, 1, 128, 191, 203; of the senses, 153–155
contingent computation, 1–8, 19, 109, 111, 197, 205, 206, 210; aesthetics of, 8, 10, 12, 144
continuity, 23–41, 75, 76, 80n66, 124, 172n12, 181; aesthetics of, 15, 30; affective, 39, 40, 136, 209; of becoming, 69, 166, 195–196; becoming of, 69, 195–196; of life and lived experience, 2, 34, 39; of life and sensation, 10, 99; ontological, 9, 27, 76; ontology of, 14. *See also* flux; impasse between continuity and discreteness
continuum, 27, 29–30, 33, 39, 120, 122, 137, 181; extensive, 76. *See also* continuity
control, 25, 37, 115, 158
corps phénoménal, 29–30
cosmology, 61, 131, 172n12
counting, 47–48, 57, 123, 127, 130–131, 137; infinity of, 126, 128–129
Cramer, Florian, 85
creation, 10, 33, 38, 43n25, 51, 67, 68, 75–71, 159, 162, 176, 184
creativity, 20n11, 39, 68, 108, 159, 188
critical theory, 2, 26, 99. *See also* Frankfurt School
Crutchfield, James P., 158

Csuri, Charles, 103. *See also* Algorists; art: algorist
cultural theory, 26, 36, 37, 99, 108, 206
custom. *See* habit
cyberculture, 28
cybernetics, 97, 155

Damasio, Antonio, 34
dance, 37, 39
Dantzig, George, 106
Darwin, Charles, 177, 179, 185
database, 107
datum of experience, 150, 169, 170, 181. *See also* given of experience
Davis, Martin, 98, 138n7
decoding, 106
decidability, 114, 115, 122, 138n2. *See also* decision; *Entscheidungsproblem*
decision, 49, 161, 178, 189, 210; and actuality, 70; capacity for, 189; and completion, 68; problem, 114, 115; rule-based, 48. *See also* decidability; elimination; *Entscheidungsproblem*
deduction, 2, 3, 84, 86, 89, 91, 97, 101, 102–103, 110–111, 118, 119, 123, 124, 126, 130, 159, 161. *See also* abstraction: deductive; axiomatics: deductive; formalisation: deductive; reasoning: deductive; thinking: deductive
Deep Thought, 87, 98. *See also* Adams, Douglas
Deleuze, Gilles, 6, 8–15, 20n11, 25–27, 30–33, 34–41, 49–58, 58n6, 59n9, 62–76, 77n4, 99, 126–127, 134–135, 137, 155, 165–168, 170, 172n12, 183, 193–195, 200n22, 203, 206–210
Descartes, René, 34, 50, 94n18, 132, 169, 172n30. *See also* Cartesianism
design, 20n11, 29, 33, 36, 48, 50, 52, 88, 90–91, 104, 114, 144–145, 148, 154, 161, 162, 179
determination, 49, 55, 69, 70, 75, 76, 87, 136–137, 148, 175, 176, 182, 183, 187, 189, 194, 197, 199, 200n22, 207–208; conceptual, 7, 64, 191, 192; double, 14; final, 136, 196; of indeterminacy, 1, 72, 75, 77, 183, 200n22; local, 181, 183; ontological, 14, 205; operation of, 14,

188; procedure of, 5, 209; process of, 6, 7, 17, 70, 72, 126–132, 133–134, 192, 197, 204; reciprocal, 40, 59n9, 65, 70–71. *See also* codetermination; self-determination

determinism, 4, 5, 16, 28, 84, 88, 89, 99, 122, 123, 147, 159, 165, 179, 186–187; total, 6, 92, 101–102, 126–132, 192

Deutsch, David, 154

diagrammatics, 74–75

difference (metaphysics), 27, 30, 33, 35, 66; philosophy of, 76. *See also* differenciation; differentiation

differenciation, 70, 200n22. *See also* difference; differentiation

differentiation (metaphysics), 9–10, 27, 30, 32, 33, 70, 200n22. *See also* difference; differenciation

digital computation, 9–10, 61, 72, 76, 100, 148, 189

digital culture, 8, 9, 15, 28, 38, 40, 44n51

digitalisation, 39, 124

digital media, 8, 23, 25, 28, 40, 49, 77n4; philosophy of, 25; studies, 23, 25, 34; theory, 23, 25, 26, 36. *See also* digitality

digitality, 15, 24, 27, 28, 29, 34, 36, 37, 38, 40, 47, 124; aesthetics of, 16, 30; experience of, 39, 41. *See also* digital media

Diophantine equation, 138n7

dipolarity, 14, 64, 72. *See also* pole

discreteness, 23–41, 26, 28, 32, 48, 61, 76, 80n66, 124, 135, 182; aesthetics of, 16, 26, 32; ontology of, 14. *See also* impasse between discreteness and continuity

discretisation, 5, 9, 15, 17, 31–32, 40, 48, 56, 165, 204, 207; abstractive, 5, 16, 204, 207–208; of infinity, 122–126, 134; of virtuality, 39, 128. *See also* formalisation-as-discretisation

Dreyfus, Hubert, 29, 52

dynamic, 30, 66, 70, 159, 194, 196, 203, 204. *See also* dynamism

dynamic system theory, 178

dynamism, 1, 3, 18, 68, 86, 208; in computation, 183, 187, 190, 191, 195, 196, 209; empty, 177–182; internal,

109, 208; virtual, 49–50. *See also* dynamic

effectiveness, 86, 146. *See also* calculability: effective; effective method; effective procedure

effective method, 115, 117, 122, 125, 138n2, 178. *See also* calculability: effective; effective procedure; effectiveness

effective procedure, 56, 107. *See also* calculability: effective; effective method; effectiveness

efficient computation, 146, 148, 155, 157, 179

elegance, 16, 85, 86, 93n11, 101, 102, 118

elimination (metaphysics), 175–176, 189. *See also* decision

embedded computing, 3

embodiment, 29, 52, 108; digital, 38

emergence, 18, 66, 158–161, 163, 170, 172n12; computational, 157–162, 163; ontology of, 179; philosophy of, 172n12. *See also* emergentism

emergentism, 18, 159–161, 164, 167, 171n6, 175, 180, 182, 194. *See also* emergence

empiricism, 6, 145, 157; British, 18, 149–151, 173, 176; computational, 18, 143–155, 157, 163–165, 168, 173, 178, 180, 181, 182, 183, 186, 193–194, 208; early modern, 6, 152, 166; Humean, 164, 166; radical, 62, 77n4, 174; sense-data, 173, 187, 192; of the senses, 13, 153; superior, 166; transcendental, 6, 166, 167; Whitehead's, 80n63

encoding, 119, 148. *See also* codification; coding

end (completion/aim), 7, 19, 66, 69, 76, 133–134, 196, 209. *See also* completion; conclusion; perishing

enframing, 17, 26, 207. *See also* Heidegger, Martin

Entscheidungsproblem, 114, 115. *See also* decidability; decision: problem

environment, 2, 29–30, 37, 53–54, 107, 129, 168

epistemology, 8, 34, 84, 86, 88, 89, 100, 124, 130, 138n3, 149, 167, 210;

associationism, 166; of British empiricism, 151; of computational sciences, 149; empirical, 149; Hume's, 165–166; of Universal Computation, 126. *See also* onto-epistemology

epochal theory of time, 75

error, 5, 76, 80n62, 85, 166, 168, 173

eternal object, 69–72, 77, 134–135, 136–137, 188, 190, 197, 198

ethics, 8, 84

Euclid, 111n1

event, 26, 61, 65–72, 76, 106, 129, 131, 155, 174–175, 188, 195; actual, 7, 19, 69, 73, 110, 114–138, 187, 188, 191, 192, 199; computational, 7, 9, 19; of thought, 132–138. *See also* eventuality; eventuation

eventuality, 7, 36, 65, 133, 155, 192; and indeterminacy, 9, 15, 191, 193, 209. *See also* event; eventuation

eventuation, 56, 167, 197, 208

evolution, 86, 162, 177–179, 181, 185, 186. *See also* evolutionary computation

evolutionary computation, 147, 177–179, 181, 183, 185. *See also* genetic algorithm

execution, 85, 107–108, 123

experience, 6–7, 13, 14, 18, 23–24, 31, 33–41, 50, 63, 84, 92, 97, 108, 127, 156n19, 163, 165–166, 168, 172n30, 173, 176, 180, 181, 183, 184, 189, 193, 207–208, 210; and abstraction, 18, 86–87, 90, 111, 120, 145, 170, 194, 206; aesthetic, 23, 63; analogue, 29; computation's own, 12–13, 14, 15, 19, 165, 192–193, 200; concrete, 74; conditions of, 10, 13, 14, 36, 40, 41, 43n39, 62, 72–77, 167, 171, 193, 194, 197, 208; of digitality, 39, 41; dipolar, 64; first-person, 29; immediate, 63, 74, 168–169, 173; intellectual, 29; intentional, 29; lived, 2, 8, 10, 11, 23, 26, 50, 54, 57, 67, 71, 75, 80n63, 103, 116, 126, 209; perceptive, 28; possible, 35, 43n39; pure, 80n63; real, 35–36, 39, 43n39, 62, 73, 75, 167, 168, 173, 208; sense, 35, 92, 120, 149–151, 170, 178, 180, 193; sensory, 153. *See also* datum of experience; given of experience

expression (metaphysics), 13, 24, 27, 34–35, 40, 50, 53, 72, 102, 191, 194. *See also* expressionism

expressionism (metaphysics), 76. *See also* expression

externalism, active. *See* Clark, Andy

externality: between subject and object, 173; between thought and sense-data, 18, 145, 150, 151, 164, 209; interactive, 181; of relations, 165

extension, 75, 94n18, 109, 168, 187. *See also* extensive continuum

fact, 18, 35, 63, 74, 77, 132, 149, 164, 169, 173, 179, 187, 194; bare, 7, 176–177, 180, 186; brute, 74; empirical, 146–148, 162, 165, 166, 176–177; and form, 7; separate, 168, 170; with no thought, 194. *See also* factuality; forms-from-facts

factuality, 7, 157–171, 173, 177, 178, 183, 185, 186; and actuality, 7, 167, 169–171, 173, 177; bare, 176, 193–194, 208; empirical, 164, 181, 184; empty, 68, 125. *See also* fact

feeling, 24, 26, 34, 36, 62–63, 64, 168, 187; causal, 175, 190; conceptual, 64, 69, 190; of ideality, 135; physical, 175; and thinking, 27–28, 36, 127, 134. *See also* thinking-feeling

Ferguson, Helaman, 103. *See also* Algorists; art: algorist

finality, 7, 19, 132, 192, 197–198, 199, 209. *See also* cause: final

finitude, 27–28, 55, 123, 199, 206

fixity, 195. *See also* permanence

flux, 38–39, 40, 53, 71, 194; aesthetic, 28–33, 136. *See also* continuity

form, 19, 41n2, 43n39, 50, 90, 98, 102, 120, 162–163, 188; computational, 91, 93n9, 103, 104; and fact, 7; as formation, 157–159; and matter, 84; of process, 191–200; subjective, 173–176. *See also* forms-from-facts

formal axiomatic system, 4–5, 13, 17, 98, 100, 115, 119, 121, 126, 129–132, 138n3, 162, 165, 183, 192, 196, 204, 208; autonomy of, 115–121. *See also* axiom; axiomatic method; axiomatics;

axiomatisation
formalisation, 5, 9, 15, 16, 17, 18, 26, 52,
    86, 88, 90, 97, 99, 100, 102, 104, 111,
    113, 118, 123–125, 152, 159, 164, 173,
    178, 186. *See also* formalisation-as-
    discretisation; formalism
formalisation-as-discretisation, 123–125,
    126–127, 133–135, 195. *See also*
    discretisation; formalisation
formalism, 100, 106, 119, 123, 165;
    abstractive, 2, 109; computational, 3, 9,
    55, 85, 89, 124–125, 129, 148, 152,
    172n12, 178, 179–180, 183, 186, 207;
    crisis of, 8, 54, 55, 56–57, 73; limits of,
    121, 207; and representation, 52–58.
    See also formalisation
formation, 38, 157, 163, 180
forms-from-facts, 163–165, 170, 180. *See
    also* fact; form
formula, 97–102, 104–105, 114, 118, 162;
    all-encompassing, 6; closed, 100;
    mathematical, 102; metacomputational,
    100, 125; simple, 1, 16. *See also*
    formulation; formulisation
formulation, 86–87, 90, 91, 92, 101, 103,
    117, 119, 120, 136, 147, 161. *See also*
    formula; formulisation
formulisation, 48, 100–101. *See also*
    formula; formulation
fracture between aisthesis and logos, 9, 32,
    49, 73, 136
Franke, Herbert W., 103. *See also*
    Algorists; art: algorist
Frankfurt School, 26, 99. *See also* critical
    theory
Frege, Gottlob, 98
Fuller, Matthew, 58n5, 93n11
functionalism, 51, 52, 59n17, 90, 95n23

generality, 115, 138n3
general purposiveness, 61, 88–89, 90, 113,
    125, 145. *See also* universality
generation, 10, 35–36, 160, 161–162, 177,
    179, 180, 184, 186, 188, 196
genetic algorithm, 152, 177, 178–181,
    184–186, 188. *See also* evolutionary
    computation
geometry, 111n1
Gestalt. See Goethe, Johann Wolfgang von

given of experience, 176, 180, 184. *See
    also* datum of experience
glitch, 85
Gödel, Kurt, 4–5, 17, 113–121, 124–125,
    127, 129, 139n12, 191, 205
Goethe, Johann Wolfgang von, 157–158
golden ratio, 84, 109, 118
Goldstein, Rebecca, 118
Goodman, Steve, 37
Guattari, Félix, 20n11, 25, 53–54, 99

habit (Hume), 6, 153, 155
Hallward, Peter, 59n9
halting problem, 5, 83, 86, 122–123, 130.
    See also incomputability
Hansen, Mark B. N., 29, 77n4
hard problem (computing), 146
hardware, 89, 105, 107, 145
Hardy, G. H., 93n4
harmony, 86, 101, 118, 175
Harnish, Robert M., 156n19
Hayles, N. Katherine, 161
Hébert, Jeanne-Pierre, 103–104. *See also*
    Algorists; art: algorist
Hegel, Georg Wilhelm Friedrich, 41n2
Heidegger, Martin, 26, 29, 42n7
Henry, Granville C., 77n4
Hilbert, David, 113–114, 115, 117, 120,
    123, 125, 129; programme, 113, 118,
    125, 138n3
Hodges, Andrew, 94n20, 117, 171n5
Hofstadter, Douglas, 139n15
Horst, Steven, 52
Hume, David, 6, 18, 35, 74, 149–150,
    151–153, 155, 164, 170, 184, 208; and
    Deleuze, 165–166, 194; and Whitehead,
    174. *See also* empiricism: British; idea
    (Hume); impression (Hume)
Husserl, Edmund, 42n7, 77n4, 120,
    139n20, 150. *See also* phenomenology

idea, 20n11, 35, 63, 69, 71, 101, 105, 106,
    120, 134, 137
idea (Hume), 74, 151, 153
idealism, 84, 90, 92, 93n3; computational,
    16–17, 83–92, 97, 100–102, 104, 108,
    110, 116–119, 125, 135–136, 161, 205,
    208

ideality, 19, 35, 63, 69, 70, 74, 87, 92, 134, 135, 137, 175, 189, 194, 195, 207; of eternal objects, 69, 70, 72, 77, 136–137, 188, 198; pure potentiality of, 17, 190
ideation, 92, 118
identity, 67, 71; of beauty and truth, 84; mind-body, 95n23; ontology of, 165; of representation, 33; self-, 175; of thought with being, 10. *See also* resemblance
image of thought, 9, 50, 53, 58n6, 135, 194, 210
immanence, 137, 188; of thought and sensation, 8–9, 10–11, 27, 35, 36, 49, 64, 127, 166, 190, 194, 205
impasse between continuity and discreteness, 9, 14, 16, 23–28, 28–29, 30–32, 33, 34, 40, 49, 76, 99
implementation, 6, 17, 105, 106–107, 108–110, 129, 178
impression (Hume), 74, 151
incompleteness, 5–6, 115–121, 124, 129, 130, 139n15, 139n21; and incomputability, 5, 113–115, 117, 119; theorems, 113, 116–117, 205
incomputability, 5, 17, 19, 56, 115, 117–118, 121, 122–135, 146, 165, 190, 198–199, 205; and incompleteness, 5, 113–115, 117, 119
indeterminacy, 1, 5, 7, 17, 18, 56, 58, 65–72, 110, 128–131, 133–136, 153, 159, 161, 181–182, 183, 189–190, 192, 198, 199, 204–205, 207; abstract, 49–50; affective, 36, 68, 127; computational, 57; conceptual, 14, 19; determination of, 1, 72, 75, 77, 183, 200n22; and eventuality, 9, 15, 191, 193, 209; external, 165, 210; formal, 5–6, 8, 11, 116, 121, 126, 128–129, 137, 165; and infinity, 11, 49; of the lived, 28; logical, 144; of material existence, 6; physical, 14, 19; quantitative, 55; of the real world, 3; virtual, 34, 40, 63, 66–67, 87, 126, 137
individuation: empirical, 117, 191, 195; as metaphysical determination, 27, 200n22
induction, 98, 156n21, 160, 174. *See also* inductivism; reasoning: inductive

inductivism, 152, 192. *See also* induction; reasoning: inductive
infinity, 10, 25, 28, 55, 56, 57, 58, 70, 119, 122, 123, 124, 130, 134, 136, 137, 206; of counting, 126, 128–129; discretisation of, 122–126, 134; of the incomputable, 128, 137; and indeterminacy, 11, 49; logico-mathematical, 124, 128; quantitative, 6, 11, 17, 57, 128, 137, 192, 198, 204, 207; virtual, 11, 49, 126
information, 20n11, 24, 37, 38, 39, 51, 55, 68, 97, 115, 124, 154, 184; processing, 28, 48, 147, 148, 160, 187; society, 30, 33, 42n8
information theory, 97
ingression: of data, 175, 190; of indeterminacy, 130, 133, 199; of infinity, 129; of potentiality, 69–71, 136–137, 197
inheritance, 28, 175–176, 184–185, 187, 189, 197–198
input, 2, 3, 4, 5, 6, 24, 32, 37, 48, 52, 59n17, 84, 92, 99, 106, 114, 115, 122, 124, 129, 130, 147, 181, 184, 199. *See also* output
instrumentalisation, 99
intelligibility, 57, 58, 72, 104, 136, 157, 163, 181, 187, 207; and sensibility, 64, 92, 164, 180
intensity (metaphysics), 25, 27, 35, 36–37, 65, 75, 80n66, 126, 135, 205
intentionality, 13, 29–30, 52, 150
interaction, 3, 29, 31, 38, 53–54, 71, 159, 164, 170, 177, 185; external, 182; factual, 177, 179, 180; human-computer, 29, 77n4. *See also* interaction paradigm; interactivity
interactive paradigm, 3, 54. *See also* interaction; interactivity
interactivity, 29. *See also* interaction; interactive paradigm
internal connection, 164, 166, 174
internal relation, 168, 173–174, 185, 187
intuition, 27, 67, 119–120; a priori, 75; categorial, 120; rational, 119–121

James, William, 62, 80n63, 167

Jaromil, 83–87. *See also ASCII Shell Fork Bomb*
Jones, Judith A., 80n66
judgement, 8, 24, 35, 103

Kant, Immanuel, 33, 34, 35, 41n2, 43n39, 62, 75, 93n6, 166, 174. *See also* post-Kantianism
knowledge, 2, 25, 30, 42n7, 42n8, 42n9, 74, 87, 88, 116, 120, 145, 149, 159, 160, 206; sensory, 8, 24, 27, 35, 41n2
Knuth, Donald, 85, 93n11
Kumar, Sanjeev, 162

language, 3, 25, 26, 55, 95n21, 150; formal, 99–100; programming, 102, 106–107
Latour, Bruno, 61–62
Leibniz, Gottfried Wilhelm, 16, 76, 87–88, 98, 101, 120, 175
life, 3, 4, 23, 28, 31, 34, 43n38, 50, 57, 83, 87, 88, 89, 91, 93n5, 108, 116, 162, 172n12, 207; 'a life', 9, 30, 67; continuity of, 2, 10, 39, 99; virtual, 11, 49, 56, 75, 127. *See also* lived, the; living, the
limit: of computation, 4, 5, 26, 57, 86, 113–138, 153–155, 196, 199; of formal reasoning, 17, 28, 57, 111, 113–138
literature, 36
lived, the, 26, 28, 36, 41, 50, 54, 56, 208
living, the, 28, 41, 54, 56, 158
Locke, John, 149–150, 169. *See also* empiricism: British
logic, 3, 32, 48, 67, 98, 99, 114, 125, 127; and aesthetics, 11, 49, 73, 136, 204; computational, 9, 84, 162, 204, 209; engines of, 2, 98; formal, 3, 9, 32, 40, 52, 57, 130, 157, 209; mathematical, 88, 115, 119; of sensation, 25, 40; symbolic, 32
logocentrism, 28
logos, 32, 56, 68, 73, 98, 127, 172n12; and aisthesis, 73; computational, 73, 86, 198, 207. *See also* fracture between aisthesis and logos
Lovelace, Ada, 1, 2
Lyotard, Jean-François, 116

machinic phylum, 53
Mackenzie, Adrian, 107
Maeda, John, 90–92. *See also* Aesthetics + Computation Group (ACG); *AI Infinity*
Manovich, Lev, 42n21
Massumi, Brian, 27–28, 33–35, 37–40, 188
materialism, 36, 204; scientific, 74, 169, 185. *See also* matter; matter-flow
mathematics, 42n9, 48, 55, 61, 98, 99, 100, 113, 114, 118–121, 122, 125, 138n3; aesthetic nature of, 93n4; ancient, 111n1; foundations of, 116, 121, 125; philosophy of, 99, 139n12. *See also* metamathematics
mathesis universalis, 16, 87–89, 94n17, 98, 101, 119, 126, 130. *See also* metacomputation; Universal Computation
Matiyasevich, Yuri, 138n7
matrix: abstractive, 74, 128–129, 133–134, 136; of discrete relations, 2, 32, 136, 198; formal, 4, 16; logical, 18, 28–33; of rationalisation, 42n8; of total determinism, 5, 132
matter, 6, 36, 53, 57, 169, 172n12, 185, 194, 207; and form, 84. *See also* materialism; matter-flow
matter-flow, 9, 32, 54, 64, 127. *See also* materialism; matter
matter of fact, 6, 68, 164
McLuhan, Marshall, 108–109
mechanisation, 2, 26, 121, 128; of reasoning, 100, 124; of thought, 5, 26, 53
mechanism, 28, 31, 58n5, 86, 97, 98, 99, 105, 121
media, 25, 37, 48, 103; art, 85; artist, 83, 108; computational, 37; practice, 108; softwarisation of, 31; studies, 29; theory, 24, 37. *See also* digital media; mediality; mediation; medium; new media
mediality, 58n5
mediation, 12, 37, 67, 72, 205
medium, 28, 36, 49, 83, 95n23, 102, 109. *See also* metamedium; medium specificity
medium specificity, 49
Meillassoux, Quentin, 78n25, 131–132

metacomputation, 5, 16–17, 87–92, 94n17, 100, 103, 104, 105, 109, 110, 116, 117–121, 124–125, 128, 130, 131, 133, 163, 189, 207, 209. *See also mathesis universalis*; metacomputing

metacomputing, 94n17. *See also* metacomputation

metamathematics, 94n17, 113, 117–118, 125, 138n3

metamedium, 48

metaphysics, 89, 116–117, 163; Aristotelian, 65; classicist, 108; Deleuzian, 67; idealist, 86; Platonist, 100; Spinozist, 35; transcendent, 89; of Universal Computation, 89; Whiteheadian, 13, 61, 62, 63. *See also* ontology

mind, 3, 52, 53, 64, 74, 86, 90, 93n3, 100, 104, 117, 118, 121, 139n21, 150, 151, 156n19, 169, 174, 180; and body, 28, 72, 76, 95n23, 126–127; philosophy of, 171n6. *See also* computational theory of mind; phenomenon: mental; pole: mental; representational theory of mind; structuring: mental

misplaced concreteness, fallacy of, 80n62, 168, 180

modelling, 52, 178; computer, 160, 162

modulation, 13, 25, 32

Mohr, Manfred, 103. *See also* Algorists; art: algorist

Molnár, Vera, 103. *See also* Algorists; art: algorist

monad, 175, 200n9

Moore, Gordon, 153

multiplicity, 26, 27, 30, 39, 66, 132, 137, 148, 166, 176, 179, 184, 189, 190, 192, 196, 197

Munster, Anna, 38–39

mutability, 54, 158, 181; algorithmic, 109; contingent, 106; empirical, 6, 18, 54, 109, 155

mutation, 42n7, 157; random, 179–180, 186

natural computing, 3, 18, 143–149, 150, 152, 153, 157–158, 160, 163, 165, 167, 169, 181, 183, 186, 191, 192. *See also* alternative computing

necessity, 84, 101, 105, 110, 131–132; aesthetics of, 17, 101, 103, 108; algorithmic, 102–105, 109; logical, 2, 5–6, 86, 89, 118, 155; metacomputational, 110, 130

Negri, Antonio, 42n8

neural network, 53, 152. *See also* connectionism

neuron, 95n23, 148, 152, 169. *See also* brain

neuroscience, 3

new media: art, 29, 37; theory, 38. *See also* digital media; media

Nietzsche, Friedrich, 27, 32, 43n25

nominalism, 100

non-classical computing, 3, 18, 143–149, 150, 152, 153, 157–158, 160, 163, 165, 167, 169, 181, 183, 186, 191, 192. *See also* alternative computing

non-contradiction, 98, 101, 111n1

notation, 85, 100

novelty, 32–33, 34, 68, 189; in computation, 1–19, 210; empirical, 159; ontological, 18, 65, 166, 197; production of, 32, 75, 99

number, 41n1, 48, 59n16, 114, 122, 123

objectification, 182, 184–185, 189, 208; causal, 176–177, 184, 186, 189, 197; perceptual, 168; presentational, 168–170, 177, 180–181

objective datum, 175–177, 189

objectivity, 29, 102, 116, 177, 188

occasion, actual. *See* actual occasion; computational actual occasion

onto-epistemology, 62, 87, 88–90, 94n17, 97, 103, 109, 127, 163, 188

ontogenesis, 34, 50, 51, 53, 56, 109, 126

ontological aesthetics, 63, 65, 203–204, 209. *See also* aesthetic ontology

ontological principle, 71, 79n54

ontological production, 1, 7, 18, 34, 67, 177, 203–204, 207

ontology, 4, 11, 24, 30, 42n9, 50, 86, 126; of computational emergence, 162, 163; of computational empiricism, 165, 194; of contingency, 1, 128, 191, 209; of continuity, 14; Deleuze's, 59n9, 66, 67, 127, 135, 163; of discreteness, 14;

emergentist, 18, 164, 167, 179, 182, 194; Hume's, 151; metacomputational, 89; of thought, 11, 135; transcendent, 89, 118, 119; Whitehead's, 12, 68, 73, 75, 76, 174, 190. *See also* aesthetic ontology; metaphysics

open-endedness, 17, 119–121, 134. *See also* axiomatics: open-ended; openness

openness, 97, 134. *See also* axiomatics: open-ended; open-endedness

optimisation, 124, 145, 146, 177, 179, 181

order, 1, 16, 19, 51, 61, 64, 66, 83, 84, 86, 89, 91, 100, 102, 107, 126, 129, 158, 159, 163, 184, 195, 196

output, 2, 4, 5, 24, 32, 37, 48, 52, 59n17, 84, 99, 106, 114, 122, 123, 124, 130, 147–148, 181–182, 184, 199

panexperientialism, 13

panpsychism, 14

Parisi, Luciana, 77n4

participation, 39, 56, 103

Peirce, Charles Sanders, 62

Penrose, Roger, 139n21

perceived, the (object), 30, 120, 166, 169, 188. *See also* perceiver; percept; perception

perceiver, the (subject), 24, 30, 169, 180, 188. *See also* perceived, the; percept; perception

percept, 24, 36. *See also* perceived, the; perceiver, the; perception

perception, 3, 14, 23, 24, 31, 32, 33, 40, 51, 53, 84–85, 151, 167, 174; analysis of, 173; conception-perception, 34; datum of, 123, 170, 193; digital, 24; sense, 120; sense-data, 38; theory of, 123–125, 174, 176, 200n6. *See also* objectification: perceptual; perceiver; percept; perception; representation: perceptual; unity: perceptual

performance, 6, 17, 105, 107–110, 129, 145

perishing, 66, 69, 195–196, 208. *See also* completion; conclusion; end

permanence, 7, 13, 71, 177, 195. *See also* fixity

pervasive computing, 3, 31

phenomenology, 15, 29–32, 77n4, 120, 139n20, 150. *See also* being-in-the-world; *corps phénomenal*; Husserl, Edmund

phenomenon, 29, 158; digital, 31; empirical, 7, 84–85, 90, 100, 103, 126, 158, 160, 162–167, 171n7, 176, 178, 179, 181, 183, 186; mental, 53; natural, 150; physical, 155

philosophy, 3, 8, 13, 20n11, 51, 55, 61, 73, 77n2, 99, 149, 168; of actuality, 7, 15, 62–63, 133, 167, 173, 182; aesthetic, 58, 64; of art, 41n2; contemporary, 26, 52; critical, 35; of difference, 76; digital, 39; of digital media, 25; of emergence, 172n12; of mathematics, 139n12; modern, 173; of mind, 171n6; Platonic, 89; speculative, 74

physical computing, 3, 37

physics, 43n36, 94n12, 144, 148, 154, 168

Piccinini, Gualtiero, 59n17

Plato, 16, 84, 86, 87, 89, 90, 93n3, 94n18, 139n12, 151, 158, 172n30. *See also* Platonism

pole: mental, 64, 69, 72, 127, 194, 198; physical, 64, 72, 127, 194; subjective, 170–171. *See also* dipolarity

Portanova, Stamatia, 39–40, 77n4

positivism, 42n7, 169

possibility, 34, 69, 78n25, 198

Post, Emil, 47, 138n7

post-computationalism, 3, 53. *See also* computationalism

post-Fordism, 42n8

post-Kantianism, 27. *See also* Kant, Immanuel

post-Marxism, 26, 42n8

post-Turing computing, 186–187

postmodernism, 31, 42n8, 116

poststructuralism, 2, 26, 42n8

potentia agendi, 27

potentiality, 2, 10, 15–16, 33, 38, 39–40, 69, 70, 71–72, 76, 78n25, 113–138, 188, 195, 200n22; pure, 12, 17, 63, 69, 70–71, 72, 136–138, 188, 190, 192, 197, 199; real, 19, 68, 69, 174, 188–191, 192, 197, 198; and virtuality, 10, 78n25 prediction, 9, 32, 33, 124, 152–153, 155, 159, 178–179, 210

preformation, 57, 67, 105, 132, 134–135, 207

prehension, 63, 68, 175–176, 195; conceptual, 12, 63–65, 68–70, 72, 120, 134–136, 190, 197–199; negative, 175–176, 200n15; physical, 63–64, 68, 72, 120, 175, 187–190, 198; positive, 175, 200n15

preprogramming, 1, 2, 16, 26, 33, 51, 54–55, 56, 101–102, 104, 108, 110, 129–130, 131, 135, 186, 191, 196, 199, 208, 209, 210. *See also* programmability; programming

presentation, 30, 99, 167, 181. *See also* objectification: presentational; presentational immediacy

presentational immediacy, 167–171, 174, 177, 180, 183, 200n6

probability, 1, 33, 34, 131, 177, 179, 181, 183, 184

problem solving, 32, 47, 88, 102, 106, 148, 177, 184

processual occurrence, 191

processuality, 10; of actual occasions, 175; affective, 135; of computation, 99, 184, 208; formal, 135; of genetic algorithms, 184; qualitative, 40

programmability, 3. *See also* preprogramming; programming

programming, 93n11, 99, 103, 106, 123, 154, 177, 179, 181; art of, 85; language, 102, 106–107. *See also* preprogramming; programmability

proof, 85, 113, 123, 138n2, 170; Gödel's, 114, 117, 118–119, 124; logical, 84, 93n7; mathematical, 93n7; metamathematical, 113, 125

Putnam, Hilary, 95n23, 138n7

Pythagoras, 84

qualculation. *See* Thrift, Nigel

quality, 27, 31, 57, 72, 75, 86, 89, 93n5, 102, 152, 164, 168–170, 174, 179

quantification, 2, 34, 40, 47–48, 89, 124, 128. *See also* quantity

quantity, 5, 40, 43n36, 61, 72, 89, 122, 124, 127, 129, 137, 152, 190, 198, 199.

See also infinity: quantitative; quantification

quantum computing, 143–146, 154

quantum theory, 62, 143–145, 154, 155

rationalisation, 2, 16, 39, 42n8, 47, 49, 56, 89

rationalism, 32, 54, 86, 88, 117, 166

rationality, 42n8; algorithmic, 86; instrumental, 42n6, 123, 210; sufficient, 101. *See also* reason; reasoning

realism, 89, 100, 169; conceptual, 117; ontological, 138n1

reason, 79n54, 117, 151, 169, 172n12; formalistic, 42n6; human, 2, 121; instrumental, 31; pure, 77n2; sufficient, 102, 131, 192. *See also* rationality; reasoning

reasoning, 28, 34, 50, 54, 55, 89, 93n6, 98, 117, 119, 151; axiomatic, 16, 101, 111; deductive, 16, 89, 114, 117, 159; formal, 17, 57, 111, 116, 171n5; inductive, 152; logico-mathematical, 117, 162; mechanisation of, 100, 124; structure of, 26, 28; universal science of, 87, 94n17, 118; valid, 32, 105, 134, 150. *See also* metareasoning; rationality; reason

reception: data, 19; external point of, 167; physical, 7, 12, 19, 173, 176, 190; sense, 7, 62, 165–166; sense-data, 18, 144, 149, 150, 153, 155, 165, 169; sensory, 164; sensuous, 92, 103, 204; source of, 170; subjective form of, 173

recognition, 25, 33, 58n6, 64, 69, 155, 161, 168, 174, 194

reduction, 12, 17, 18, 49, 57, 124, 136, 150, 160, 166, 173, 190, 207, 210; of complexity, 54, 129; epistemic, 2, 50, 127; representational, 12, 63; symbolic, 11, 119, 189. *See also* reductionism

reductionism, 136, 159. *See also* reduction

reflexivity, 6, 30, 163

relativism, 116

representation, 25, 27, 33, 34–36, 47, 50, 58n6, 68, 72, 74, 145, 169, 172n12, 190; a priori, 12; cognitive, 9, 26; cognitivist, 185; critique of, 2–3, 8; and formalism, 52–58; perceptual, 168;

predetermined, 157; symbolic, 56
representational theory of mind, 52–53.
  See also computational theory of mind
resemblance, 67, 151, 153. *See also*
  identity
Robinson, Julia, 138n7
robotics, 3, 54
Russell, Bertrand, 61, 77n2

Schattschneider, Doris, 93n7
scientific materialism. *See* materialism:
  scientific
script, 41n1, 83, 85, 93n2, 106, 108, 180.
  See also code
searching (computing), 107, 177, 179
Searle, John, 52
selection, 103, 107, 152, 178–179, 189
self-actualisation, 7–9, 14, 17–18, 18,
  132–134, 183, 186, 187, 191–192, 195,
  196, 198–200, 204–205, 207–208. *See
  also* self-determination
self-causation, 196–198. *See also causa sui*
self-creation, 67, 71, 176
self-determination, 7, 14, 16, 18, 19, 71,
  182, 185–186, 205, 207–208, 210. *See
  also* self-actualisation
self-organisation, 161, 162
self-sufficiency, 2, 17, 42n8, 110,
  130–131, 191–192, 196–197, 209
sensation, 11, 14–15, 24, 26, 27, 28, 32,
  33–41, 56, 67, 75, 87, 137, 151, 173;
  abstract, 6; and affect, 9, 13, 23, 64,
  209; bare, 168; digital, 24; force of,
  207; and life, 10, 99; logic of, 25, 40;
  science of, 36, 193, 203; and thought,
  8–9, 12, 27–28, 35, 36, 63, 73, 166,
  190, 194, 203
sensationalist principle, 18, 167, 168, 171,
  173, 176
sense-data, 18, 38, 144, 145, 149, 150, 151,
  153, 155, 164, 165, 166, 168–170, 173,
  179–180, 187, 192, 209
sensibility, 6–7, 9, 12, 13, 16, 31–32, 35,
  40, 57, 58, 72, 73, 105, 127, 134, 155,
  163, 164, 166, 167, 170, 197, 204, 207;
  and intelligibility, 64, 92, 164, 180;
  theory of, 27, 41n2, 43n39
sensus communis, 35
Shaviro, Steven, 43n39, 62–64

signification, 27, 37, 116, 166
Simondon, Gilbert, 26, 31, 42n7
Simplex method. *See* Dantzig, George
simplicity, 1, 5, 7, 16, 54, 57, 84, 86,
  90–92, 101, 104, 115, 118, 129, 132,
  146, 151, 155, 159–162, 175, 178,
  181–183, 190, 207
simulation, 29, 88, 161, 178, 186, 187;
  computer, 36–37, 149, 160; of
  empirical reality, 6, 147, 183, 188
situated action. *See* Suchman, Lucy
situatedness, 3, 30, 53, 57
software, 85, 89, 104, 107; art, 37;
  designer, 162; free-, 83; industry, 122;
  program, 55; studies, 108
softwarisation of media. *See* media:
  softwarisation of
sorting (computing), 107, 177
sound, 36, 37, 44n51
space, 75; computational, 90; memory,
  146, 160; multidimensional, 106;
  search, 179; and time, 7, 65, 169, 174
Spinoza, Baruch de, 35, 43n38, 196. *See
  also* Spinozism
Spinozism, 27, 35, 36, 41, 42n11, 62, 64.
  See also Spinoza, Baruch de
structuring, 41, 204; abstractive, 128;
  conceptual, 58; logical, 40; mental, 68,
  127
subject-object relation, 175–177, 188
subjective aim, 197
subjectivist bias, 170, 172n30, 176
subjectivity, 13, 27, 37, 54, 98, 170, 176,
  189
Suchman, Lucy, 53
superiority of the analogue. *See* analogue:
  superiority of
symbol, 48, 52, 91, 99, 115, 120, 124;
  manipulation, 52, 119–120, 125. *See
  also* logic: symbolic; reduction:
  symbolic; representation: symbolic;
  symbolic reference; symbolism;
  symbolisation
symbolic reference, 200n6
symbolism, 92
symbolisation, 99–100
synthesis, 157, 170, 192; asymmetric, 27;
  rational, 39

systematisation, 56, 68, 99, 113, 149;
cognitive, 173; of computation, 1;
discrete, 49; final, 57, 114, 117, 119,
123, 125; formal, 2; mechanical, 160;
metacomputational, 124; procedures of,
131; quantitative, 56; rational, 90; of
reality, 16; techniques, 27

tangible computing, 37
taste, 8, 24, 108
technoscience, 28, 55, 94n12, 147, 183
Terzidis, Kostas, 51
theism, 14
thinking, 2, 10, 11, 23, 24, 26, 27, 32,
34–35, 41n2, 42n9, 50, 51, 52, 58n6,
63, 64, 72, 120, 124, 135, 151, 159; and
feeling, 27–28, 36, 127, 134. *See also*
thinking-feeling; thought
thinking-feeling, 36, 68, 72
thought, 10, 11, 16, 18, 26, 32, 33–41,
43n25, 49–50, 51, 53, 58n5, 63, 64, 68,
69, 74, 94n18, 99–100, 102, 114, 121,
124, 127, 135, 145, 156n19, 162, 166,
170, 172n12, 195, 206; and aesthetics,
10, 12, 27, 62, 210; automation of, 88,
210; computational, 210; deductive, 2,
117; events of, 132–138;
mechanisation, 5, 26, 53; ontology, 11,
135; representational, 52, 55, 57, 109;
and sensation, 8, 12, 27–28, 35, 36, 63,
73, 166, 190, 194, 203; shock to, 50,
127, 155. *See also* externality: between
thought and sense-data; fact: with no
thought; image of thought; thinking
Thrift, Nigel, 31–32
time, 37, 49, 69, 74, 77n4, 83, 107, 122,
146, 151, 168, 177, 179, 185; non-
deterministic polynomial, 156n7; and
space, 7, 65, 169, 174. *See also* epochal
theory of time
togetherness, 76, 182
transcendence, 86–87, 89, 90, 97, 104, 110,
120
transducer, 13, 31. *See also* Simondon,
Gilbert; transduction
transduction, 12, 31, 57, 64. *See also*
Simondon, Gilbert; transducer
travelling salesman problem (TSP), 146

truth, 1, 3, 28, 43n25, 99, 114, 116, 120; of
abstract reality, 118–120; and beauty,
16, 83–87, 88, 90, 101, 103, 108, 109,
116, 118; logical, 16, 85, 97, 118
Turing, Alan, 4–5, 17, 47, 48, 52, 54, 56,
59n16, 88, 89, 94n20, 98, 113,
113–115, 117–119, 122–123, 125–126,
127, 128, 171n5, 199. *See also* Turing
machine; universal Turing machine
Turing machine, 16, 48, 52, 90, 94n20,
114–115, 122, 123, 147, 156n11,
186–187. *See also* universal Turing
machine

ubiquitous computing, 3, 25, 29
uncertainty, 54, 67, 157, 181
unconventional computing, 3, 18,
143–149, 149–150, 152–153, 157–160,
162, 164, 168–169, 179, 181, 183, 186,
191, 192. *See also* alternative
computing
undecidability, 114, 123, 130–131
understanding, 2, 24, 35, 52, 74
unification, 66, 75, 176, 184, 193, 195,
198–199, 208. *See also* unity
unity, 35, 38, 42n7, 53, 64, 75, 77n2, 84,
86, 176, 182, 187, 192, 195–197, 199.
See also unification
Universal Computation, 16, 87–90, 94n18,
97, 98, 100, 101, 103, 104, 109,
116–118, 125–126, 129, 163; See also
mathesis universalis; metacomputation
universal Turing machine (UTM), 88, 90,
94n20, 95n21, 115. *See also* Turing
machine
universalisation, 50, 98
universality, 42n7, 88, 89, 92, 103, 126,
147. *See also* general purposiveness;
Universal Computation; universal
Turing machine
univocity, 123, 148; of being, 30, 194; of
the virtual, 137
unknown, the, 56, 69, 131, 134–135, 136,
198, 207, 210; virtual, 67, 126
unpredictability, 3, 130, 147, 155,
159–160, 181, 183, 186
user, 3, 6, 10, 13, 29–30, 31, 41, 86, 108,
123, 130, 209

virtualisation, 10, 15, 39, 40, 77, 77n4, 127, 167

virtuality, 10, 11, 13, 33–34, 36–41, 50, 55, 57, 63, 66–67, 70–71, 75, 109, 126–127, 137, 166–167, 193, 205; and actuality, 39, 59n9, 65, 69, 70–71; discretisation of, 39, 128; of life, 11, 49, 56, 75; and potentiality, 10, 78n25; pure, 35, 71. *See also* virtualisation

vitalism, 13, 32, 172n12

Viterbi algorithm, 106

Viterbi, Andrew. *See* Viterbi algorithm

wearable computing, 37

Whitehead, Alfred North, 1, 7, 8, 11–12, 13–14, 15, 17, 18–19, 58, 61–77, 120, 127, 132, 133–137, 167–171, 173–177, 180, 182–200, 205–210

Williams, James, 71

Wilson, Stephen, 104

Zeno of Elea (paradoxes), 76

About the Author

M. Beatrice Fazi is Research Fellow at the Sussex Humanities Lab (University of Sussex, United Kingdom). Her primary areas of expertise are the philosophy of computation, the philosophy of technology, and the emerging field of media philosophy.

Made in the USA
Coppell, TX
01 December 2020

42503946R00146